THE
MURDER
OF THE
CENTURY

THE MURDER OF THE CENTURY

THE GILDED AGE CRIME
THAT SCANDALIZED A CITY
AND SPARKED
THE TABLOID WARS

PAUL COLLINS

CROWN PUBLISHERS ❂ NEW YORK

All rights reserved.
Published in the United States by Crown Books, an imprint of the Crown
Publishing Group, a division of Random House, Inc., New York.
www.crownpublishing.com

Crown and the Crown colophon are registered trademarks of Random House, Inc.

Library of Congress Cataloging-in-Publication Data

Collins, Paul, 1969–
The murder of the century : the gilded age crime that scandalized a city and
sparked the tabloid wars / Paul Collins—1st ed.
p. cm.
Includes bibliographical references and index.
1. Nack, Augusta. 2. Murder—New York (State)—New York—Case studies.
3. Crimes of passion—New York (State)—New York—Case studies.
4. Tabloid newspapers—New York (State)—New York—History—19th century.
5. New York (N.Y.)—History—19th century.   I. Title.
HV6534.N5C66 2011
364.152'3092—dc22
2011009390

ISBN 978-0-307-59220-0
eISBN 978-0-307-59222-4

Printed in the United States of America

Book design by Gretchen Achilles
Jacket design by W. G. Cookman
Jacket photograph © Bettmann/Corbis

1 3 5 7 9 10 8 6 4 2

FIRST EDITION

To Mom and Dad,

who let me read the mysteries from their bookshelf

CONTENTS

V. THE VERDICT   209

SOURCES   271

A NOTE ON THE TEXT

The tremendous press coverage of this affair, with sometimes more than a dozen newspapers fielding reporters at once—not to mention the later memoirs of its participants—allowed me to draw on many eyewitness sources. All of the dialogue in quotation marks comes directly from conversations recorded in their accounts, and while I have freely edited out verbiage, not a word has been added.

—P. C.

I.

THE VICTIM

A & B — KNIFE WOUNDS.

D — SHOWING WHERE BREAST WAS LACERATED

E — PORTION OF BODY FOUND NEAR 17th ST.

PORTION OF BODY INDICATED IN STRONG BLACKLINE FOUND AT EAST 11th ST.

1.

THE MYSTERY
OF THE RIVER

IT WAS A SLOW AFTERNOON for news. The newsboys along the East River piers still readied themselves on a scorching summer Saturday for the incoming ferry passengers from Brooklyn, armed with innumerable battling editions of Manhattan's dailies for June 26, 1897. There were sensational "yellow papers" like Pulitzer's *World* and Hearst's *Journal*, the stately flagships of the *Herald* and the *Sun*, and stray runts like the *Post* and the *Times*. By two thirty, the afternoon editions were coming while the morning papers were getting left in stacks to bake in the sun. But there were no orders by President McKinley, no pitched battles in the Sudan, and no new Sousa marches to report. The only real story that day was the weather: OH! YES, IT IS HOT ENOUGH! gasped one headline. The disembarking ferry passengers who couldn't afford lemonade seltzer from riverside refreshment stalls instead downed the usual fare—unsterilized buttermilk for two cents, or sterilized for three—and then headed for East Third Street, where Mayor Strong was giving the dedication speech for the new 700-foot-long promenade pier. It was the city's first, a confection of whitewashed wrought iron, and under its cupola a brass band was readying the rousing oompah "Elsie from Chelsea."

Weaving between the newsboys and the ladies opening up parasols, though, were four boys walking the other way. They were escaping their hot and grimy brick tenements on Avenue C, and joining a perspiring crowd of thousands didn't sound much better than what they'd just left. To them, the East Eleventh Street pier had all the others beat; it was a disused tie-up just a few feet above the water, and surrounded by cast-off ballast rocks that made for an easy place to dry clothes. The boys took it over like a pirate's landing party, claiming it as their own and then lounging with their flat caps and straw boaters pulled rakishly low. It was a good place to gawk at the nearly completed boat a couple of piers over—a mysterious ironclad in the shape of a giant sturgeon, which its inventor promised would skim across the Atlantic at a forty-three-knot clip. When the boys tired of that, they turned their gaze back out to the water.

Jack McGuire spotted it first: a red bundle, rolling in with the tide and toward the ferry slip, then bobbing away again.

"Say, I'll get that!" yelled McGuire's friend Jimmy McKenna.

"Aw, will you?" Jack taunted him. But Jimmy was already stripped down and diving off the pier. A wiry thirteen-year-old with a powerful stroke in the water, he grabbed the bundle just before the wake from the Greenpoint ferry could send it floating away. They'd split the loot; it might be a wad of clothes, or some cargo toppled off a freighter. There was no telling what you'd find in the East River.

Jimmy dragged the parcel up onto the rocks with effort; the boys found it was the size of a sofa cushion, and heavy—at least thirty pounds, tightly wrapped in a gaudy red-and-gold oilcloth.

"It's closed," Jimmy said as he dripped on the rocks. The package had been expertly tied with coils of white rope; it wouldn't be easy for his cold and wet fingers to loosen it. But Jack had a knife handy, and he set to cutting in. As kids gathered around to see what treasure had been found, Jack sawed faster until a slip of the knife sank the blade into the bundle. Blood welled out from inside. He figured that meant they'd found something good; all kinds of farm goods were transported from the Brooklyn side of the river. It might be a side of fresh pork.

"I'm going to see what's in there," he proclaimed, and dug harder into the ropes. As they fell aside, Jack peeled back the clean new oilcloth to reveal another layer: dirty and blackened burlap, tied with twine. Jack cut that away too, and found yet another layer, this one of dry, coarse brown paper. Annoyed, he yanked it off. And then, for an interminable moment, the gathered boys stopped dead still.

On the rocks before them was a human arm. Two arms, in fact. Two arms attached to a muscular chest—and nothing more.

THE POLICE KNEW just who to blame.

Medical students, they muttered as they examined the sawn-off torso. The riverside boys had dithered for half an hour over the grisly and headless find, deciding what to do—though Jack had hastily tossed his knife into the river, afraid of catching any blame. But there was no real cause for alarm; a patrolman arrived and dragged the parcel up onto the dry pier, followed by two detectives from the Union Market station. In no great hurry, they eventually put in a call to the coroner's office to note that the med students were up to their usual pranks. The city had five schools that were allowed to use cadavers, and parts of them showed up in the unlikeliest places: You'd find legs in doorways, fingers in cigar boxes, that kind of nonsense. By the time the coroner bothered to pick up the parcel, it had been on the East Eleventh Street pier for three hours, exposed to the curious stares of the entire neighborhood. Meanwhile, boys had eagerly taken to diving into the water trying to find, as one observer put it, "every floating object that might by any possibility be part of a human body." They gleefully dragged waterlogged casks, boxes, and smashed timbers onto the pier, but alas, nothing more.

The morgue driver finally arrived. He wrapped the cloth back around their gruesome find, tossed the whole package aboard his wagon, and trundled it away with a signal to his horse. The city had yet to buy its first horseless carriages; it had been only two years since the first one had been seen in New York, and they remained such a rare sight that Manhattan still hadn't even recorded its first auto fatality. Every other kind of fatality, though, ended up where this one did, fifteen blocks north in Midtown, at the morgue's squat brick building on Twenty-Sixth Street.

They all came here: any skipping child struck by a dairy wagon, any organ grinder downed by apoplexy in the middle of Central Park, any wino found expired in a Bowery gutter, any sporting gentleman stabbed in a saloon. The Bellevue morgue was the haunt of the dead and the deadlined; newsmen were always around, because with about twenty unclaimed bodies a day thudding in—more during a good cold snap or a heat wave—you were always guaranteed some column inches for the late edition.

Even before the latest heat wave, Bellevue had been especially rich in news; its old morgue keeper had been arrested after twenty-seven years of illegally selling bodies to the local med schools at $5 a pop—selling so many, in fact, that he'd accumulated a $100,000 fortune on his morgue salary of $60 a month. The lowlier attendants were more cheaply bribed. A cigar or a pouch of shag tobacco would get a reporter the run of a windowless building some sixty by eighty feet wide, lined along one side with marble slabs, the other with chest-high tiers of cooled body drawers.

To wander through this library of corpses was a dubious privilege. The dead room's only respite from the gloom came from a single sky-light, and the occasional nudge from a resident tomcat. There were no fans, and flies buzzed constantly over the marble slabs where the latest deliveries reposed naked, awaiting identification. A thin mist of icy water was kept running over the slabs in an ineffectual attempt to keep the bodies fresh and to shoo the flies away. The effect was that of a dark, dripping cave filled with the broken bodies of Manhattan. It was, by universal assent, the most miserable place in the city. Worst of all were the mangled and bloated remains of bridge jumpers and failed swimmers pulled daily from the river.

"That horrible place—God!" novelist Theodore Dreiser would later recall of his days there as a *World* reporter. "Daily from the ever-flowing waters of New York there were recaptured and washed up in all stages and degrees of decomposition the flotsam and jetsam of the great city—its offal, its victims, its *what*?"

The *who* and *what* were always the questions for these nameless corpses. But the source of the oilcloth-covered bundle that had arrived that evening was not so hard to guess at.

"Medical students," an attendant seconded, noting its arrival in the ledger.

Probably cut from one of their own bodies here in the morgue, maybe off a cadaver sold just a day or two earlier. Well, now whoever it was had come back. They'd wait the obligatory seventy-two hours, of course, and then send it on to the coffin room, where another attendant hammered together cheap plank boxes. Anyone left unclaimed for three days went there—the body photographed, the clothes stored for laggardly friends or relatives to make a later identification, any money or jewelry on the body quietly pocketed—and then the newly filled coffins were disgorged out the back of the building onto the pier. Each day a dead-boat pulled up for a final stygian journey up the East River to a waiting trench in the potter's field on Hart Island.

That, no doubt, is where this misbegotten parcel would go, and nobody would ever hear of it again.

BY THE TIME Bellevue superintendent Dr. Thomas Murphy and city medical examiner Dr. George Dow arrived on their evening rounds, there were reporters from the *World,* the *Herald,* and the *Evening Telegram* all gathered in the morgue, waiting for their day's quota of Dreadful Cases and Awful Tragedies. They'd already gotten a good one out of Bellevue that day when Diamond Jim Brady forcibly checked his mother in to the insane ward next door. But the reporters could always hope for more, and as the two doctors made their obligatory check of the day's casualties, they froze before the river parcel, exchanging significant looks.

Dr. Murphy closely examined the oilcloth-wrapped package: the well-muscled chest and shoulders of a white man, its arms folded across in an X with the hands lying on its shoulders. The head, wherever it was now, had been rather raggedly hacked off at the larynx, while down below, the torso had been cleanly cut under the fifth rib.

"There is a mystery here," Dr. Murphy muttered cryptically.

Dr. Dow nodded. He felt the tone of the body's skin, and lifted the arms to reveal that an irregular horseshoe-shaped chunk had been sliced away from the chest. But it was the saw marks at the neck that most immediately caught his eye.

"No medical student would have done this," he announced. It was simple, Dr. Dow explained to the reporters: This body was no more a med-school cadaver than you or I. "A saw, and not a knife, was used to sever the head and the body," he explained. That was the mark of the untutored; professionals saw bone and slice flesh.

"I am pretty familiar with the methods employed by the different colleges," agreed Bellevue's superintendent. "None of them does this kind of work. The removal of the flesh from the breast has a very suspicious look." It might have been done, he ventured, to dispose of a telltale tattoo. But without a head or an identifying mark on the body, how could they describe it?

"Let me see . . ." Dr. Murphy brightened. "The height of the average man is that of arms extended and measuring from the tips of the fingers." He turned to a morgue assistant. "Measure the arms and fingers."

The assembled men watched as the orderly eased the headless trunk down from its drawer and laid it out at full length on the floor, then ran the measuring tape along the arms.

"Five foot eleven," the assistant announced.

Dr. Dow continued to examine the body and added his own guess. "I would not want to be quoted as expressing a positive opinion," he warned the reporters, "but I should think the man when alive weighed 190 pounds."

The muscular body the oilcloth enclosed, the *Herald*'s reporter wrote in some admiration, showed "a man of magnificent physical development." The hands were remarkably soft and uncalloused— genteel, even, with the nails carefully manicured. Dr. Dow pressed on the flesh of the arms and found it still soft and supple; he moved the fingers back and forth, and they yielded and straightened easily. Rigor mortis had not even set in.

Word spread quickly among the Bellevue buildings; a dozen physicians from the hospital piled into the morgue, each wanting to poke and prod the mysterious cadaver. The city's coroner was roused from his house. But as for Dr. Dow, he'd already seen enough. The medical examiner stood over the severed trunk and rendered his professional judgment.

"The man of which this formed a part," he informed the startled room, "was alive twenty-four hours ago."

2.

A DETECTIVE
READS THE PAPER

IT WAS A GLORIOUS Sunday morning. Julius Meyer was home in his Harlem tenement on 127th Street, enjoying a day off from his job as a mechanic.

"Papa, let's go cherrying!" pleaded his eight-year-old son. He could hardly say no, and so the father and his two boys—little Edgar and strapping teenaged Herbert—made their way up toward Ogden's Woods. Getting there meant a forty-block train ride north to the Highbridge station, and then a ten-block walk into the northern reaches of the borough—out toward the Bronx, that drowsy region of farms, apple orchards, and placid dairies.

Up here, between a densely wooded crescent bounded by Undercliff Avenue and the Harlem River on one side, 170th Street and the Washington Bridge on the other, one could forget the city altogether. These were the hinterlands, thick with pines and huckleberries and cherries but scarce in people; you could stand on Undercliff Avenue for an hour or more without seeing another soul. Just one house was visible along this lonely stretch of road, with nary another shack for a quarter mile around. As Julius and the boys wended their way into the woods—a good twelve-foot drop from the main road—it was as if they'd shimmied down into another country.

While Julius and Herbert pressed forward through the swatting tree limbs and the thick brambles, Edgar was able to snake through the tangled brush and scamper ahead of them—too far, almost. They'd entered down by Sedgwick and 170th Avenue, but Edgar, an ebullient boy, was charging into wild and thorny depths, far from any entrance.

Julius could no longer see his boy.

"Edgar!" he called out. "Edgar?"

SUNDAY AT the Highbridge station house was neither challenging nor especially rewarding police work—at least not for someone like Detective Arthur Carey. Once a rising star at HQ, he'd been caught in a department power struggle, knocked down a couple of pay grades, and exiled to the sticks. For two years Carey had been deprived of the murder cases he'd once landed downtown; testifying to packed courtrooms and seeing his name in the paper weren't part of his job in Highbridge. "I was walking a post," he'd explain without irony, "where, according to police tradition, a patrolman helped tend the goats."

That's what everyone in the department called it: Goatsville. It wasn't on any map, but every officer knew where it was. Goatsville was where you got sent when you shook down a gambling house too hard, or busted a local ward boss in a brothel, or when your service revolver discharged in an unfortunate direction. For Carey, it was for hitching himself to the wrong star; a few years earlier, a corruption scandal meant that some heads had to roll. Carey hadn't been implicated, but his mentor—the mighty Inspector Thomas Byrnes, the most famous police detective in America at the time—had stepped down, and another faction took over the Detective Bureau at the police headquarters on Mulberry Street. Carey had been in Goatsville ever since.

Inside his station were Julius Meyer, his sons, and the parcel they'd accompanied on the police wagon. It was turning into quite the Sunday adventure for the two boys.

Detective Carey listened carefully to their story. Little Edgar, they recounted, had yelled back excitedly to his father from the foot of Undercliff Avenue's steep retaining wall. He'd found a peddler's pack. There, on a small shaded ledge that jutted out just before the forest sloped away, was a tightly bound bundle, the sort that a linen or notions dealer might waddle under from one house to another, ready to untie it to lay out his wares. But it was heavy—easily a hundred pounds. A tug on one end had drawn out a putrescent waft. Meyer didn't know what it was, but he knew something was amiss. He left his boys to guard the find while he flagged down some mounted policemen. They'd needed a stretcher and towing ropes just to hoist the mass up from the ravine.

Detective Carey and Captain Thomas Killilea carefully appraised the package. The station captain was another Byrnes appointee sent up to Goatsville. He'd been on the force since the Lincoln administration and held a double claim to the precinct: He was also tangled in yet another corruption fiasco just a year earlier, accused of renting out on-duty police to work as security guards at football games. The former police commissioner Teddy Roosevelt had tried pushing Killilea and his cronies out altogether, getting so many top officers under indictment one year that the annual police parade was canceled. Still, even an old-timer like Killilea retained enough of a fondness for his old downtown beat to read of the latest doings beyond Goatsville. And to him, the red-and-gold-patterned oilcloth already looked plenty familiar; in fact, the captain knew exactly where he'd spotted it before. He'd seen it, he explained, in that morning's *New York Herald*.

Detective Carey cut the baling cords and pulled back layers of red oilcloth, burlap, and twine-secured brown paper. Inside was the midsection of a man—and it was very clearly a man—hewn between the ribs up top and about four inches below the hip joints at the bottom. *Medical students*, others at the station house shrugged. They figured the officers at Tenth Street had been right, and the morning's newspapers were just out to make something out of nothing.

Carey wasn't so sure.

The bundle would be sent onward to the morgue at Bellevue, of course—an officer was already making the phone call—but Carey wanted a closer look. This wasn't the cat-up-a-tree work of his precinct that he had before him; and even if nobody else in the station thought so, to Carey it had the feel of something big.

The detective examined the inside of the parcel. The layer of dirty burlap was secured with faintly pink-colored string, and Carey had seen spools of it before: It was a sort druggists used, a variety called seine twine. Below that was a brown paper wrapping, and then the body. The revolting smell was filling the station house. But Carey wasn't quite finished: He wanted just one more look before they loaded it up onto the wagon again. Carey rolled the limbless trunk over for a better view.

There, in the small of the back, adhered another piece of brown paper—a slightly different, smaller piece. He delicately peeled it away and examined it. The paper bore a single, small ink stamp— and the detective knew, in that moment, that he had to return to his old precinct.

Murder, mused Carey darkly, *followed me here*.

THE TRIP from the cows and orchards of the north down to the corner of Houston Street and Bowery was only about ten miles, but Arthur Carey might as well have been traveling to another world. These were his old haunts from his rookie days on Byrnes's detective squad: a ramshackle and roiling retail polyglot of hagglers, banjo players, dime museums, beer gardens, fruit stands, and discount crockery shops. You could walk full blocks down Bowery and fill your arms with newspapers hawked by newsboys, each one a different title, and none of them in English. It was one of the city's oldest streets, its name a mocking remainder of the land's old Dutch farms or *bouwerij*—but now a cheap, noisy, and beery cacophony of drunk bums and sober business.

If you didn't mind the occasional fisticuffs or dead body, it was a swell place for an officer—a little too swell, maybe. Teddy Roosevelt had found the neighborhood so obliging to his men that he went around pouncing on on-duty officers for quaffing pints in oyster houses and dive saloons. In their place came recruits who had to pass fitness tests and undergo weapons training, and it was said that you could tell the old and new officers apart by sorting the fat from the slender. But the old sins remained, and then some; there was real money to be had in this neighborhood. The Bowery Savings Bank was improbably becoming one of the world's largest savings institutions, and for police the temptation to dip in at less reputable businesses was everywhere. Even Carey's well-regarded old boss retired with a fortune of $350,000—something not easily explained when a typical yearly salary on the force was $2,000. Some departmental accomplishments, perhaps, were better left unsung.

The Bowery's packed streets and low-slung tenements overflowed with Germans and Poles, and the storefront of Kugler & Wollens was emblematic of the changing neighborhood. John Jacob Astor IV owned the poky two-story brick building at 277 Bowery—in fact, the Astors owned much of the block, as their long-dead patriarch had made his first land buys a century earlier along this very street. For decades the building had been occupied by a clan of butchers and grocers, the Marsh family; but by the 1870s, as the neighborhood acquired umlauts at an impressive rate, it became a German beer saloon, and then a hardware retailer.

On this block of narrow brick buildings, hardware in every variety was hawked by Germans. The mighty Hammacher Schlemmer hardware shop held down one end, selling everything from mechanic's tools to piano fittings. At the other end was the domain of Ernst Kugler. Herr Kugler had been here more than twenty years, outlasting a previous partner, watching the passing of the Bowery Boy gangs, and seeing the latest immigrant wave turn the Bowery Theater into a Yiddish venue. Kugler and his employees knew their business well enough that when a detective turned up with a piece of paper stamped Kugler & Wollens, they knew exactly what it was for.

At some point, *someone* connected with that bundled body had been here. It might have been any time and for any purchase from a handful of wood screws to a brass keyhole escutcheon. Like every hardware store, they kept a large roll of brown paper, a stamp, and a reel of twine for wrapping up all manner of purchases. But the shape and condition of this piece was distinct.

It had been used to wrap a saw.

SO CAREY HAD ONE CLUE. The other—his only other, really—was the oilcloth that the trunk had been wrapped in. The fabric was still so new that it smelled of the store. But the piece found in Ogden's Woods had been about four feet wide and fourteen and a half feet long. Unless you had a baronial dining room table, you weren't buying sheets that long for a tablecloth. Someone had bought this with a task in mind—maybe, given its red color, for catching dripping blood. But where would they have bought it?

Finding someone in the Bowery who knew about oilcloth wasn't hard. The street was filled with exactly the kind of peddlers who used the stuff, people who immediately knew where to locate the nearest distributor: Henry Feuerstein, a sharp-eyed Hungarian who wholesaled yarns and fabric just three blocks away on Stanton Street. An Orthodox Jew, Feuerstein was contentedly working in his warehouse on the Christian sabbath; he personally examined the swatch and identified the maker of the brightly colored red-and-gold floral pattern. "A. F. Buchanan and Sons," he said. He even knew the pattern number. "Diamond B, number 3220."

It was a cheap and unpopular pattern—a leftover from last year's stock, in fact—and just too gaudy and vivid to sell well. He hadn't unloaded a roll of it to any store in four months. Most dry-goods customers for oilcloth, Feuerstein explained, preferred something a bit lighter in color.

Of course, the detective could check the other distributor that Buchanan & Sons used—there was also Claflin & Company, over on Church Street. But that wouldn't happen without a warrant; its proprietor, John Claflin, had been arrested weeks earlier after dodging a jury summons. He was not known to be overly fond of police. But Feuerstein, you understand, was a reasonable man.

The merchant threw open his ledgers, tracing out the network of dealers and distributors. And once they tallied up all the dry-goods shops and general stores they distributed this stuff to, it became clear: Carey would have something like fifty more shops to visit. Here, right in Feuerstein's books, you could see how far even an unpopular cloth went. There was a Mr. Bernstein on Belmont Avenue in Brooklyn; a Mr. Bratzenfelder on Avenue D; a Mr. Theimer uptown at Seventy-Second Street; a Mr. Prencky . . . It went on and on. A roll of Diamond B #3220 even went to the store of Ignatz Rucmark, over in Hoboken. You'd need to hit all five boroughs and then some to track this cloth down. That would take time—and men. Aside from Detective Carey, though, barely anyone else on the force had moved into action yet.

But if the police weren't on the case, Carey found, somebody was. Because someone *else* had been coming here and asking Feuerstein these very same questions.

Reporters.

3.

THE JIGSAW MAN

SUNDAYS WERE ALWAYS a bit slow at the *New York World,* and Ned Brown just about had the place to himself. Walking along a vast Park Row newsroom so crammed with rolltop desks that it was nearly barricaded, he read panel after panel on walls placarded with exhortations:

ACCURACY, ACCURACY, ACCURACY!

And:

WHO? WHAT? WHERE? WHEN? HOW?

And:

THE FACTS—THE COLOR—THE FACTS!

These continued around the perimeter of the room, so that in every direction a reporter looked, the *World* credo was shouted at him. But on this day the room was quiet; only the stale cigar smoke hinted at last night's fury in getting the June 27 *Sunday World* out.

From the windows between the placards, Ned could see out over the rooftops—over every rooftop, in fact—clear out to the East River. The teeming city below had nearly doubled in size over the last generation; it vaulted upward with newly invented elevators, and outward with hurriedly built elevated railways. Towering above it all were the eighteen-story offices of the mighty *New York World*, the crowning achievement of Joseph Pulitzer.

A lanky Hungarian immigrant, Pulitzer had enlisted in the Union army, ridden cavalry in Sheridan's Shenandoah Valley campaign, and then drifted into New York at the end of the Civil War. On the very site of this newspaper office had once stood French's Hotel, and Pulitzer, then a penniless veteran, was thrown out of it. Two decades later, in an almost operatic act of revenge, a wealthy Pulitzer returned from out west and razed the hotel to the ground, erecting on the spot the city's tallest building: *his* building. He'd lavished two miles of wrought-iron columns to support the world's largest pressroom and placed his offices on the soaring top floors beneath an immense 425-ton golden dome. The reflection of its gilded surface could be seen for miles out to sea; for immigrants coming to America, the first sight of their new land was not the Statue of Liberty but Pulitzer's golden beacon. Inside, his sanctum was decorated with frescoes and leather wainscoting; one of his first visitors, emerging from the elevator and into his office, blurted: "Is God in?"

But when Pulitzer had bought the paper from Jay Gould in 1883, the *World* was scarcely godlike at all. It was an arthritic operation with a circulation of twenty thousand, and it bled money. Pulitzer fired the old staff, bought a blazingly fast new Hoe press, and dragooned the best reporters and editors, pushing them mercilessly to reinvent the era's drab uniform columns into bold headlines and sensational woodcut illustrations. No longer would shipping news and market results count as front-page stories; as much a showman as a newsman, Pulitzer unapologetically courted women and immigrant readers with a heady mix of bombast, sentiment, and attention-grabbing promotions that rode on the latest fads. When Jules Verne was on everyone's nightstand, Pulitzer ordered daredevil reporter Nellie Bly to travel around the world in eighty days; she accomplished it in seventy-two. In the midst of the craze over Martian canals, Pulitzer even considered mounting a giant billboard visible to "readers" on Mars. Rather more pragmatically, the rags-to-riches immigrant seized the moment when the newly built Statue of Liberty lacked a pedestal: a flag-waving *World* campaign among housewives and schoolchildren raised more than $100,000 to buy one. And Emma Lazarus's "huddled masses" inscription? That came from a *World* contest.

The facts—the color—the facts! Circulation had risen fifteenfold since he'd bought it, making the *World* one of the largest dailies in the world. The paper itself had swollen, too, its immense three-cent Sunday edition becoming a thing of sensational beauty. Pulitzer had created the world's first color comics section, featuring the antics of a bald tenement kid with ears like jug handles: the Yellow Kid. His popularity inspired competing papers that year to scoff that the *World* was comic-strip journalism—*yellow journalism*, they called it. Perhaps, but it was an absolutely brilliant hue of yellow. Past the day's front-page grabber from the East Eleventh Street pier—BOY'S GHASTLY FIND—the paper was bursting with an exposé of a Chicago diploma mill, an account of a Maine aeronaut taking flight with a giant kite, fashion tips for women, and ads for everything from Hoff's Malt Extract to Dr. Scott's Electric Hair Brush. A thick periodical section promised "More Reading Material Than Any Four Magazines" and was fronted by a thundering headline on unregulated "baby farm" orphanages: NOTHING SO CHEAP IN NEW YORK AS HUMAN LIFE!

At the front of the newsroom was the ringmaster for this printed circus: the city editor, who regularly bellowed from a wooden platform for more copy. But today it was just the substitute editor enjoying the luxurious lull of Sunday afternoon.

And then the phone rang.

Ned Brown was motioned over. A second oilcloth-wrapped body part had been found up by the Bronx and was due to arrive at the Bellevue morgue any minute. Ned was to run over and meet up with Gus Roeder, the *World*'s crack morgue correspondent.

"Do whatever Gus tells you," the editor snapped. "The *Journal*'s probably got forty guys there already."

The competition! The newly launched *Evening Journal* had been nipping at the paper's heels for months, and here the emptied *World* offices would get caught flat-footed on the story. It could be a new victim, or a second helping of yesterday's East River find; either way, it was sizing up to be another front-pager, and the editor knew they'd have to grab it.

"If the pieces fit, it's the same stiff," he declared, and hurried his rookie to the door. "If it's part of a different stiff, then the guy with the red oilcloth has murdered them both."

RUNNING FROM THE EL STATION to the Bellevue morgue, Ned Brown was a sight: A short and stringy bantamweight, his blond hair swept up in a pompadour like his boxing heroes, he sprinted along Twenty-Sixth Street while dodging newsboys and Sunday strollers. The nineteen-year-old NYU student had been angling for any news assignments he could get over the summer. Today was his break, his first real story.

Gus Roeder was waiting for him when he flew into the morgue. So were Deputy Coroner Philip O'Hanlon's findings on the river bundle, the result of several hours of painstaking autopsy. Gus—a dour, red-faced German with a thick accent—bustled into the crowd of reporters to listen to Dr. O'Hanlon, while Ned went to examine the arms and shoulders found by the pier. By the skin he could immediately see that the victim was probably fair, about thirty-five years old; judging by his soft hands, he was not a manual laborer.

But who was he, and who had done this?

"At first," O'Hanlon admitted to the gathered reporters, "it looked to me as though it were the fore section of a body prepared for photography so as to show the position of the heart and lungs, as might be done in a medical college. But I do not believe so now."

Observe: not only did the torso still retain all its organs, the body contained no trace of any preservative. On the contrary: inside the broad chest of a powerfully muscled man, the tissue of the lungs was still spongy and the heart was filled with blood—the very blood that had stopped flowing after a knife was plunged between the victim's fifth and sixth ribs.

What?

The reporters looked closely at the body. The flesh stripped away from the chest—and, perhaps, an identifying tattoo along with it— had also quietly hidden two previously undetected stab wounds on the body. A casual observer would not spot them among the gore— but O'Hanlon had.

"They must have been inflicted *before* death," he flatly stated.

Making incisions around the stab sites, the deputy coroner found that blood had entered into the surrounding tissue—that is, it was pumped into them. That only happened in the living; a stab or incision made on a dead man created different internal damage than one on a living body. He'd also looked *inside* these stab wounds. A stab will typically show threads of clothing driven into the wound; but this one had none. So the victim, O'Hanlon concluded, had been alive and naked when stabbed.

"Both wounds were made with a long-bladed knife," O'Hanlon continued, "and both cuts were downward, as a man would strike while standing. One was above the left collarbone, and the other above the fifth intercostal space. The latter penetrated the heart . . . this alone would cause instant death."

Only, Dr. O'Hanlon realized, it *hadn't*. True, the fatal wound had been driven deep into the heart at a nearly perpendicular angle—plunged into the victim from above, possibly while he was sleeping. But the victim was a powerful man, and the assortment of nonfatal wounds—the other stab wound under the collarbone, a glancing cut to the left hand, blood under a fingernail, and boot-shaped bruises on the arm—these told the story of a horrific struggle. The victim had cut his hand in trying to grab the attacker's knife, the deputy coroner theorized, and had made an attempt to stand up and fight back in a terrifying but already doomed final effort.

"That he was knocked down I think is proved by the imprints of the boot," O'Hanlon theorized. "He struggled to his feet and was standing erect when someone, who I think must have been very muscular, stabbed him in the collarbone with a big knife. The blood under his nail shows that he struggled hard, or else that he clasped his hand to his bosom after he had been stabbed."

And with that, the deputy coroner—and the headless torso—had told their story.

The morgue doors slammed open. From outside, orderlies heaved in another load of cargo: a red-wrapped parcel that took two men to carry. Without the preserving cold of the East River, and after a spell sitting in a summertime forest, it was offensively rank. The morgue keeper ignored the smell to unwrap the bundle and lay it out: the midsection, male and muscular and circumcised. A mass of reporters watched as the two segments were pushed together on the marble slab.

They fit perfectly.

AT SIX P.M. on June 27, the body had its first claimant.

Bellevue was hardly the place to spend a Sunday evening, but Miss Clara Magnusson's friends and neighbors had been urging her to visit ever since the story in the previous night's *Telegram*. She lived just three blocks away, yet it had taken until now for her to make the journey over to this dismal place; her neighbor Gustav accompanied her to help with the identification and to provide a steady shoulder. She explained that her brother-in-law, Max Weineke, had been missing for a month: he was a thirty-four-year-old Danish scrap-metal dealer, and the descriptions of the morgue's find had her friends on East Twenty-Eighth Street wondering. Coroner Tuthill led the two over to the marble slab, and to the legless and headless segmented man who lay nude upon it.

There was a scar on Max's back, she recalled, and that would surely identify the body. But as she watched the attendant turn the body over, her heart sank; it had been sawed through *exactly* where the scar should be.

It's him, her neighbor Gustav decided. He was sure of it. Max had been a moody fellow—industrious, but he drank a bit at times— and . . . well, there's no telling what could have happened to him, really. He'd had $30 on him when he disappeared—more than a week's pay—and that right there was enough motive for a man to be killed.

And yet the body did not seem *quite* right. Max had been missing for more than a month, but this body was fresh. Then there was the matter of those strong but supple hands—so soft, so smooth and pampered. These were not the hands of a scrap-metal dealer. And there was a scar on the left hand—and an old fingernail injury where it had been partly cut away—that neither of them recognized or could account for.

For Bellevue's superintendent, it was the scar on the finger that did it. "If they had only been able to account for the scar on the finger." He sighed. "I should have thought the body was that of Weineke beyond a reasonable doubt."

Gustav and Clara stepped back out into the fading evening light, leaving just as much of a mystery as when they'd arrived.

WHILE THIS PUZZLING DRAMA played out, the morgue had received another visitor. A few among the reporters took notice: *Art Carey?*

They hadn't seen Byrnes's exiled protégé in ages. The detective was energized, back in his element. He walked briskly around the body—the segment he'd unwrapped earlier that afternoon now reunited like a jigsaw with its top half—and examined the matching red-and-gold oilcloth of both segments. He'd come to know it well, though maybe not as well as the newspaper reporters who'd scooped him on finding the fabric wholesaler. In fact, the newspapermen had been ahead of the police force all day.

I knew it was a murder all along, Captain Hogan had blustered earlier, claiming that he'd blamed it on medical students out of a concern for public safety—keeping the citizenry, you see, from panicking. The reporters were incredulous. Was Hogan joking? It took a *Telegram* reporter to actually get the first crime scene's facts right, since the patrolman's report claimed that the bundle included the abdomen but no organs—a patent falsehood to make it sound like a med-lab cut-up. And the police hadn't done anything since; it was a *Herald* reporter who had fetched the coroner the night before and escorted him to the morgue, and a *World* reporter who started knocking on doors even later that night to interview groggy oilcloth dealers around the city. The police hadn't secured the crime scene at the pier, hadn't assigned any extra men to the case, hadn't even admitted it was murder until the coroner telephoned and *insisted* they do something.

Well, Hogan ventured, the murder had probably been committed among a ship's crew, and so maybe it was out of their jurisdiction.

Wait, a *Herald* reporter had asked. Didn't the hands lack the kind of calluses a sailor would have?

Hogan didn't really have an answer on that one.

In fact, there was a lot the police didn't have answers for. They'd already been on the defensive all weekend, even *before* this case; one of their captains had led sweeps of women guilty of little more than walking along Broadway after midnight, filling the courts with the tragic injured respectability of sobbing baker's assistants and late-shift shopgirls. When one cop was asked for his evidence, he'd scarcely sputtered, "I saw her walk up and down the street a few times" before being cut off by a magistrate's bellow of "Discharged!" Reporters had been having a field day with it; a new murder was the last thing the department needed that day.

But Carey was different: He knew this was a homicide case, and he was making it *his* case. He even had his own pet theory. The murder, he mused aloud to a reporter, might have been committed in Long Island or Brooklyn. The killers—for it would have required more than one to cut up and dispose of the body so quickly—had taken a ferry and dumped the first piece. But then they'd panicked. Maybe they thought that they'd been seen. That's when they went back and fetched the larger piece with a wagon, drove over the Washington Bridge, and dumped it onto the loneliest stretch of road they could find. Of course, this was just a hunch—half a hunch, really. And as for who did it, or who the victim was . . . well, there was no way to tell yet.

Taking one last look at the body before he headed back to the World Building with Gus, though, young Ned Brown wasn't so sure about that. When he examined the headless corpse's hands, an unnerving sense of recognition crept over him. Those well-muscled arms and smooth fingers—they were like something he'd seen somewhere before.

But where?

4.

THE WRECKING CREW

ON MONDAY MORNING, New Yorkers awoke to find a hand shoved in their face. HAND OF THE HEADLESS MURDERED MAN—EXACT SIZE, crowed the June 28 *New York World*. There, above the fold, the life-sized fingers splayed across the morning paper—a dead man reaching out of the page to grab readers by the collar. RIVER MYSTERY GROWS IN HORROR, bellowed *Press* newsboys, while the high-minded *Herald* fretted over "the strangest and most brutal murder of the century." Even the immigrant sheets took notice, with the staidly Teutonic *New Yorker Staats Zeitung* trumpeting the latest on *Der Kopffabschneider*—"the Headcutter." But none topped the *World*'s engraving—procured, it boasted, "from a flashlight photograph made in the Morgue last night." The illustration irresistibly invited readers to place their own hand across the dead man's—to clasp their fingers across his—and wonder at his identity.

An overnight autopsy of the second parcel by Coroner Tuthill furnished some intriguing hints. The victim, as one reporter put it delicately, "may have been a Hebrew." He had no alcohol in his stomach, which discounted a drunken brawl. Nor was there food in there—so it had been at least three or four hours since his last meal. But among this minutiae, one of the coroner's consulting physicians had made a sensational finding: *The leg stumps had been boiled.*

"It appears to me," he'd confided to an *Evening Telegram* reporter, "that an attempt has been made to dispose of the body by boiling it. It is possible the murderers thrust the legs into a kettle hoping to boil the flesh off, but found they could not do it quickly or easily enough, and that they then cut up the remains."

Well, that was one way of looking at it.

CANNIBALISM SUGGESTED, the *Herald* announced. Or was it something more subtle—quicklime or a harsh deodorizer on the skin, the remains of a failed attempt at a hasty cover-up? The most fascinating solution offered up in the morgue came from a *Times* reporter: Weren't butchers in the habit of scalding stuck pigs to loosen up their skin? The suggestion was compelling; a butcher's handiwork might account for the curious quality of the murderer's saw cuts—more skilled than an amateur, yet cruder than a med student.

"A butcher may have done it," Coroner Tuthill mused aloud. "Or, perhaps, a carpenter."

Yet the scalding seemed to favor a butcher, and reporters and morgue employees alike could hardly keep from thinking of the Luetgert case—a recent Chicago murder where a local sausage maker dropped his wife into one of his factory's vats. Luetgert's case was a peculiar one, since there was no witness and no victim left to produce. But this Manhattan mystery provided a horrifying and neatly packaged clue—a body with skin, a *Herald* reporter marveled, that was "as white as marble." That, the coroner explained, was because "the body had been washed, and the blood removed before it was wrapped up."

But who would do such a thing? The victim might not have been drinking, a *Press* reporter suggested, but the killer surely had been. Not just to commit the deed, mind you, but to steel himself to venture into the Bronx woods at night. "His nerves must be of iron," he speculated, "and probably he fortified himself with liquor for the ordeal." Even just the sawing would have been exhausting, awkward work. On this the coroner spoke from some experience, after all—in cutting through the trunk, he explained, you'd need somebody to hold the arms so that they wouldn't keep getting in the way. And that meant an accomplice.

Or, perhaps, an entire gang.

The *World* knew just the man to ask about the case: Andrew Drummond, the former head of the U.S. Secret Service.

These days he was running a detective bureau at the foot of Newspaper Row, and he'd been following the case closely. "I believe that this most atrocious murder was committed by a foreigner," he huffed to a *World* reporter. Its ferocity, he deemed, was the work of men hailing from warm and lusty climes. "The murderer is a Sicilian, or possibly a Spaniard or Cuban. Maybe a Spanish spy has been put out of the way by the Cubans. The most likely one is that it is the result of a family feud among Sicilians. I know the ways of the Mafia."

To Drummond, the clincher was the oilcloth. What murderer would call attention to his deed by wrapping it in lurid red cloth? Ah, but attention was the *point* with a Mafia hit. And of course, as Drummond reminded readers— "Sicilians love bright colors."

Even as scores of reporters were fanning out across the city, beating the bushes and shadowing the police along the riverbanks and in the Bronx woods, Drummond was sure of one thing: Whether the head was burned, buried, or sunk in the river, they wouldn't like what they'd find. "When the head is found," he warned, "it will be seen to be horribly disfigured."

But where some saw horror, others sensed opportunity.

EVERY DAY OR SO for the last couple of years on Newspaper Row, a mob of mustachioed, derby-hatted men would come tumbling out of a low brick building, the first of them saddling up onto their squeaking bicycles even as they ran, and then careening wildly past City Hall; then a second group, more raggedly bohemian with their leather portfolios and wooden camera tripods, would clamber aboard carriages and go clattering madly after the bicycles. Behind them, editor Sam Chamberlain could be heard roaring from his desk.

"Get excited. God damn it, *get excited*!"

This was the Wrecking Crew.

The appearance of the Wrecking Crew meant just one thing: that a splendid story—a lover gunning his society sweetheart down on Broadway, a passenger ferry upending itself, or a rollicking downtown building collapse—was to appear in the next edition of the *New York Journal*.

You could tell when New York was having a peaceful day, it was said by friends, by how despondent *Journal* publisher William Randolph Hearst looked. But give him a murdered lad or tragic maiden, and Hearst joyfully revived. And a man dying at the hands of a maniac who scattered parts all around the city? He was ecstatic.

For their newly created *Evening Journal* edition—meant to be even saucier and more shameless than the morning *Journal*—it was pure homicide gold. What a way to launch! And so the word came down from the top: Do whatever it takes. Hearst editors sent reporters off to tail detectives and swipe evidence from the scene if necessary, the better to run it in the *Evening Journal* first. Photograph the Meyer boys, map the spot where they found it, show the twine and the knots and the pattern of the oilcloth around the torso. Get diagrams of the nude body. Get graphics and put it on page 1. That morning the Wrecking Crew seemed to be rushing in and out of the *Journal* almost nonstop; it was like nothing anybody had seen before.

"Events seem to indicate that men, like dogs, go mad at certain seasons," Hearst mused as he surveyed the day's news. There were race riots in Key West, idiots stealing electricity off high-voltage streetcar lines in Ohio, and two millionaires fighting over a $15 dog here in New York. But this story, *this* was something more than ordinary madness. It was already getting picked up by the wires and running across the country. And so the order came from Hearst's offices: Hire four launches, and set them to dragging the bottom of the East River—immediately.

Find that head, the chief wrecker commanded.

CAPTAIN O'BRIEN COULDN'T ward it off anymore, not with every newspaper headline on his way in to the Mulberry Street headquarters yelling at him. After two days of hopeless stalling by the police, several detectives were sent trudging over to the morgue in the early-morning hours to take down names and addresses.

They had a long day ahead of them. The steps and wooden porch leading into the death house were crowded with bereaved families—scores of people, all convinced their lost loved ones were inside—as well as local curiosity seekers, lounging surgeons from the neighboring hospital, and legions of reporters. The detectives and the coroner could barely make their way inside. The first two visitors to squeeze in gave their names to a detective as John Johnson and Adolph Carlson of 333 East Twenty-Eighth Street. They were fellow boarders with Max Weineke. As men living in close quarters, they'd seen Max nude a number of times; there was a mole on his shoulder, they said. There wasn't one on the body, so that settled that.

But then, marveled a *Herald* reporter, three "Japanese—or at any rate, Orientals" pressed their way to the front and were led to the slab. They announced that it *was* Weineke. Who were they, and how did the three of them know a Danish scrap-metal dealer? They wouldn't say. Another mysterious visitor correctly described, sight unseen, a surgical scar on the abdomen; the fact had not been announced to the public, and he was quickly led to the slab. He identified the body as Weineke; but the fellow wouldn't identify *himself*, and promptly melted back into the crowd. So now they had five positive identifications of Weineke—four by men who refused to name themselves— and three negative identifications of the very same body.

The morning had only just begun at the morgue.

Next came the presumptive widow of Mr. Robert Wood. She was regal in her floral-decked hat and dark mourning dress, waiting with her attending minister amid all the tumult and weeping outside. Wood, it seemed, was a Long Island City butcher who had gone missing after leaving his shop with a $150 bankroll in his pocket, and his empty wagon had been found abandoned in front of a Greenpoint saloon. His description, the location, the motive—they all matched the body pretty well. Mrs. Wood and the minister were led inside, and the headless and legless body—further decomposed and sliced into by two autopsies—was revealed to her. She fell into a dead faint.

It was too much—too much. She slumped into her minister's arms and was carried into a morgue office and revived. She wanted to try again. There was a scar on his left hand, she recalled, and so the morgue attendants covered up the remains, leaving only the forearm and hand undraped on the table. Mrs. Wood and the minister approached quietly, while the crowd inside kept keen watch from a close but respectful distance. She held the cold, lifeless hand in her own and examined the nails of the man she believed to be her husband—and a man with a distinctive scar on his middle finger. This body also had a scar on its finger . . . the index finger.

It is not him, Mrs. Wood announced.

It was also not missing Mafia murder witness Agguzzo Baldasano; neither was it a missing young Mr. Levaire of 106th Street, nor the Brooklyn gas engineer Charles Russell. But it *was* Brooklyn bartender John Otten, or Brooklyn printer John Livingston, or perhaps New Jersey carpenter Edward Leunhelt. The body also, apparently, belonged to a Manhattan bricklayer.

"It is surely George," his brother assured the morgue attendants.

On and on the identifications came, all day, like an endless handkerchief pulled from a magician's pocket. Watching outside was a young man dandling an infant; when asked by a *World* reporter what he was doing there, he refused to talk; all questions for him had to go through the gentlemen over *there.* The reporter turned to find himself face-to-face with the assembled forces of the *Evening Journal.* They were a formidable sight. Hearst was fond of giving his reporters bicycles, so that his crew were like another regiment of "scorchers"—the lunatics who barreled through city traffic on Sylph cycles, Lunol racers, and greased Crackajack bikes, their futuristic bronze headlights ablaze and slopping kerosene. There were enough of these wildmen riding up the sidewalks and getting horsewhipped by irritated carriage teamsters that Hearst retained a specially designated "bicycle attorney" on the paper's staff.

Cycles tossed aside, the Wrecking Crew pushed their way in. Their witnesses, they told detectives, were the nephew and niece of one Louis Lutz, a cabinetmaker who had disappeared from his Upper East Side home on Wednesday. His namesake nephew examined the left hand for a scar.

"I feel sure it is my uncle's body," he proclaimed.

The attending detective wasn't impressed.

"They are too willing," he muttered.

"The finger of the dead man looks like my uncle's marked finger," young Lutz insisted—whereupon a morgue attendant leaned in and wiped away the scar with a rag. It had been a streak of dirt. *Now* was Lutz sure?

He wasn't so sure.

As the Lutzes filed out, a hysterical woman passed them on the way in.

"Oh, Dick! Oh, Dick, why did you go away and leave me?" she wailed, and was led sobbing over to the body. It was her husband, she moaned—Richard Meggs, a retired liquor dealer of West Fifty-Second Street. He'd left on Thursday for a card game with $500 in his pocket, never to return. When shown the scarred finger on the left hand, she broke down again. "Dick had a scar right there," she sniffled.

The detectives and coroner's assistants weren't quite convinced. Did her husband have any other unique characteristics? Why yes, she recalled. Her husband had a very distinct scar on his groin. The attendants dutifully displayed it to Mrs. Meggs's full view.

It was not Dick.

IN THE DOORWAY of a redwood-paneled office at the *New York Journal,* a dapper young man could be seen dancing a little jig. Then, as page proofs were laid out over the floor of the war room, he'd indulge in another little dance—tapping over the day's stories, snapping his fingers like castanets. He might well dance: He was becoming the most powerful publisher in New York.

LOUIS A. LUTZ THE VICTIM? his evening edition demanded. Lutz wasn't, of course, but that hardly mattered. The important thing was that the *Journal* had a great story. "The public," he reminded his staff, "likes entertainment better than it likes information."

A generation younger than Pulitzer, William Randolph Hearst represented everything his Park Row neighbor was not: He was young, native-born, and the scion of a California senator and mining baron. Hearst seemed to have careless wealth written upon him, right down to the $20 gold piece he used for a tiepin. At Harvard he'd shown more interest in newsrooms than in his studies, and after presenting his professors with piss pots emblazoned with their portraits, he was booted out of the school. But no matter; he slummed around as a freelancer for the newly launched *World*, carefully observing the business. Pulitzer, he believed, had invented a whole new way to make a fortune from journalism.

"I am possessed of the weakness which at some time or other of their lives possesses most men," he wrote to his father. "I am convinced that I could run a newspaper successfully."

A decade later, he'd lifted Pulitzer's ideas to remake the scrawny *San Francisco Examiner* into the country's fourth-largest paper and bought the near-worthless *New York Journal*—"the chambermaid's delight," some called it—to turn it into a juggernaut of high-speed presses and color graphics and sensational headlines. He mocked rivals as doddering dinosaurs stuck "in the Silurian era." His comics pages were blazingly ornate and complicated print jobs; perfecting them chewed through equipment, though demolishing new presses was a price that Hearst was happy to pay. "Smash as many as you have to, George," he instructed his printer. Now Hearst had the best color Sunday supplement in the country—page after page of *The Yellow Kid*, the adventures of *The Katzenjammer Kids*, and *Happy Hooligan*—"eight pages of iridescent polychromous effervescence," his paper boasted, "that makes the rainbow look like lead pipe."

His headlines were equally colorful, especially for the wilder *Evening Journal* edition. THE MAN WITH THE MUSICAL STOMACH, proclaimed one, while a particularly fine science story announced that A GENIUS HAS CONCEIVED A PLAN FOR A MACHINE THAT WILL KILL EVERYBODY IN SIGHT. A good headline could always be ginned up; even a bizarre old 1856 French undertaker's patent for the "Application of Galvanoplating to the Human Flesh" might yield the splendid DROP DEAD AND HAVE YOURSELF PLATED. It wasn't the best quality journalism, granted, but it was the best *quantity* journalism. At an unheard-of cover price of one cent, the paper could proudly display its motto: "You Can't Get More News; You Can't Pay Less Than One Cent."

And that night, you couldn't get more on the river murder. Hearst proudly looked over an *Evening Journal* whose front page boasted lavish illustrations of both sides of a dead man's hand, the entire forearm—and a close-up of the wounded fingernail—*and* a "butcher's diagram" showing exactly how the body had been cut up. The next page was given over to a pictorial tour of the infamous Ogden's Woods and the East Eleventh Street pier, plus a complete list of current missing persons with their identifying marks. Column after column of crew reporting covered witnesses, the police chief, the coroner, and the invaluable Mr. Lutz.

Hearst barely had time to enjoy his grisly triumph when word arrived of the upcoming four o'clock *World*.

He had his spies in neighboring pressrooms, of course—he liked to know what his competitors were about to publish. But that evening's final edition of the *World*, stuffed with illustrations and columns about the case, had a real shocker right up front:

$500 REWARD

The *World* will pay $500 in gold for the correct solution of the mystery concerning the fragments of a man's body discovered Saturday and Sunday in the East River and in Harlem. All theories and suggestions must be sent to the City Editor of the *World*, in envelopes marked 'Murder Mystery', and must be exclusively for the *World*. Appearance of the solution in any other paper will cancel this offer of reward.

It was a jaw-dropping amount—a year's pay for the clerk who could recall selling the oilcloth; several thousand bottles of cheap claret for the proprietor in whose establishment the deed was hatched; a personal horse and carriage for the commuter who might have overheard it. It was $500, for that matter, to *any* reader who could deduce a solution, just like readers had been doing with the Arthur Conan Doyle stories that the *World* ran. Now they could do more than just read Sherlock Holmes; they could *be* him.

This was going to be a sensation.

Hearst ordered his pressmen into action: Run an Extra Final Edition, timed to appear just minutes after the *World*'s $500 reward. He had an utterly devastating headline to run atop his *Evening Journal*, and the words rolled deliciously off the tongue.

$1,000 REWARD . . .

5

JILL THE RIPPER

ONE READER ALREADY KNEW who the culprit was: *Hearst.*

The body was the work, a *Journal* reader wrote in, of "some enterprising newspaper or group of men who wish to test the efficiency of the local detective force, which has been called in question quite often under its present management."

As letters piled into the *Journal* offices on Tuesday morning, other reader guesses included tramps killing a peddler (conveniently "using rope and oilcloth from the peddler's pack"); bickering butchers ("probably employed in one of the slaughter houses on the East Side or in Harlem"); a nefarious cabal ("I think the man was tattooed or branded with the marks of some secret society"); and, of course, "fiendish" Spaniards who "hacked him to pieces with their machetes." Some suspected a woman of the deed, since only "jealousy could have terminated with such terrible results." Still others invoked Sherlock Holmes, who seemed the best guide to such a baffling case. Alas, Arthur Conan Doyle had recently killed off his great detective. "If he were still alive," one reader mourned, "Sherlock Holmes would surely earn your thousand-dollar reward through deduction."

Still, the suggestion of Hearst himself topped them all. "It would be a comparatively simple matter," the reader insisted, "for a newspaper to secure through a physician a suitable cadaver and to dispose of the portions effectively, yet theatrically, so as to secure the widest possible publicity."

The *Journal* had a good laugh and ran the letter; if only they'd thought of it themselves! Hearst loved promotion; he'd already run bandwagon signs and sandwich-board men around the city and advertised his paper's one-cent price by mailing out sackfuls of pennies to New Yorkers. He'd invaded the city, as one editor put it, as quietly "as a wooden-legged burglar having a fit on a tin roof."

And the roof he most loved to dance on was the *World*'s. When he'd rolled into New York, Hearst stole his old paper's crown jewel by grabbing *Sunday World* editor Morrill Goddard, a daredevil journalist who'd made his name as a London correspondent covering Jack the Ripper. "Take all or any part of that," he'd told Goddard, tossing him a crumpled Wells Fargo bank draft for $35,000. Then, for good measure, Hearst immediately bought the rest of the *Sunday World* staff as well. An outraged Pulitzer purchased them back, only to find his repatriated *World* men emptying their desks yet again and walking back to the *Journal*. Hearst had stolen them *twice*. The Park Row sidewalk between the two papers, newsmen joked, was wearing thin.

Now, rallying his pirated staff from his barber's chair as he took his morning shave, the young millionaire was ebullient. "We must beat every paper in town," he declared.

His first blow for the *Journal* would beat them all—maybe even top the sensation created by the reward. It would be something nobody had ever seen before. He had his pressroom chief working up a special color illustration. Not for the Sunday comics supplement, mind you—but for that day, Tuesday.

And if that didn't knock the competition sideways, his next idea would: an elite band of Wreckers dedicated to homicide coverage. Backed by veteran crime reporter George Waugh Arnold, they'd be even *better* than the NYPD's rudderless Detective Bureau, which had been adrift ever since Inspector Byrnes was forced out. Not so George and his men. They'd carry their own badges, pack licensed pistols. They'd make arrests, they'd *get things done*. Hearst even had a dandy name for them, one that might have sent that suspicious letter writer into a tizzy: the Murder Squad.

———

CROWDS POURED into the morgue that morning, ready to identify the city's most famous body, but they were made to wait; the coroner had scheduled yet another autopsy. Three days had now passed since the body's first discovery, and reporters were growing jaded about the odds for any more would-be identifiers. "One might as well have tried to identify a particular Texas steer by the sirloin hanging in a butcher's shop," a Hearst man dryly observed.

Some guesses had certainly been less helpful than others. Occultists plied their way into the city morgue, including at least one phrenologist apparently undeterred by the absence of a head; that morning's *World* ran a palmist's not particularly edifying judgment: "Did love or jealousy have aught to do with the tragedy? Perhaps." Not to be outdone, the *Journal* hired the country's most famous palm reader, Niblo, who swanned into the morgue and performed a reading on the dead man's hands. Among his pronouncements: the victim had been murdered for love rather than money, and the killer might be a "female Jack the Ripper."

Oddly enough, it looked like Niblo might be on to something. Inside the Bellevue morgue, five men gathered around the dissecting table: Deputy Coroner O'Hanlon, three consulting physicians, and pathologist Frank Ferguson of New York Hospital. Dr. Ferguson had seen this kind of case before; three years earlier he'd been in this very same room, at this same table, examining the headless and limbless body of Susie Martin, an eleven-year-old girl who vanished from her Hell's Kitchen tenement. Twelve days later her remains were found in a cellar just blocks away, identifiable only by the clothes the killer had used to bundle her body into. The crime had gone unsolved; and now, reading the details of this new case in the papers, Ferguson sensed a chilling familiarity.

Look, he pointed to two stab wounds: one to the left lung, the other from a downward thrust to the collarbone. Both made with a long, narrow blade.

The same had been done to Martin.

The sawing along the neck and atop the legs?

The same.

Dr. Ferguson directed their gaze to a previously ignored wound—a faint cut into a rib, where the saw had glanced off the body. It was a crucial clue, for unlike the stumps, it was here that you could determine the width of the saw.

"The same kind of saw was used," he surmised after measuring the cut. "The blade of the saw is only a millimeter in thickness. A butcher's meat saw is about that thickness. A carpenter's saw is thicker." In fact, the angling of the cuts told a story of their own. "By examining the marks made by the saw and the knife," he said, "I can tell about how the murderer went at it to carve up the body." The body, disassembled under the terrible light of the dissecting room, bore mute witness as Ferguson envisioned its fate.

"I can almost see him in the room with his dead victim," he told his transfixed audience. "I can see him tearing off the clothing, if he had any on when he was slain. I can see him turn the body bellydown, so that the wild eyes should not stare at him. I can see him sever the flesh of the neck and then use the saw on the vertebrae. The murderer stood on the right-hand side. The marks of the teeth of the saw on the shoulder prove that there must have been a twisting motion as the sawing was finished."

The backbone had also been sawed from the right-hand side, and with the body still facedown; the left leg had been severed from the left side. The head had been sawn off not in one downward cut but rather around in a circle. These were the same actions the Martin killer had made. And there was an even more troubling similarity: the boiling of this body's legs. The body of Susie Martin had *also* been boiled, and a sliced-off bone fragment showed signs of at least some of its flesh having been consumed.

This, Ferguson announced, was the work of the same killer—a cannibal.

ALERTED BY FERGUSON'S FINDINGS about the saw, detectives coursed uptown to inspect the cellars of local butchers. But a lone cub reporter could be seen walking determinedly to Forty-Second

Street, notebook in hand, his blond hair pompaded high under his hat. Ferguson hadn't been the only one with an unnerving feeling that there was something familiar about that body in the morgue.

Those well-muscled arms and soft fingers: they were something Ned Brown had seen before—*felt*, even. It was a combination found in just one place, among the muscled masseurs of Turkish baths. The baths were where revelers would go after a night of hard drinking in Midtown; with rooms heated to 120 degrees, they were thought to evaporate the alcohol—and even to cure bites by mad dogs. Ned Brown had been known to work off a few shots in Murray Hill Baths, a long and narrow Times Square establishment on Forty-Second Street. A Romanesque space with white marble floors and a delightfully long swimming pool, it advertised itself as "the Most Handsome and Perfect Baths in the World." The locals had another name for it: "The House of a Thousand Hangovers." After signing up for a steam bath and massage there, Ned idly let a question drop. Had anyone slacked off from showing up for work that week?

That would be *Bill*, snapped an attendant.

"He took Friday off because he was going to look at a house in the country with his girl—or so he said . . . Guldensuppe is his name." He hadn't been back in since then, the attendant added, though someone had called him in sick on Sunday. "Drunk someplace, of course."

"I must have seen him around here," Ned ventured, "but I can't place him in my mind."

"He's just built like a big Dutchman. He has the upper half of a woman tattooed all over his chest—used to be a sailor on one of them Heinie windjammers when he was a kid."

If you see him, the baths' cashier warned as he rang up the $1 ticket, *tell him he's fired*.

Bill lived somewhere around Thirty-Third and Ninth Avenue, it was thought—a German and Irish neighborhood of low brick tenements. Ned joshed his way through the nearest bar there, knocking back a couple of beers and posing as a long-lost pal of Willie's. Had anyone seen his old buddy?

Not lately, the saloon's cook said, but try the apartment over Werner's drugstore, where he'd shacked up with his landlady.

"She got plenty of cash." He winked from behind the bar. "She treats him good."

"He's a hot sketch!" Ned quickly agreed. "Always after the dames."

"You bet!" The cook laughed. Strangely enough, though, he hadn't seen Willie around in the last few days.

Ned Brown knew he had to think fast.

How would he get inside the apartment? Pleading ten bucks from the *World,* he bought a suitcase of expensive twenty-five-cent soaps and made his way through the tenements around Werner's building, posing as a salesman with a five-cent trial offer. The air stung with the smell of cooking sauerkraut and the clatter of tin washtubs; hausfraus inside leaned out windows to gossip as they strung laundry over the fire escapes. They knew good sandalwood and verbena soap when they saw it, and at a nickel a bar, they didn't care if it was a trial offer or just plain stolen. Word was passed around quickly, and by the time Brown reached the apartment over Werner's, he was down to his last bars.

In the center of the apartment door was a brass nameplate:

AUGUSTA NACK

LICENSED MIDWIFE

That was rich: New York didn't license midwives.

He knocked and heard a faint commotion inside; the door opened to reveal the midwife herself, a dark-haired woman in her late thirties with a curiously sensual presence and the glow of an afternoon of exertions. Ned went into his spiel—wondrously soft, satisfaction guaranteed!—but she didn't wait to hear out his sales pitch.

"Give me the soap now," she demanded.

Well, it's a funny thing, Brown said—turned out he had used up all his cakes. But for *her* he did have two left, because he did need a testimonial for their next ad . . . "If you could give the soap a trial now, while I wait," he added, "I'd be glad to let you have one."

She regarded the bars; their fragrance brought release from the disorder of the apartment around her, which appeared to be halfway packed for a move; rugs lay rolled up on the floor.

"All right." She motioned him over to a black leather chair. "Give me the soap."

As Ned heard the water running in the next room, he continued his sales patter—"Let your hands soak in it! You will feel each finger separately caressed . . ."—and looked hungrily around the room. An object, any incriminating object, anything to set up as a chalk engraving and run in the next edition of the *World*. On a small side table, he spotted it: a portrait of a muscular beau, blond with a turned-up mustache. He quickly snatched the photo and thrust it into his jacket just before she reentered the room.

She liked the soap, she said, but she didn't want to be quoted for his ad.

Quite all right, quite all—

"Now you give me the other soap also," she demanded. "Here is a dime."

She hadn't noticed anything missing.

It was, perhaps, the sweetest single coin he had ever earned. He pocketed the dime, passed an angry-looking fellow on his way back downstairs—not the man in the picture—and noted the address: *439 Ninth Avenue.*

"IT WAS A GOOD DAY'S WORK, kiddo," Roeder admitted when young Ned returned to the World Building. "Thanks."

He'd gotten his first big scoop.

As he made his way to the El station that Tuesday evening, bound for home in Flatbush and a well-earned rest, the streets around Ned were strangely dotted with blotches of red—hundreds of them, *thousands* of them. It was the new issue of the *Evening Journal*. THE REAL CLEW TO THE MURDER MYSTERY, the front page proclaimed. "Facsimile in Colors of the Oilcloth Which Will Aid in Getting the $1,000 REWARD."

It was stunning—not the clue, but the *printing*. Hearst had outdone himself again: For the first time ever, color was being used on a breaking news story.

And yet everything else about the competition revealed them as safely clueless. Papers still fixated on Max Weineke, noting that his wife had insurance on him, and that she was a bad mother to boot: "I learned from some neighbors," a *Telegram* reporter huffed, "that Mrs. Weineke had gone out and left her babies alone many times." Rather inconveniently, though, a slender *Times* reporter attempted to try on one of Max's suits and couldn't struggle into it, so it certainly wouldn't fit the body in the morgue.

Ah, the *Times* theorized, that's because the secret of the crime was that two escapees from the state lunatic asylum had turned on each other—that "Mutilation Maniac" Olaf Weir had murdered his fellow maniac William O'Neill. Weir had been a carpenter with a suspicious talent for sawing. It was a fine theory, save for one problem: O'Neill's family didn't recall him having any markings on his chest or fingers.

As for the police, an afternoon's rummaging uptown in butchers' basements and along roadsides had netted but a single find. An abandoned bag—without, alas, a head inside—was scooped up, emptied out for clues, and proclaimed THE DEAD MAN'S VALISE in the newspapers. The *Evening Journal* lavished a dozen illustrations on its mysterious contents: writing slates, clothes, a thimbleful of tacks, a rolled-up newspaper. All terribly interesting, but none of it was Guldensuppe. The closest anyone had gotten was a chance comment to the *Journal* by William Pinkerton, musing that the use of dismemberment hinted at the killer's nationality: "The German seems to regard that as the best means of disposing of a body." If that was the best they could do, then Ned felt reassured; his find on Ninth Avenue belonged to just him and tomorrow's *World*.

THE COMPETITION'S COLOR PAGE was no gimmick at all.

Like Detective Carey, the head of Hearst's Murder Squad thought the oilcloth really *was* the clue to the mystery. "The solution of the whole matter hangs upon the oilcloth," the paper declared. Innumerable New Yorkers might lay claim to the body—and without a head, who was to disprove them?—but only one or two could claim that oilcloth. The body was one of two million New Yorkers, part of a constant and fluid population; the oilcloth was tangible, unequivocal, traceable: two sheets from just 6,000 yards manufactured upstate by A. F. Buchanan & Sons between June and December 1896. George Arnold knew Detective Carey had covered Manhattan and Brooklyn but hadn't made it to Queens or Long Island yet. So *Journal* men had swamped Newspaper Row saloons, hiring unemployed reporters on the spot as day labor, throwing *thirty men* into tracking the oilcloth. Thirty reporters—now armed with three hundred thousand color copies of the oilcloth.

They flooded across the boroughs as Ned Brown took his train home in innocent contentment. And before the sun set, a *Journal* team at the dry-goods store of one Max Riger had found an oilcloth purchase of Diamond B-3220. The name in the customer-accounts book pointed to just one address.

439 Ninth Avenue.

II.

THE
SUSPECTS

6.

THE BAKER IN
HELL'S KITCHEN

BY LATE MORNING Ninth Avenue was already getting hot and dusty, the first grim signs of another heat wave. A wagon from the Astoria Model Bakery threaded through the ice deliveries and brewers' trucks, its horses clip-clopping along the daily rounds to grocers with graham loaves, doughnuts, and raisin bread. The driver was an unshaven and tough-looking fellow, with a flat cap yanked low on his head, sweating as he guided his wagon team around a busy streetcar line and past the drunks staggering out of saloons. He was in the worst stretch of Hell's Kitchen, a couple of blocks from the hideout of gangster Mallet Murphy—so named after his favorite implement for braining victims. When two men clambered aboard at the corner of Fortieth and Ninth, Herman Nack knew it wasn't to buy pumpernickel.

One of them pulled himself up to the driver's seat. "Mr. Nack?" he inquired.

"What do you want?" the driver replied brusquely.

"Captain O'Brien wants to see you."

Nack gave him a violent shove, sending the man sprawling off the running board, then took off down Ninth Avenue. The loaded bakery wagon swerved wildly onto Thirty-Ninth, and then onto Tenth Avenue, loaf trays clattering as the driver looked back and swore. The two men were in hot pursuit on bicycles.

Stop! Stop! they demanded.

The mad trio flew past tenements and ash barrels, past the Salvation Army crowds on Thirty-Sixth Street, and straight toward the Garfield Drug Company on Thirty-Fourth, where regulars were already congregating for sodas to escape the heat. A patrol cop by the drugstore took chase after them, and in another block one of the pursuing cyclists leapt aboard.

You're under . . .

Nack slashed him with his horse whip, and the second cyclist vaulted on, trying to wrest control of the vehicle.

. . . arrest.

The cop came crashing in from the other side of the carriage, and the delivery driver roared and struggled desperately until the three men forced him down onto the ground. There the patrolman made his collar—not of carriage-jackers Oscar Piper and Walter McDevitt, who were Hearst reporters attempting a citizen's arrest—but of delivery driver Herman Nack, on suspicion of murder.

HE TRIED ESCAPING twice during the five-block ride to the precinct house.

"I have absolutely no idea why I have been arrested!" the driver yelled from the back of his own bakery carriage.

Walt and Oscar thought otherwise, and the officer wasn't buying it either. The night before, nine coworkers from the Murray Hill Baths—some brought on the sly by the *World*, the rest sneaked in equally secretively by the *Journal*—had identified the body as William Guldensuppe's. Why, all Nack had to do was look at one of that morning's papers: VICTIM THOUGHT TO BE THEODORE CYKLAM, declared the *World*.

Well, perhaps not at *that* paper.

Ned Brown's breakthrough piece for the *World* had been elbowed aside by Pulitzer's ace reporter Ike White, a man famous for once identifying a suicide bomber by a single charred button off the man's suit. Ike's pet theory this time centered on cabinetmaker Theodore Cyklam; he'd been missing from his job in Long Island since the previous Thursday. Cyklam owned a valise like the one found in the woods the day before, and the contents checked out. He'd owned two writing slates for charting shifts at his factory, and the can of tacks was common to cabinetmakers. And the injured index finger? A banged nail holder, the universal ailment of woodworkers. What was more, Ike tracked down one Diamond B-3220 oilcloth to a Mr. Cunningham, a peddler who also sold the same kind of cord used to tie the parcels. He worked a circuit near Cyklam—and, the *World* noted darkly, lived just a block from where little Susie Martin's body had been found three years earlier.

It was a splendid theory; everything fit perfectly. Except . . . except that it had no *motive*. And no witness. And no crime scene. And no time line to put Cunningham and Cyklam in the exact right place at the right time. Ike's story was beautiful—and useless.

Ned Brown's big scoop had been shoved into just a couple of inches of space at the bottom of page 2 under the deeply unremarkable headline ANOTHER IDENTIFICATION. Another indeed; in fact, there had already been a *Herald* reporter on this exact story. It was not unknown for reporters to tail detectives, for detectives to tail reporters, and for competing reporters and detectives alike to tail one another—anything for a good lead.

But this was different. The *Herald*, it seemed, had boozily stumbled into the Guldensuppe story all on its own. Several Murray Hill Baths coworkers had been drinking after work at a Third Avenue saloon, *also* idly wondering whether Willie Guldensuppe might be the guy in the morgue. They were overheard by reporter Joe Gavan, who dutifully reported the theory to the police, and in that morning's *Herald*: "Suspicion pointed to a jealous husband as the instigator of the crime. It was said that the man was a shampooer in an uptown Turkish bath. . . . This man, it is said, had been living with a baker's wife." But Gavan couldn't identify any of them; police detectives had immediately demanded secrecy to pursue the lead.

The *Journal* happily stole their thunder.

Incredibly, within hours three newspapers had all independently converged on the same victim. But Hearst alone made a personal visit to the Murray Hill Baths, and Hearst alone commanded a Murder

Squad to trail Herman Nack's morning delivery route. The *World* and the *Herald* had bobbled and dropped the lead of the year. Not only had Hearst's *Journal* nabbed the story, they'd nabbed the *man*.

THE DRIVER REMAINED ADAMANT. What did they want with him? He was just an honest immigrant delivering bread.

Nack was booked at the Twentieth Precinct station house and then quickly sent downtown with his *Journal* entourage to a building that was, as one police commissioner mused, "that antique and shabby palace, that sepulcher of reputations, that tomb of character, that morgue of political ambition, that cavern of intrigue and dissimulation—the Police Headquarters on Mulberry Street."

The *Journal* men had to be discreet going inside. The headquarters rose up four stories in a lopsided and grimy old marble hulk from Little Italy's labyrinth of cobbled alleys, tenements, and street vendors, and it was under constant watch by the competition. The *World* kept an apartment across the street, where reporters and photographers played cards to pass the hours between cases. One *World* reporter was always posted to the window to watch for colorfully agitated incoming suspects—or, better still, even more colorfully agitated police commissioners. That always meant a good story. Next door the *Tribune* kept an office that also spied through HQ's windows; so did most of the big papers, for that matter.

Their suspect was quietly hustled inside and through a lobby and dingy anterooms crowded with men in blue uniforms. Mulberry Street was a bewildering place, the nerve center for more than 100,000 arrests a year and uniformed officers issuing curt commands from the telegraph offices in the basement all the way up to the Lost Children Department on the top floors. The exterior of the building bristled with wires to every precinct house, firehouse, and hospital in the city; the interior was a constant flow of sour and sharp-looking hard cases—bunco men, badger schemers, wife stabbers. Shuffling newcomers were startled by the yells of "Mug him!" This, they would discover, meant they were to be photographed for the police files.

But today was different. Nack was not bound for the usual

fine-grinding wheels of mugs and glowering sergeants. He and the *Journal* reporters were led to the private office of Captain Stephen O'Brien, chief of the Detective Bureau.

O'BRIEN SAT PATIENTLY, letting his man sweat. The chief had more than 250 detectives serving under him, but a case this infamous required intervention from the top. O'Brien was the successor to chop-busting Inspector Byrnes himself—as famed for his honesty as Byrnes was for graft, and newly appointed by Teddy Roosevelt just before that reform-minded police commissioner left for a promising political career. The move had been so sudden that the paperwork for his new rank hadn't even gone through yet; he was a captain ordering other captains around, a downright comical situation to old-timers. And so the former inspector's presence lingered; the very walls and floors of the office had been carefully muffled on the old man's orders, the better to cuff prisoners around while interrogating with "the third degree"—a term the old inspector had coined himself. Captain O'Brien was more subtle than his predecessor but no less ruthless. He'd been on the force for more than twenty years, many of them spent breaking up waterfront gangs. A surly bakery driver was no match for what he'd dealt with.

Wasn't he married to Augusta Nack, of 439 Ninth Avenue?

Yes, the driver admitted, he had been—or rather, he still was on paper. They never divorced, but they'd lived apart ever since the last of their three children had died two years ago. She lived on Ninth Avenue, but he lived over in Astoria now—and he hadn't spoken to her since.

Did he know a Mr. William Guldensuppe?

Nack certainly did. Bill had been their boarder, back when he and Gussie lived together, just as things were falling apart, and she ran off with him. The *Journal* reporters wrote quickly and eagerly; a sketch artist busily drew Nack's sullen face and bushy blond eyebrows. The real question now hung pregnant in the air.

Where was he last Friday?

"I went to work at two o'clock on Friday morning," Nack said sullenly. "I got my load of bread and left the bakery at four o'clock. My work was finished by two thirty in the afternoon."

And then?

"I don't know where I went after that."

O'Brien was unimpressed.

"I guess I was drunk," Nack sneered—and his alibi for the next day was not much different.

"I get up at about 1 or 2 and go over the ferry to the bakery. I hitch up and then start to deliver bread. I get through about 4 p.m. Then I go on a spree."

"A spree?"

"Oh, I go to Strack's and I bowl with the boys and drink beer. I get back to my room in Eighty-Second Street about 10 o'clock. I had a good load on when I went to bed Saturday night. Haw! Haw!"

And the next day?

"I was so drunk that I had to stay in bed nearly all of Sunday."

"When did you last see the murdered man?"

"I don't remember exactly, but I guess it was three or four months ago. I saw him on the street at Ninth Avenue and Thirty-Fourth."

Captain O'Brien puzzled over the man before him. A brute, a drunk—yes, yes—a spurned husband with a perfect motive. But Nack didn't give a damn about his ex-wife, and bachelorhood seemed to suit him just fine.

"What the deuce do I care?" The suspect shrugged.

And it checked out: Word came in that not only could Astoria Model Bakery's owner vouch for Nack's working and drinking schedule but that on the fateful Friday night the bakery foreman and Nack had actually led Strack's saloon in belting out an entire set of drinking songs. *He's not it*, O'Brien quietly decided. Herman Nack's story just didn't fit the case.

But someone else's did.

AUGUSTA NACK WAS READY for the next steamer to Hamburg. She'd spent the previous afternoon with four hired men rolling rugs, packing furniture and bedclothes, and washing the curtains for the next tenant in her six-room flat over Werner's Drug Store. This was the last day on her $20 monthly lease; she'd given notice to Mr. Werner two days earlier, and with all the quarreling that had gone on in the place, the short notice didn't seem to trouble him. She'd even had to sleep in the apartment of her upstairs neighbor overnight, as nearly everything short of her portmanteau was packed.

The visit from the detective now sitting on her sofa was most inconveniently timed.

"Do you know William Guldensuppe?" he asked.

Mrs. Nack looked keenly at Detective Krauch, and then at the chair—which should have been readied for storage but was instead seating another detective. Then she shifted her gaze over to the doorway, where yet another detective stood with his back to the door, keeping any movers from coming in and Mrs. Nack from going out.

She hesitated. "Yes, I know him. He is my man. At least he *was* until Friday morning, when he came from the bath and made me give him fifty dollars. Then we quarreled over a woman, and he went away."

Detective Krauch watched her carefully as she spoke. She was not exactly a Gibson girl anymore, but she had dark eyes and the presence to fluster one observer into describing her "pleasing, yet repellant, appearance." Her man, she claimed, had been wooed away by the wanton widow of a grocer. She'd caught them in the parlor mirror the week before when they thought her back was turned. Why, just that very day that grocery hussy had come by to collect more of his worthless possessions.

"I gave her a bit of my mind," she snapped, "and told her she had stolen William from me." So now she was putting her own goods in storage and heading back to Germany and her mother, and—couldn't she just leave now?

No, they informed her, she could not.

For the detectives knew two things that Mrs. Nack didn't. First, that Detective Krauch had been watching her apartment, and neither the mistress nor anyone else had come up her stairs that morning. And now they also knew that she wasn't going to be making it to her Hamburg steamer that day.

SITTING IN CAPTAIN O'BRIEN'S OFFICE at the Mulberry Street headquarters, the midwife looked more like a wronged woman than a suspect in a murder case. Her chair was moved over to the window, suffusing sunlight over the fashionable tulle-trimmed hat that she'd quickly donned when detectives hustled her from the apartment over Werner's Drug Store.

"My name is Augusta Nack," she stated carefully for the record. "I am thirty-eight years of age. I have been living with William Guldensuppe for sixteen months."

She was, by her account and by her accent, a German immigrant. She'd married Herman Nack in 1883 in Lauenburg, on the Elbe. They'd moved here in 1886, whereupon Herman had squandered a series of jobs—in a pottery works, as a bologna-store proprietor, and finally as a grocer—all on account of his drinking. He was gone, their children were dead, and now she worked as a midwife and kept the occasional boarder, one of whom had been Guldensuppe.

What, O'Brien wanted to know, had happened to Guldensuppe after their argument the previous Friday, when he'd demanded money from her?

"The last time he was in the house Friday was about two p.m. He did not come home that night. Saturday morning between six and seven he came into the house." Mrs. Nack continued her account steadily, carefully choosing her words. "'Where did you come from?' I asked. 'None of your business,' he told me. 'Have you got that money?' . . . I then went to the Franklin Savings Bank at Forty-Second and Eighth Avenue and drew fifty dollars. This was about eleven o'clock Saturday morning. From the bank—"

Speak louder.

"*From the bank* I went to a confectionery store on Eighth Avenue and had some ice cream soda water. From there I went to the dry goods store of McPartland & Flaherty, and reached home about noon. I stayed until Willie came in, which was between three and four o'clock. The first thing he did was ask for the money. 'Here it is' I replied, throwing it on the kitchen table. Willie picked it up and went out, and I have not seen him since."

O'Brien and his detectives listened and took notes carefully. Home on Saturday afternoon; that was several hours after the first find in the East River. The implication was that Guldensuppe was still alive. Which, of course, he might be; after all, the body still didn't have a head or legs, and the morgue had filled again that day with people identifying the pieces as belonging to any number of other men.

So, can we talk with him?

Well, she explained, that's just it. Willie hadn't been back home since then. He'd sent notes asking for more money, though. Just yesterday, come to think of it. Probably spending it all on a woman somewhere.

"Monday afternoon I was convinced that Willie would not come back to me, and made up my mind to go to Europe—"

Louder.

"*Go to Europe* and see my mother, who was sick. Willie had asked me to draw my money from the bank and give it to him, saying he would accompany me to Europe, but this I had refused to do."

The last she'd heard from him, she said, was the day before—on Tuesday.

"About ten o'clock," she continued, "a man came to the house with a note from Willie asking for his clothes. I wrote on the back of the note, in German, *No; if you want your clothes come and get them yourself.* About two o'clock in the afternoon two other men, who were dirty and disreputable looking, and spoke English, came and said Willie wanted his clothes. . . . I put them in a brown valise and gave them to the men. That was the last I heard of him."

The room lapsed into an unnerving silence. O'Brien motioned to a woman he had hidden just outside his office door. It was Pauline Riger, dry-goods proprietress of Astoria, and she had been listening all along.

"This is the woman who bought the oilcloth," Riger said as she eyed Mrs. Nack. The proprietress had a hawklike countenance, and her face was sharp and pinched in concentration. "I am sure of her."

"You haven't the slightest doubt?" a *Journal* reporter pressed.

"No! It is the lady. I know it. . . . I remember her well because she was a fine looking lady, and better dressed than most people who come to my store."

Captain O'Brien maintained his disquieting gaze at Mrs. Nack. "This woman has identified you as having purchased oilcloth from her," he said evenly. "Which would seem to connect you to the murder of William Guldensuppe."

"That is impossible," the midwife shot back. Guldensuppe, she maintained, was still alive.

She didn't know where Willie was now, she didn't know this Mrs. Riger, she didn't even know any stores in Astoria. But as she spoke, word passed among the detectives that a new piece of evidence had arrived at headquarters; it had just been fished out of the Brooklyn Navy Yard after it came bumping up against the USS *Vermont*. And as they stood up to leave, Captain O'Brien coolly swung open the door for Mrs. Nack.

There, in the middle of his hallway, were two severed human legs—sawn halfway through, then snapped off.

"*Do you know those?*" he gloated.

They were hideous objects—rotted from five days in the river, and still nestled in an opened bundle of oilcloth. O'Brien waited for Mrs. Nack to faint, to shriek, to break down. But the midwife merely turned to him with a look to freeze the marrow.

"How should I know?" she asked coolly.

7.

THE UNDERTAKER'S NEIGHBOR

WILLIAM RANDOLPH HEARST wheeled into action—literally.

Jumping onto a bicycle, Hearst sped up the fifty blocks from Printer's Square to Mrs. Nack's apartment building at Thirty-Fifth and Ninth. He marched past the peppermint-stick displays into Werner's Drug Store looking for the owner, and he was in luck: Franz Werner's indispensable assistant was vacationing in Larchmont, so Werner himself was in charge.

Didn't Mrs. Augusta Nack's lease run out today?

Indeed it did.

The young millionaire made the landlord an offer on the spot: He'd pay handsomely to rent out Nack's apartment—right now. Werner was delighted, and Hearst quickly conferred with the Wrecking Crew, which had finally caught up with him. Because he was such an upstanding new tenant, the publisher decided to post staff to all the entrances as complimentary doormen. Another group of Hearst reporters was sent out to the neighborhood hotels with instructions to take over every pay-phone booth. By the time Pulitzer's men caught on to the Nack arrest and arrived, they found a cordon of Wreckers around 439 Ninth Avenue that, as it so happened, allowed only the police and fellow Hearst reporters into the building.

It was only the latest indignity for the *World* men. The morning's triumphant Cyklam story was already being dethroned, and the kind of grandstanding that Hearst was doing here was exactly what Joseph Pulitzer would not and *could* not do. His eyesight and his nerves shot, over the past few years Pulitzer had increasingly taken to isolating himself in his Fifth Avenue mansion. All the day's papers were read to him, so that his presence remained constant and ghostly; nitpicking commands were brayed by telephone, telegraph, and memos. And with the *Journal* savagely attacking the *World*'s circulation, the messages from Pulitzer were getting harsher.

"We must smash the interloper," one memo commanded.

Other newspapers were looking endangered as well. The *Times* had briefly gone bust the previous year, and over at the stately *Sun*— the paper whose respectability the *Times* still only aspired to—an even more dire drama was now unfolding. It was being whispered that editor Charles A. Dana, after having helmed the *Sun* for more than fifty years, had stopped coming to his office in the previous week. Only imminent death could be keeping the old man from his desk in the middle of the year's biggest crime story. New York newspapers without Dana were nearly unthinkable—indeed, Pulitzer himself had trained under the *Sun*'s publisher before turning on him.

The irony was not lost on the denizens of Newspaper Row. Pulitzer had made his fortune by attacking his old colleagues at the *Sun* as dinosaurs, and he then went after James Gordon Bennett's equally celebrated *New York Herald* by undercutting its newsstand price. Now Hearst, trained in his college years at the *World*, was doing the exact same thing.

"When I came to New York," one editor heard Pulitzer say with a sigh, "Mr. Bennett reduced the price of his paper and raised his advertising rates—all to my advantage. When Mr. Hearst came to New York I did the same. I wonder why, in view of my experience?"

The *World*'s unmatched circulation of more than 350,000—an audited figure it proudly advertised atop its front pages by proclaiming CIRCULATION BOOKS OPEN TO ALL—was now in danger of being overtaken by the *Journal*. And as the two pulled perilously close in record-setting circulations, the city's other papers were getting shoved further aside. A future owned by yellow journalism was not one most reporters wished to contemplate. Some libraries had already barred the *World* and the *Journal* from their precincts, with one Brooklyn librarian sniffing that they attracted "an undesirable class of readers." Rival papers were quick to agree, and laid into the salivating coverage of what the *World* had dubbed the Missing Head Mystery.

"The sensational journals of the city have now become scientific and publish anatomical charts and figures, solely in the interests of science, and to supply a want which the closing of the dime museums in the Bowery creates," mocked the *New York Commercial Advertiser*. A *Times* reporter bemoaned the sight of the yellow journals co-opting the case from a bumbling police force: "The freak journals, those startling and irrepressible caterers to the gross and savage side of human nature, are having a particularly fine time with their new murder mystery . . . and putting all the celebrated detectives of fact and fiction to shame." Worse still, he admitted, they were good at it: "Yet it seems that in an enlightened age criminals might be brought to justice in a manner less demoralizing to the whole community."

But it was another observation by the *Times*, one being quietly made all down Newspaper Row that day, that contained the real sting for Pulitzer's men.

"The *Journal*, by the way," they wrote, "is generally doing better nowadays. The pupil is taking the master's place now."

It was all too true. Ned and Gus and the rest of Pulitzer's newsmen were barred from the very crime scene that *they'd* been the first to uncover. Locked out of Nack's building while a joyous Hearst scampered about inside, infuriated *World* reporters marched off to the neighborhood pay phones to call the newsroom and complain. But when they picked up the earpieces, nothing happened.

Hearst's men had cut the cords.

WHILE PULITZER'S JOURNALISTS fumed in disbelief outside, the police carefully picked through Augusta Nack's apartment. Detectives Price, Krauch, and O'Donohue, the three who had taken Nack in, spent the next few hours unpacking and rifling through the hastily packed boxes. It wasn't easy. Nearly everything had been readied for storage, and by Nack's own account, she'd been busily brushing and sponging the apartment down before moving out. But was it to get her deposit back, or to wash away evidence?

Amid the crates of crockery and bedclothes there remained intriguing hints of life at 439 Ninth Avenue. Photographic albums immediately went into the evidence pile; so did a large number of letters, including the telegram that had arrived on Sunday, the day after the first bundle was found in the river. It was signed *Guldensuppe*, something that occasioned more than a little skeptical commentary among the detectives.

More policemen spread out onto the other floors of the building. There was, almost unnoticed in the fuss upstairs, a small trapdoor in the ground floor of the stairwell. It led to a basement, where their torches shone upon a motley assortment of barrels and stray wooden planks; against the wall stood a large wooden display cabinet, one of its doors fallen off onto the floor, filled inside with an array of bottles. An eerie spot, perhaps, and yet there was no particular sign of any scuffle or recent activity.

Upstairs was a different matter. Neighbors watched from the adjacent buildings to see a hatch atop Werner's roof thrown aside. Then, climbing a ladder from the top of the stairwell, officers and reporters emerged onto the roof, blinking in the sunlight. Normally the only noteworthy attraction up there was a small Werner's Drug Store billboard, but on this day a more humble object caught their attention: an overturned tub. It was exactly what one might need to boil a body. They grabbed it as evidence, though not before Hearst artists ran up a sketch of the suspicious tin hulk for the paper.

Looking down from the rooftop, they could see an avenue that was turning increasingly chaotic; word had gotten out, and police were holding back more than just competing reporters now. But in the neighboring tenements and stores, resourceful newsmen from the *World*, the *Times*, and the *Herald* were all conducting their own searches—and finding plenty. An undertaker's assistant up the block, George Vockroth, had rented a horse and surrey to Nack on Saturday morning; she'd come by at ten a.m. to arrange it, and then a mustachioed German stopped by at three thirty p.m. to pick it up. It wasn't Guldensuppe, though; this fellow was shorter, moodier, and darker-haired. Mrs. Nack's other neighbors had a notion of who that might be. They murmured that *another* boarder had lived in the apartment for while—a mysterious German barber known only as Fred, though that wasn't thought to be his real name. Mrs. Nack had been more than friendly with *both* of her boarders, until back in February when Guldensuppe had beaten his rival so badly that the barber was left with a black eye. He had moved out after that.

But if "Fred" was back, why was he picking up carriages on behalf of Mrs. Nack? Back inside her kitchen, the detectives had a good guess. One of them reached into the recesses of a cupboard and found that it was not empty. His hands emerged holding a butcher's knife, a broken saw, and then a revolver. And held up to the light, by the hammer of the pistol there appeared to be a dried spray of blood.

WORLD REPORTERS WERE TAUNTED all the way to Mulberry Street by Augusta Nack's visage staring out from below that evening's *Journal* headline:

MURDER MYSTERY SOLVED BY THE JOURNAL
Mrs. Nack, Murderess!

Crowds of commuters swarmed the pint-sized newsboys to grab precious copies of the *Evening Journal*. The paper, ginning up the publicity, ostentatiously sent out beefy guards to tamp down any riots by customers. To complement four full pages breaking open the case and the sensational find of the legs that afternoon, Hearst also whipped up portraits of everyone from Augusta and Herman Nack to William Guldensuppe and the oilcloth seller Mrs. Riger. That night he'd outdone the police, he'd outdone the *World*, and he'd very nearly outdone himself.

"When patting oneself on the back for a recent achievement, it is a reprehensible thing to boast," the tycoon began modestly. "But in an instance like an overwhelming victory over its rivals in the Guldensuppe murder case, the *Journal* comes to the front, sweeps the curtain away from the mass of doubt connected with the case, and exposes almost every detail of the crime." If his neighbors on

Newspaper Row still didn't get the message, Hearst was happy to elucidate: "All this was done, of course, with the main purpose of exhibiting the *Journal*'s superiority over its rivals."

Inside police headquarters, evidence kept piling up. The telegram in Mrs. Nack's apartment, dated from the day after the murder, was signed Guldensuppe, which was what *other* people called him—and not Gieldsensuppe, which was how the victim himself spelled it. Detectives poring over Mrs. Nack's bank account and purse couldn't find missing money she claimed to have given Guldensuppe just a couple of days earlier—it was all still on her, for a jail matron found it hidden in her corset.

The alibi literally didn't add up.

The matron also noticed bruises along Mrs. Nack's upper arm—signs of a struggle, perhaps—and called in a doctor to have a look. From their faded color, they were judged to be about five or six days old. Mrs. Nack couldn't account for those, either. Captain O'Brien made a great show of having her fingernails pared and scraped out—if there was any foreign blood or tissue there from a fight, he assured her, they'd find it.

Sitting in his office later that night with a crowd of reporters, O'Brien was pleased indeed. He had the putative murder weapons laid out on his desk, nearly a dozen identifications on the body in the morgue, and the prime suspect in a jail cell upstairs.

"Do you believe that Mrs. Nack killed the man whose body is now in the morgue?" one reporter asked.

"If that body belonged to William Guldensuppe, I believe she did, or is implicated."

It was a dramatic turnaround in just one day. That morning he'd had only two people in custody in connection with the case, and both were clearly useless. One was a Bowery waiter who'd seen two men carrying awkward packages on a streetcar—as if that were newsworthy in New York City—and the other was a babbling metal-polish peddler who'd led the police on a wild-goose chase after claiming to spot an eyeless and toothless severed head in a vacant lot. The "head" was nothing but an old hat. The peddler was booked purely out of pique, and returned the favor by giving a home address that proved to be a lumberyard.

"He is a freak," O'Brien had to explain earlier that day to an inquiring *World* reporter.

But now the chief of the Detective Bureau had a real suspect. And maybe, he mused contentedly, she was the only one he'd need.

"She has a temper—an awful temper, I believe," O'Brien said, though he hesitated to give specifics on her capacity for vengeance. He didn't need to: A *Herald* writer heard Herman Nack claim that his ex-wife had indeed once threatened to kill him.

"She is strong enough?" a *New York Press* reporter asked.

"Oh my, yes," O'Brien joked. "She has arms larger and more muscular than mine."

BUT MRS. NACK was not without friends.

Late that day, one of the city's top defense attorneys, Emanuel Friend, had marched into the Mulberry Street HQ. Manny was fond of asking awkward questions, and this case had plenty. Where was the victim's head, and how could they make a positive identification without it? Since none of Mrs. Nack's neighbors had heard or seen any struggle at all the week before, just where was the scene of this so-called crime? And what was her motive, exactly? Why hadn't they found this "Fred," who *did* have a motive?

In fact, it wasn't quite clear what *Manny's* motive was. Was he even Mrs. Nack's counsel, and who had hired him? He wouldn't say, but Murder Squad writers harbored their own suspicions about who might want to undermine the *Journal*'s case against their prime suspect. Badly burned by their bet on the Cyklam theory, the *World* editors were doubling down late that night with the next morning's headline:

THE MURDER MYSTERY IS A MYSTERY STILL
Not Sure of Identification
Police Losing Faith

"The detectives of the Central Office have very little faith in the case against Mrs. Nack," the paper insisted. The *World* found a few men who knew Guldensuppe—including drugstore owner Franz Werner, now profiting nicely by both papers—who were willing to testify that the body was not his. Alas, only one of them had actually been to the morgue to see it. A more serious challenge came from a woman identifying the headless body as belonging to *her* man, a soldier named Alpheus Clark, whom, she claimed, was killed "by a Spaniard named Julian." She seemed utterly certain of this, until a few probing questions were asked. Mrs. Clark, it turned out, had been caught up in a divorce with her now-missing husband and was trying very hard indeed to have him declared dead.

The coroner was not impressed by her story.

While the *World* kept rowing in circles, Hearst had more men shuttled over into the morgue to make positive identifications on the body, and blitzed the Murray Hill Baths with *Journal* reporters. A picture was beginning to emerge of Guldensuppe and his fate. He was a ladies' man, his boss said—"always mixed up in several affairs" with women, so much that it was a running joke that he'd get into trouble someday. But the man who really knew Willie's secrets—his best friend at work—was his fellow masseur, Frank Gartner. And when the *Journal* reporters sat down with Frank, a whole new story began to unfold.

THEY WORKED LONG HOURS there in the baths, nearly naked, sweating, feet calloused from the heated marble floors. And between jobs, they'd get to talking—especially about women and money. The previous Wednesday night, Frank said, Guldensuppe had a name on the tip of his tongue, and asked him if he'd ever heard of a Long Island town that sounded something like *Woods*.

"Well, there are three that I know of," Frank offered. "Woodbury, Woodhaven, and Woodside. Do you recognize any of those names?"

Guldensuppe wasn't sure, but he'd find out. On Thursday night, he told Frank just what *Woods* was about.

"I think," he confided, "that I am going to make something good out of that Long Island matter. A woman whom my wife performed an operation on about two years ago and for which she gave my wife four hundred dollars cash came to our house again this afternoon and told my wife that she would need her services again. She is a pretty little woman, twenty-two or twenty-three years old, and she's married to an old man."

Frank didn't need to read between the lines much. Everybody knew the illicit service that some midwives quietly provided: abortion. And in an old-fashioned May-December marriage, it wasn't hard to guess why the young wife needed one.

"This *voman* owns a small house on Long Island," Willie continued in his accented English, warming to the subject. "Her husband did not know that she owned the house, and I think she used it as a rendezvous. She told my wife that she had no ready money, but that she would sell her this house in Woodside for $1,500 cash. The remainder would, of course, be my wife's fee."

It was the deal of a lifetime, and Willie didn't have to do anything but go and look at the house with his wife.

"How do you get out there?" he asked Frank. "I think my wife went there this afternoon. . . . If she likes it, why, I'll go out there tomorrow afternoon."

"I know a little about Woodside," Frank offered. "If your wife does not want to go with you Friday afternoon, I'll go over with you Saturday morning as soon as I get through here, and we'll see if the place is worth $1,500."

But in his mind, Willie was already buying the house. "This woman who owns the house is in a tight fix," he theorized. "I am only going to offer her *vun*-thousand dollars for the place. I'm tired of working here."

And with that, there was a call on the phone for him.

"Is that you, Gussie?" he answered. After a happy pause, Willie came back over to Frank, beaming. "It's all right," he said. "She was there today with a friend of hers, and says the house is well worth the money. I will take tomorrow night off and go there with her."

The masseur worked the rest of the night quietly, happily contemplating the new home awaiting him. When he finished his shift, he turned to Frank and the other masseurs on his way out: *"Vell, good-bye, gentlemens."*

And that, Frank said, was the last anyone ever heard from William Guldensuppe.

8.

THE WIDOW'S FRIEND

WHEN CAPTAIN O'BRIEN MADE IT to the office on Thursday, July 1, he found that he was a captain no more. Word had come down from the top: He'd finally been promoted to acting inspector.

It was a strange morning, amid all the backslaps. O'Brien wasn't born to the force like some men were; he'd spent his first few years out in the world as, of all things, a composer of novelty tunes. It was a local pol who talked him into trying for the police force. A life of patiently arranging notes and an easy familiarity with saloons had given him, oddly enough, just the right mindset for a good detective.

This morning he was orchestrating for an audience of one; on the table and chairs in O'Brien's office lay a revolver, a saw, a broken knife, and a washing boiler dismantled from a Ninth Avenue rooftop. Before these implements, sweating and tight-lipped in the rising heat, sat Augusta Nack. O'Brien had arranged the tools into an accusatory choir, facing her from whichever way she looked, while he questioned her about the events of Friday, June 25.

But Nack still wasn't budging.

"She is," marveled a *Brooklyn Eagle* reporter, "the most cold blooded woman in the world."

Her nerve was a thing of wonder, so much so that alienists wandered in and out of O'Brien's office to scrutinize Nack for telltale facial characteristics of criminal degeneracy. Doctors, after all, now looked for the devolution of mankind; they had neatly flipped Darwinism on its head, and then measured that head with craniometer calipers. They sought the inherited stigmata of criminal tendencies, and *Evening Journal* readers were treated to close-ups of Mrs. Nack's prominent chin, her ears, and her "dull and shifty eye."

Another doctor, though, observed the interrogations more quietly.

"I made an especial study of her facial and bodily peculiarities," Dr. Edward Spitzka told a *Herald* reporter. He was the city's top alienist, famed for discovering "masturbatic insanity" and for presiding over the electric chair's rather messy debut. And while Dr. Spitzka didn't know whether Mrs. Nack was guilty, he knew she had a guilty *look*. "A very coarse-minded animal creature," he pronounced. "Brutal, frozen and stolid, extremely selfish, with small mentality, yet with a certain amount of low cunning."

He listed the damning evidence: "Her ears are her most animal features. The lobules are of the short, stumpy, fleshy variety so often seen in state prisons and penitentiaries. . . . A pyramidal neck. . . . Her hands are remarkable for their breadth. In the old times an examiner in obstetrics would never have passed a medical student as being fit for that branch of medicine if the measurement of the hand at the finger line extended beyond three inches."

She had masculine hands, in other words—and bad ones at that.

"Did you know," a reporter ventured, "that she has never reported a live birth to the Bureau of Vital Statistics?"

Spitzka knew perfectly well what the reporter meant. "She might have been in the habit of disposing of the bodies of children stillborn or prematurely born in exactly the way in which she disposed of Guldensuppe's body," he agreed. Her likely sideline in abortions, he surmised, was why O'Brien's gambits were doomed. "I cannot understand how detectives could expect such a clumsy trick to succeed as showing the severed legs, the suspected tools and the wash boiler to a woman whose occupation has long deadened her."

But Inspector O'Brien was undeterred. He had detectives in hot pursuit of the *Journal* reporters headed for Woodside, and he still had one more surprise to spring on the midwife. A dignified gentleman in dark clothing was ushered in to the office, his bearing speaking of his profession; he was Mr. Streuning, the undertaker Mrs. Nack hired her surrey from. He'd identified her from a lineup and could point officers to the very carriage and horse that she'd used.

I did not hire a surrey, the lady insisted quietly.

Did she not even know who this gentleman was?

Not at all.

O'Brien was flabbergasted.

"She is a decided liar," he informed reporters afterward. She dissembled at every opportunity. Why, she'd returned the carriage the previous Saturday night with the complaint that the horse was balky—even though the animal was exhausted and sweating and the carriage muddy from a long run. And now she claimed that she'd never met the undertaker in her entire life? This very undertaker, the inspector explained, was a longtime neighbor and acquaintance of the Nacks, all the way back to when Herman and Augusta had lost their own five-year-old daughter to diphtheria. And he was not just any old acquaintance, either.

"Streuning buried a child of hers," he said incredulously.

HEADQUARTERS WAS the usual mess of cases the rest of the day: a servant girl who let burglars into a bandleader's house on Seventh Street, a would-be parachute inventor found dangling comically from a bridge arch, a severed black-stockinged leg netted from the East River. And there were the suicides—the druggist who hanged himself from a hotel transom, the lovelorn young man in Harlem who turned on the gas—there were always those.

The inspector paced his office and stayed focused on his subject.

"You will remember," he mused aloud to colleagues, "Mrs. Nack told me she had seen Guldensuppe three or four times on Friday, and that the last time he called to see her was on Saturday afternoon between three and four o'clock. That was the time she said she gave the man fifty dollars."

Before him in his office was a prim, dark-haired woman in her thirties and her angelic blond ten-year-old daughter, Amelia. And in these two witnesses, O'Brien saw the midwife's doom.

"My name," the mother began, "is Sophie Miller. I have known

Mr. and Mrs. Nack for about five years. I worked for the Nacks in their delicatessen store on Tenth Avenue."

After the Nacks' business and marriage both went under, Miller became a cook at Buck's Hotel but stayed close to Gussie. She knew Willie Guldensuppe well, and even knew about the fight he'd had with their boarder "Fred" back in February. The boarder was a silent and brooding sort, she said—a barber, apparently—and had been thrown out by Willie months ago.

"The last time I saw Willie was on Thursday," she recalled. "He came into Buck's and went upstairs with Mrs. Nack . . . . On Saturday night I went shopping in Eighth Avenue and took Amelia with me. We stopped at Mrs. Nack's house between 9 and 9:30 p.m. and rang her bell, but got no answer. A lady standing at the door of the house next door said . . . 'I don't think you will find her home. She has been out all day. I saw her shade down and her windows shut.'"

When she ran into Gussie later that evening at a grocer's down the street, Guldensuppe was nowhere to be seen.

"She said, 'Willie has not been home since Friday.' I said, 'What is the matter? Have you quarreled?' She said, 'No.' Between 1 and 2 p.m. on Sunday Mrs. Nack came to Buck's . . . . We were all at dinner when she came in and Mr. Buck invited her to join us. We all asked her did she hear anything from Willie. She said: 'No, not since Friday.'"

O'Brien was triumphant; he'd caught Nack in another lie. Better still, Sophie Miller knew the real name of the mysterious boarder called Fred. A lurking *Journal* reporter caught it, a scoop so close to press time that Hearst's print room hastily jammed the two crucial words into the one remaining opening in the layout—the front-page headline:

MARTIN THORN

THERE WAS NOBODY that night who needed a shave less than O'Brien's old partner, Detective James McCauley. The new inspector's right-hand man had spent the afternoon working barbershops for leads on Thorn, and barbers being the kind of fellows they were, the best way to really get them to talk was over a shave. By the time he reached Vogel's Barbershop on Forty-Seventh and Sixth, Mac had taken so many straight-edge shaves around Midtown that his face was raw with razor burn.

He took a deep breath and got into the barber's chair once again.

Vogel's was the sort of men's sanctuary one expected in a good Manhattan barbershop. It was redolent of cigars and bay rum, with leather-covered barber's chairs and a wall of long mirrors. The counter before them was well stocked with the myriad tools of the trade: Diamondine straight razors, Sanasack strops, tubes of Benitz's Waxine, bottles of Rezo Hair Tonic, jars of sweet-clover pomade, and heliotrope brilliantine. Nearby a shelf held dozens of enameled shaving mugs, elaborately emblazoned with customers' names and insignias of their professions: firefighters, bartenders, butchers. There were ruffled copies of the daily papers and the inevitable barbershop bible—the illustrated weekly *Police Gazette*—always full to bursting with boxing, murder, and cat-fighting dance-hall girls.

Listen, did he know of a barber by the name of Thorn?

Martin Thorn? Sure, Vogel knew him. He'd worked here, though he'd quit on the spot last week, and hadn't been seen in the shop since.

You don't say?

McCauley was in luck, though: Thorn's coworker Constantine Keehn was in that day. Keehn was a handsome, slicked-down Berliner, his mustache curled up like ram's horns in the German style— not unlike Thorn himself, actually. Keehn knew Thorn better than anyone else at the shop did. But, he mused as he slid a cold steel straight razor across the detective's face, their personalities could not have been more different.

And Keehn already knew why the detective was there.

"As soon as I saw in the papers that Nack had been arrested," he said, "I thought right away of Thorn."

Why?

"Martin was very *friendly* with Mrs. Nack," Keehn explained as he lathered. Thorn had been a brooding sort, but he was a first-rate barber, an even better pinochle player, and an absolute cad with women.

I always told him it would get him into trouble, another barber piped in.

"Thorn was a queer man," Keehn agreed. "He told me that for years he had been in the habit of hiring furnished rooms from women. If he learned that his landlady had money, he would make advances to her. If she repulsed him he would move away from her house and try someone else."

He had a particular fondness, Keehn said, for widows. He even used to advertise in German-language newspapers like the *Morgen Journal* for them. McCauley made a note of that. Mrs. Nack had taken to listing herself in the city directory with the notation *Widow*—a claim that would have been news to Herman Nack—and so she must have looked perfect to Thorn. There was just one thing in his way: her boyfriend.

"He used to laugh at Guldensuppe," Keehn recalled, "because for months Guldensuppe did not suspect his relations with Mrs. Nack." That changed when Thorn's suspenders turned up in her bedroom. Soon he was out of the house, and exiled to an apartment on Twenty-First and Third Avenue.

So why hadn't Nack just ordered Guldensuppe out instead?

"She was tired of him." The barber shrugged. "But he said the woman was afraid of the big fellow—that he was a powerful man, and that he threatened to kill both of them." They'd kept their trysts going until Guldensuppe caught on. "While they were drinking in there Guldensuppe rushed in and began to punch Thorn. Thorn had been expecting something like this for a long time, he said, so he always carried a revolver. He drew the revolver and tried to shoot Guldensuppe . . . "

Scrape—scrape—scrape.

"'The damned pistol wouldn't go off,' Thorn said to me. 'I pulled and pulled and it wouldn't work. The rubber took it away and pounded me with it. That's how he blackened my eyes and smashed my nose. Then he threw me out. That taught me a lesson. No pistol for me after this. I'm going to get a dagger or a knife. I'll catch him some time when he isn't expecting me, and then I'll fix him.'"

It was an angry brag one might laugh off, except that Thorn wasn't the sort of fellow to laugh at, and he wasn't joking.

"He asked me if I knew where he could get a stiletto. I told him my brother-in-law, a police captain in Berlin, gave me one years ago. He wanted me to sell it to him. . . . For about three days he was at me all the time. One day he went downtown, however—I think it was in the Bowery—and bought a stiletto like mine. The stiletto had a yellow handle, and a yellow leather case."

A few months passed, but Thorn just couldn't let the idea go.

"Barbering is not my regular business," Keehn admitted. "I was a dentist in the old country. Thorn knew that, and he was always asking me about different poisons. He wanted to know how to give chloroform. I told him there were different ways. You could put it in a sponge, saturate a towel with it and put it up to the nose."

He'd gotten uncomfortable, Keehn said, when Thorn started asking about other poisons and then started showing up to work with little bottles in his vest. But how could Thorn think that he had any chance with Gussie, especially after that beating?

"Why, the man was always dreaming." The barber laughed. He'd even talked of marrying her. "Thorn had Mondays off. He used to talk about trips he made out to Long Island with Mrs. Nack, looking for a house where she could set up a baby farm and he would run a barber shop."

Really?

Mac kept a poker face. The *Journal* and the Detective Bureau had been sitting tight on Frank Gartner's story about a Woodside house—a lead that hadn't made it yet into any of the newspapers.

"He said," Keehn added innocently, "she had one thousand dollars in the bank and she would furnish the money for the whole business."

"He wanted to be a boss for himself," another barber agreed.

Thorn certainly had the ability to run a shop, the barbers concurred, if he just put his mind and a bit of money to it. But Detective McCauley had heard enough. He walked out into the summer evening, his face prickling painfully as theater-bound crowds swirled around him, emptying into and out of the multitude of tenements and houses of the teeming city. The detectives still hadn't found anything over in Woodside, but all the signs pointed to someplace across the river.

Thorn had fixed his rival, all right—but where?

9

THE DISAPPEARING
SHOEMAKER

THE FARMER FROM WOODSIDE was insistent: Weren't the police interested in the extraordinary coincidence that he'd discovered in connection with their murder case?

"I noticed last Saturday morning," he explained earnestly, "that several of my ducks were sick."

Yes, of course he had.

The case was becoming a headache. Not only was it attracting curiosity seekers, but the newspapers were taking their circulation fight into the case itself. *Journal* and *World* reporters were tampering with witnesses, trampling crime scenes, and making wild accusations. The headline of yesterday's *World* bellowed, THE IDENTIFICATION UPSET—but the only dissenting identifier was unnamed and "refused to talk any further," the *World* claimed, "after being threatened by a *Journal* reporter." *World* reporters in turn humiliated Mrs. Riger, attacking her over accepting $30 in Hearst blood money, and rattling the Astoria storekeeper with a surprise lineup to identify a confederate who had just shopped there.

THE WORLD DESPERATE, the *Journal* shot back in a headline. "If Guldensuppe is dead, the *World* feels that it is going to be dead, too." One of Nack's neighbors signed an affidavit alleging overtures from the *World* for testimony favoring Mrs. Nack; outraged *Journal* reporters claimed that Pulitzer had a $10,000 slush fund dedicated to perverting the case. But it was becoming apparent along Newspaper Row that while Pulitzer and his editors were dictating hostile headlines, their crime reporters had few doubts left about the murder. The denials from up top were becoming such an embarrassment that the *Journal* had taken to simply reproducing its rival's front page with the devastating caption STILL TWENTY FOUR HOURS BEHIND THE NEWS.

On this morning, July 3, just as they were gearing up for a blowout Sunday holiday that would see half the city tipsy and shooting off fireworks, the police were having to field questions about the latest stunt by the papers. After *World* editors wisely decided on a new strategy, a pair of their reporters hired Mrs. Nack's surrey and horse, promptly dubbed the Death Carriage, and galloped around asking if anyone recognized it. An impressionable young lady in Long Island said she did, and a nearby campsite offered up an old handkerchief and a few scraps of paper. This, the paper loudly announced on the front page, was surely where Guldensuppe's clothes had been burnt. It then helpfully directed the police to a "murder den," largely on the evidence of it being a frightful-looking old house.

And now this fellow wanted to talk about ducks. His name was Henry Wahle, and he lived in Woodside over by Second and Anderson. There was a two-hundred-foot-long field between his place and the next house, and his ducks had crossed it—toward Mrs. De-Beuchelare's dairy, you see, but not all the way down to the next street, where Mr. Jacobs kept that greenhouse, and . . .

Yes, they said. *Go on.*

"They had eaten something that they could not keep down," he explained with alarm. And it got worse. "I knew they had been swimming and paddling about in the open drain in Second Street, across the way. I went over to investigate . . . right at the end of the drainpipe that comes from the house on Number 346, Second Street."

The cottage, Wahle said, was a vacant one. That's why it was so strange to see that ditch full on a hot summer day. "Water was running out of the drain-pipe as if it had been left turned on in the empty house," he mused aloud.

Was that so? Officers took notice; maybe there was something to this. But Wahle still wanted to talk about his ducks.

Yes, the ducks. When they came out of that ditch, something had been running off their feathers—perhaps the very thing that had made them sick. A substance that was pooling into the mud by that drainpipe.

"Red stuff," the lamplighter confided.

FOUR MANHATTAN DETECTIVES marched off the New York & Queens County trolley at eleven that morning, accompanied by a sharp-eyed *World* reporter who'd at last gotten a jump on the Hearst men. It was hard for Woodside residents not to notice the group. They were out of their neighborhood, out of their jurisdiction, and out of the city altogether.

Detective Price surveyed the scene before him. He'd come from searching Mrs. Nack's place in Hell's Kitchen to . . . this?

Woodside was one of the sleepiest villages within reach of the city, a precinct of lonesome farmhouses and overgrown marshy lots, a place where churches were still the tallest buildings. A general store by the trolley stop sold hay and groceries, while up the street the local Greenpoint Avenue Hall offered wholesome rube entertainments like bowling and a shooting gallery. The city detectives swatted away insects as they strolled over to the village center, where the fire chief and a coroner were convenient neighbors. The local police captain was summoned as well—they were now in Queens County, after all, in his jurisdiction.

Did they know the way to 346 Second Street?

Sure, the detectives were told. *We'll walk you over there.*

Second Street held little more than a placid dairy and a flower nursery that supplied Broadway swells across the river with carnations for their lapels. Just up the street stood three cheap new wood-frame houses—two stories apiece, flat-roofed boxes with nearly windowless, unadorned sides. The eight men walking up to them hadn't gone unnoticed; a scowling woman was waiting in the nearest one, at number 344.

"Mrs. Hafftner," she introduced herself.

She was the caretaker for these three houses. The owners, the

Bualas, ran a wine shop over in the city. And yes, she said, someone had been in 346 recently—a couple from the city who had wanted to rent it—a Mr. and Mrs. Frank Braun. She'd warned them that it was a little desolate out here.

"On the contrary," Mrs. Braun had assured her, "I like to be where it is quiet."

The *World* reporter thrust a photo forward. *Is this her?*

Mrs. Hafftner examined the unlabeled photo of Augusta Nack. Yes, she said, that was the very image of Mrs. Braun.

The crew eyed the block around them. It was a good place to get in and out of quickly, if you were coming from the city. It *looked* rural, but near one end of the block was the stop for the NY & Queens County trolley line. A couple of blocks in the other direction was Jackson Avenue, which was a straight shot down to the East River ferries.

The couple had signed a year lease and paid the first month's rent, Mrs. Hafftner said, but after coming to their new house a few times, they'd disappeared.

"They promised me they were to move in yesterday or today," the caretaker fretted. "But I haven't seen them."

She unlocked the door of 346, and the detectives strode into the empty building, their footsteps echoing. It was a dreary little house, coated in cheap brown paint; its seven rooms sat vacant, the gloom unrelieved by the rays of light filtering in through the shutters. Someone *had* been here, it seemed, because crammed in among the ashes of a stove there lay the remains of a man's shoe. Just the steel shank was left, the leather having been consumed into fine ash. Someone had stoked the fire as hot as they could get it. Interesting. But that could have been the previous tenants, who'd left a couple of months before.

Detectives fanned out into the empty bedrooms upstairs, and one of the doors along the southeast side creaked open into a bathroom. There was nothing in the eight-by-ten room but a large zinc bathtub. It was spotless. Yet the pathologist, Frank Ferguson, had claimed there was some scalding on the body. Was this where it had happened?

The bathroom didn't look quite right, somehow. It was clean—*too* clean, for a place that had been vacant for nearly two months. There was no dust on the floor. Kneeling down, the detectives found a splatter of dark drips on the planking between the bath and the wall, and some hard-scrubbed sections of flooring around them; something had soaked into the wood, impervious to any effort at cleaning. They procured a carpenter's plane and, as the property's caretaker waited helplessly, shaved samples off the floor. Inspector's orders: that stuff was going to NYU's Loomis Laboratory for analysis. Another detective followed the drain line to the ditch outside and scooped up a bucket of the mud around the mouth of the drainpipe; it, too, would go the lab for testing.

As more men dug out the cellar and probed the cesspool in vain for Guldensuppe's head, a crowd gathered outside. Word had gotten out around the block and then back on Newspaper Row as well. Reporters were pouring over on the East River ferries, hungrily circling the local residents.

Why, yes, neighbors said, they *had* heard a strange cry last Friday. Something like—*"Help! Help! Murder!"* One of them had even poked his head outside to investigate. But he hadn't heard anything more, and, well, you hear all sorts of crazy things from neighbors' homes. But a trio of local busybodies—Mrs. Buttinger, Mrs. Ruppert, and Mrs. Nunnheimer—had indeed noticed when Mrs. Braun and another fellow stopped by here a week earlier.

"I clean my windows every Friday afternoon," recalled Mrs. Nunnheimer, "and somewheres about three o'clock, I noticed while at this work the trolley car stop at our corner. I turned my head and saw a nicely dressed man get off. He held his hand out and received a small yellow hand bag from the lady who sat next to him, and then he gave her his hand and helped her down. What fixes it in my mind is that he was so polite and nice about it.

"In *fact*," she added chidingly to her husband, "I said to my *husband* that night when he came home that I was jealous of such niceness and that I wished he had such *elegant* ways."

Another neighbor said she'd seen a second dapper gentleman enter the house the previous Friday, well before the couple arrived.

So *two* men had gone in there. Now that she thought of it, that seemed like a strange thing.

She'd only seen one come out.

WORLD WIDE HUNT FOR MARTIN THORN, the *Evening Journal* declared from the sidewalks as the detectives made their way back to the city. While they were gone, Inspector O'Brien had cabled Washington and asked the State Department to put out an alert for Thorn in all U.S. and foreign ports. Newspaper readers worldwide had been deputized into the dragnet:

WANTED—For the murder of William Guldensuppe, Martin Thorn, whose right name is Martin Torzewski. Born in Posen, Germany; thirty-three to thirty-four years old; about 5 foot eight inches in height, weighs about 155 pounds, has blue-gray eyes, very dark hair, red cheeks, very light-brown moustache, thick, and curled at the ends; slightly stooped shoulders, small scar on the forehead, and red blotches around the lower part of the neck. He is a barber by trade. Speaks with a slight German accent. Wore, when last seen, a dark-blue suit of clothing, a dark-brown derby hat, and russet shoes; is an expert pinochle player and a first-class barber.

Suspicious that Thorn had already fled the country, the inspector had his eye on two ships in particular.

"Cable dispatches have been sent to Europe this afternoon," he explained, "for authorities to intercept the arrival of passengers on the steamers *City of Paris* at Southampton, and the *Majestic* at Liverpool, in order to cause the arrest of Martin Thorn, if by any chance he should have sailed."

But the detectives had a different destination that night: the hulking five-story building at 410 East Twenty-Sixth Street, where NYU maintained its newly built Loomis Laboratory. True, most police only resorted to a place like this when the third degree failed; tweezers were for the evidence that a nightstick couldn't reach. But the forensics lab represented the future. The first guide to preserving crime-scene evidence had been issued in Austria just a few years earlier, and the first book on cadaver fauna—the hatching of maggots and other bugs on a body—was issued not long afterward in Paris. New spectroscopes could find arsenic in blood, and high-powered optics could match the microscopic shells on a dead man's muddy boot with a specific ditch. A careful practitioner might even extract the wadding from a gunshot wound—that is, the paper used in a cartridge to tamp down the powder—for if some old incriminating scrap had been reused to pack a homemade cartridge, he could read the writing on it.

For reporters and cops alike, the Loomis Lab was an intoxicating blend of theoretical science and visceral practice. It was the kind of place that, crammed with the latest instruments of pathology and detection, also featured asphalt floors for easy hosing down after especially bloody cases. And for the expert on those cases, the detectives knew just where to take their evidence: the second-floor office of Dr. Rudolph Witthaus, professor of chemistry and toxicology.

With his round spectacles and an immense white mustache that drooped like tusks, he embodied one *World* reporter's judgment of him: "Witthaus looks like a sea-lion." But the man was a real-life Sherlock Holmes, and a Sorbonne scholar. Witthaus could discourse on book collecting while detecting cyanide hidden in some mail-order patent-medicine stomach salts, or a fatal dose of arsenic and antimony in the moldering exhumed remains of a dead husband. The author of the standard text *Medical Jurisprudence*, Witthaus had quite literally written the book on science and crime. And yet he owed much to his fictional counterpart; it was the immense popularity over the previous decade of Holmes and Watson, after all, that had nudged the public into expecting some scientific acumen in modern policing.

A trip to Witthaus was as good as a new Conan Doyle story, though, and detectives already knew his work well. Long before tracking down the oilcloth used to bundle Guldensuppe, Detective Carey had collared a physician suspected of poisoning his wealthy wife to feed his brothel-and-gambling habit. It was Professor Witthaus who'd gotten the goods on that one. He'd deduced that the wily doctor had poisoned his wife with morphine, and then applied atropine to her eyes to cover up the telltale dilation of her pupils.

But the professor was also, well . . . peculiar.

An ardent art and book collector, he was well known for possessing such gems as the original handwritten manuscript of Robert Louis Stevenson's *Strange Case of Dr. Jekyll and Mr. Hyde.* The story might well have been his own. Witthaus, it was whispered, could be a bit of a Mr. Hyde himself. Even as the detectives delivered their Woodside samples to the professor, Witthaus was battling an allegation of attempted murder. His wife was demanding a divorce because, she claimed, he'd been poisoning her. A bottle of malaria medicine he'd prepared for her was the damning proof: Under analysis, it had been found to contain a massively toxic concentration of quinine—a poison, as it happened, on which Professor Witthaus was the world's greatest authority.

But he was the best expert in the art of murder they had, even if he was a little *too* expert. They'd already brought him some suspected murder weapons the day before, and for starters, he could tell them that O'Brien had been going at it all wrong with his interrogations.

This is not blood.

The pistol, saw, and knife found at Mrs. Nack's flat on Ninth Avenue? There wasn't a speck of blood on them, he determined. The saw and knife weren't even the right fit for the cuts made on the body. It was no wonder that she had been so unimpressed when O'Brien made her sit in a room with the "evidence": He'd laid out the wrong weapons. He might as well have tried to frighten her with tea cozies.

The scrapings taken from under Mrs. Nack's fingernails might prove useful, though; that strategy had secured a conviction six years earlier in the East River Hotel disembowelment of Carrie Brown, a Bard-quoting prostitute nicknamed "Shakespeare." The case remained controversial. Inspector Byrnes had publicly dared Jack the Ripper to set foot in his precincts, and some suspected that the fellow had crossed the Atlantic to take up his challenge. With his career on the line, Byrnes roped in a hapless Algerian sailor nicknamed "Frenchy" and had his scrapings and clothing analyzed.

They revealed the telltale viscera of dismemberment—bile from the small intestine, tyrosol from the liver—plus roundworm eggs, blood, and stomach matter resembling the corned beef and cabbage that the victim had eaten earlier in a hotel bar. Frenchy was sent to Sing Sing for life, though more than a few observers had been left unconvinced by Byrnes's ulterior motives in using this strange new form of evidence. This time, though, there was less doubt; nobody was blaming the new inspector for this murder, and along with the mud and wood shavings from the Woodside house, such evidence might look convincing indeed.

Still, they'd have to wait for results, and the warm summer air and firecrackers outside hinted at why: An entire city was about to knock off work for July 4.

HOW COULD THEY BE ASKING these questions at a time like *this*?

Charles Buala was bustling around his wine shop on West Twenty-Sixth Street; it was where Parisian expatriates could still find an old-fashioned *cabaret*, the kind of place with sawdust floors and rickety tables, where you could split a bottle of cheap Spanish red with a neighbor and play dominoes into the hot summer evenings. But this was a Saturday, the busiest night of the week, and the eve of one of the busiest holidays of the year. New Yorkers stocking up for the next day's picnics and parades streamed in for bottles of champagne, sauterne, and sweet muscat; some were already well sauced.

Charles Buala didn't have time to talk, not about their new tenants or anything else. Mrs. Buala, though, was a kinder sort; her beauty and ready smile were not the least of the store's charms for its habitués.

"I do not remember these people very well. I thought they were German Hebrews," she said in her French accent. That's why the German caretaker, Mrs. Hafftner, had done so much of the talking with them. "The woman was fleshy, but I cannot remember more. If she was light or dark I do not know."

Talking in English was still a bit difficult for Mrs. Buala. Her thirteen-year-old niece was eager to help.

"Auntie says she couldn't even tell how the woman was dressed," the niece piped in.

"The woman was about thirty-five or thirty-six. The man the same. He was *good*-looking." Mrs. Buala smiled. "With a light-colored moustache, but I do not remember if it was straight or curly. He was a good-looking man, though—I remember that."

The trolley bells rang from the lines at either end of the block, and more customers piled in. Mr. Braun, she remembered, said he was a shoemaker in the next town over, on Jackson Avenue.

"They wanted a house to live in. The rent is fifteen dollars a month. They said they would take it. . . . They were nice looking people, and I thought it was all right. They said they might move in last Tuesday, if not, then Thursday."

She was still puzzled by the whole affair. "It is very strange," she added. "They said they would move in. Why did they not?"

But Mr. Buala had a pretty good idea why. Breaking away from his rush of shoppers, he dug out a letter and passed it over to the detectives. He'd received it that morning:

Mr. Buala:
On account of sickness in my family I will not move into the house before another week or ten days.

Respectfully,
F. BRAUN

The handwriting was immediately recognizable to the detectives—it was the same as in the "Fred" letters to Mrs. Nack—the very ones they now knew to be Thorn's. And this one from "Frank Braun"? It had been postmarked only yesterday at the West Thirty-Second Street post office, six blocks from where they now stood.

Martin Thorn was still in the city.

10.

THE SILENT CUSTOMER

THE FOURTH OF JULY wasn't much of a holiday for Detective J. J. O'Connell. While his colleagues across the river were taking the Sunday off, going to church, or settling in for parade duty and fireworks accidents, he and his partner, Detective Boyle, were arriving in Queens for another search of the crime scene. Newsboys hawked thick Sunday editions the whole way over.

MURDER TRACED IN DUCK TRACKS, roared the *Herald*.

THE HOUSE OF DEATH! declared the *World*.

HAIR PULLING MATCH! added the *Press*. Well, some local news staples didn't change much.

Woodside had hung out its bunting for the holiday. A blazing sun rose over the village's preparations, promising a fine day in root beer and cider sales for the local merchants. But not, it seemed, on account of the Independence Day parade. Something strange was happening in the sleepy neighborhood of Woodside. It began slowly as the detectives walked up Second Avenue—a smirking urchin here, a girl screaming with hilarity there—and slowly gathered force. They came by ferries; they came by trolleys; they came up the roads with their flat caps and angelic curls, with penknives and cheap lockets, dusty rock candy in their pockets and blades of grass between their teeth.

The streets were filling with children.

Boys and girls, some brandishing their flags, thrashed around behind the house—the Den of Murder, the press called it—and into a field of cattails where cows grazed. Others went wading into the local pond, feeling for the mucky bottom. Still more beat the bushes and jabbed sticks into malarial ditches by the roadsides. A rumor had spread of a $1,000 bounty on William Guldensuppe's severed head, and the city's children were hooting with delight. A thousand dollars! It was Easter in July—a delightful, appalling Easter egg hunt.

O'Connell and Boyle forced their way forward to the Bualas' house, where a local constable struggled to keep the masses at bay.

Where's Mrs. Hafftner?

Nobody knew where to find the caretaker or the owner; the police didn't have a key to the place. The throngs of children and adults alike grew behind them. Scores became hundreds, their weight pressing against the fence around the property. If they didn't collect evidence now, they might never get it.

Let's go.

O'Connell and Boyle wrenched open a window and boosted themselves through. In a stroke of luck, the crowd was briefly distracted by a street show: Streuning's infamous "death carriage" and horse came trotting up to its old Second Avenue haunt. The police had lifted a page from the *World* and returned with the surrey to jog townspeople's memories. The duck farmer next door was one of the first to recognize it.

"Yes, that's the same rig those people had," Mr. Wahle said. "I remarked at the time on the black horse and the dark painted carriage, and thought it looked like an undertaker's rig."

The caretaker's husband, having belatedly arrived after the detectives, was quick to agree with his neighbor.

"That's the same carriage," Mr. Hafftner confirmed. "When I saw that man and that woman come here on Saturday in a carriage I was rather astonished, because Mrs. Buala had told us he was a shoemaker. It seemed strange that a shoemaker could afford to leave his business on a Saturday and hire a horse and carriage just to drive over from Jackson Avenue."

The house itself remained as vacant and unremarkable as ever, save for two previously unnoticed clues in an upstairs bedroom: an empty wine bottle and a small cardboard bullet box discarded in the back of the closet. Detective Boyle busied himself with testing planks to find any that might have been recently pried open to hide a body. But Detective O'Connell still had his mind on that ditch outside. Before landing a job on the force, he'd worked as a plumber, and the drainage described by the duck farmer gave him an idea.

I'm taking out the trap, O'Connell announced as he deftly exposed and disassembled the plumbing under the upstairs bathtub. There was a pastelike sediment in the drain—not hair, not black mildew, but a sticky mush with an awful, deathly smell. Another sample for the lab, O'Connell decided.

The bathroom window now looked out over a sea of children. More than a thousand of them were romping through the fields and ditches of Woodside, at least one for every dollar of the imagined reward. The borough was swarming with bicycling parties as well. Spurred by the fine weather and a day off, cyclists were getting drunk and crashing wildly into the undergrowth, all looking for the ghastly prize.

"Between drinks," a *World* reporter dryly observed, "this crowd dodged into the woods and sought for the head. Within the depths of these thickets are cat-briers that demand of each that passes through either blood or raiment. Profanity arose with the passage of each."

O'Connell tried to ignore the hubbub and stray fireworks outside and focus on the water. The drainage outside didn't look right. How could it have filled up like that in the middle of the summer? They called over Citizens Water Supply, a local supplier that pumped fresh water out from a spring in Trains Meadow. The water meter showed a whopping 40,000-gallon spike in the last month for the empty house.

"The amount of water," the utility's superintendent said incredulously, "is *three times* the amount that an ordinary family would use in a year."

There were no leaks in or around the premises, either; the water meter hadn't budged since they'd arrived that morning. As evening descended and the disappointed children and boozy holiday cyclists gently wended their way homeward, the inconspicuous device bore a mute testimony that no grisly find in the fields could have given.

"The only way I can account for it," the water representative said with a shrug, "is that all the faucets were open continually. For days."

BRING OUT THE BODY, came the order to the night-shift morgue keeper. Even after the tumult of Independence Day, a steady stream of identifiers still came to the morgue each day to view Guldensuppe's remains. As Bellevue's superintendent stood nearby, the latest visitor's credentials were checked and an assistant sent to fetch the remains.

The staffer came back to the morgue's front desk, disbelief written over his face.

"The legs . . . ," he stammered to the superintendent, "are not in the morgue. The arms and trunk are, but . . . I don't know where the legs are."

The superintendent nearly fainted.

Morgue staff threw open paupers' coffins, while reporters took frantic notes. How could they just vanish?

"Guldensuppe has gained more fame by his death than he could gain by living a million years," one *Herald* writer reported drolly. "But for a pair of legs, detached and supposed on expert testimony to be dead, to make a clean escape from the Morgue—that was a mystery."

Maybe they were just out for a walk, one wag suggested.

"One of the theories," a reporter mused, "was that they had gone to help Acting Inspector O'Brien find Thorn."

In fact, the inspector's search was already going quite well. He'd even taken to praising the newspapers for the fine work they'd done. "I desire," he announced grandly, "to thank the newspaper men who during the past week have aided me so in bringing about the conclusions which I have reached."

It wasn't often that the Detective Bureau even grudgingly allowed that kind of praise, but it was true: The papers had outdone themselves. Hearst was already boldfacing praise from the coroner, police commissioners, and Mayor William Strong across his pages—"The *Journal* deserves credit" the latter admitted—and just that night announced the recipients of his $1,000 reward for identifying the body.

The case had been solved by many people at once, really, but half went to a Murray Hill Baths customer who'd overheard some attendants discussing Guldensuppe's absence; the fellow sent in what proved to be the first correct wild guess. The other half of the reward was split between Guldensuppe's coworkers, who had been key in the actual discovery. None, of course, would go to Ned Brown—or anyone else at the *World*.

But Pulitzer's paper was now basking in some fine publicity itself. After a week of humiliations by the Murder Squad, it had begun to regain its footing. The *World* was the first paper on the scene at Woodside, and lavished its first three pages on the case for the July 4 issue. And the next day the *World* once again had the best scoop—literally. They'd surreptitiously gouged a stain out of the floor in Woodside and rushed it to an analytical chemist ahead of the police.

BLOOD IN THE HOUSE OF MYSTERY, crowed its front page.

Their chemist, Dr. E. E. Smith of Frazer & Company, had cannily used the Teichmann test, one of the few ways to analyze a sample like this one. It was a tricky procedure: He dissolved the stain in an ammonia solution, then precipitated some brown crystals with common salt, acetic acid, and evaporation. Under the microscope, the rhomboid crystals revealed their telltale identity: hydrochloride of haematin.

"They are absolutely characteristic of blood," Dr. Smith announced.

Under the hammering of discoveries by both O'Brien's detectives and Hearst and Pulitzer reporters, Mrs. Nack was beginning to waver. She denied any murder—denied that Guldensuppe was even dead—but was now hesitantly admitting to O'Brien that, well, she *had* hired that surrey . . . and that she *had* been involved with Martin Thorn . . . and that she *had* seen him the week before. In fact, the two had been spotted at a saloon just before her arrest. Thorn had been spied reading about the case in a newspaper—purely as a disinterested party, you understand—and Mrs. Nack admitted that, yes, they had discussed Ferguson's theory on the then-unidentified victim's legs being boiled.

So Thorn was still in town, and in the habit of reading newspaper coverage of the case. Being friendly to reporters now made perfect sense: They were O'Brien's key to luring Thorn into the open. After flattering the journalists, the inspector fed them a steady stream of misinformation for the next two days. Thorn, he assured the *Journal* and the *Tribune*, had surely left the country on a steamship—probably, he added to the *Press* and the *Brooklyn Eagle*, escaping via Canada. To the *Mail and Express*, he was "positive" that Thorn had already fled.

Finding the murderer would still be harder than, say, finding Guldensuppe's legs. *Those* had turned up later that evening in the morgue's pickling vat; the afternoon shift had forgotten to mention that they were there to their hapless colleagues. The reporters had a fine wheeze over the incident, unaware that O'Brien was quietly laying out his bait in the columns of their newspapers. The inspector was lulling Martin Thorn into a false sense of safety; now all his fugitive had to do was make a mistake.

MY HUSBAND'S SEEN HIM, said a nervous woman the next day in the Central Office. Perhaps the beads of sweat on her brow were just due to the heat. It was getting past one in the afternoon, and with the hottest July 6 on record, the police were logging one sunstroke case after another: the ironworks owner who'd left his home that morning crying, "The heat! The heat!" who was later found raving in a cab for a ride "to the gates of heaven"; the fellow who went berserk on Broadway, hallucinating that he had turned into a cable car; the ladies who simply removed their flowered hats and crumpled out in the sun.

He's seen him, she insisted.

Of course he had. Thorn was everywhere and nowhere, a heat mirage. Two suspicious look-alikes had already been swept up from city streets, and they were indeed criminals, it turned out—a fugitive Louisville embezzler and a Brooklyn con man named Sleeping Jake—but, alas, neither was Thorn. A suicide found in a Jersey City cemetery, who'd swallowed acid and died in agony over a grave, surely *that* was Thorn. And what about the body that veteran stage actor George Beane found in the water while yachting off Staten

Island, its face blown off at close range? Headlines wanted to know: IS THIS MARTIN THORN?

Why should someone walking in off the street know any better? The suspect's own kin couldn't even be sure.

"I don't suppose I would know him if I saw him now," Thorn's younger sister Pauline told a *Journal* reporter who had tracked her down to an apartment on Forty-Second Street. The last time she'd seen Martin, she explained, was on July 4 . . . nine years earlier. "I have never heard from him to this day," she added. "He was at that time suffering nervous troubles, and he wrote to a doctor in Boston about it two or three times."

Not to be outdone, *World* reporters located Thorn's older brother John in Jersey City. Not only hadn't he heard from his brother Martin lately, he hadn't even heard from the police.

"I can only hope that the police are mistaken in their belief that Martin is implicated in it." He sighed. "But about that I have my misgivings. The description fits him."

He'd always despaired of his brother, he said.

"There are four boys and two girls in our family," the older brother explained. "Martin is the black sheep of the flock. As long as fifteen years ago I had trouble with him. I gave him money so that he could learn the trade of barber, but he did not appreciate my efforts to make a man of him. He preferred to loaf. . . . When I got married I forbade him from my house."

No, he didn't know where Martin was now. But his last encounter with him, after years of silence, made him fear the worst.

"I did not see him again until a year ago. He came into my store under the influence of liquor and I ordered him out. He had a revolver on him and he showed it to me.

" '*See that,*' he said. '*Well, some day you will hear of me using this on someone.*' "

The accounts in the paper that day made detectives look at one another significantly: Pauline had been married to one Ludwig Braun. And the shop that John Torzewski ran? It was a shoe repair. Pressed for a false identity, Martin Thorn had grabbed the closest materials at hand—his brother's profession and his brother-in-law's surname. And the disguise had worked well. The last confirmed sighting of Thorn was by a moving company that he'd tried to hire exactly one week earlier—the previous Wednesday, in the hours before Mrs. Nack's arrest. As soon as news of her arrest hit the streets, he'd vanished.

But the woman in the Detective Bureau's office seemed insistent. *My husband,* she explained, *is John Gotha.*

The detective on duty sat bolt upright. Gotha was a tall and lanky German barber, and one of Thorn's old pinochle friends. O'Brien had hauled him in on Saturday for questioning, to which the barber had innocently protested that he hadn't seen Thorn in a fortnight.

Well, Mrs. Gotha explained, that was true—he hadn't. But *now* . . .

They raced back uptown with Mrs. Gotha. She didn't want to make a scene at her husband's workplace, so detectives waited impatiently at the 125th Street El station while Mrs. Gotha walked over to Martinelli's Barber Shop. Her husband already knew what she was going to pester him about.

"I can't go back on a friend," he complained when he saw his wife.

"Put on your coat and hat and come with me," she said flatly. "I've told them everything."

Back downtown in Inspector O'Brien's office, his story came tumbling out. Thorn had come out of hiding to confide in him. He wasn't ratting out his friend—really, he wasn't!—but his wife had *made* him come down here.

When did you see him?

Yesterday, Gotha explained. He'd been waiting for a customer in Martinelli's when a man entered, sat in his chair, and uttered a single word: "Haircut."

Gotha looked up at the mirror and into the face of the country's most wanted murderer. Martin had changed his appearance a bit—shed his usual brown derby for a white fedora and shaved off his luxuriant mustache—but there was no mistaking the eyes or the old fighting scar along his nose. The barber clipped in absolute silence, neither of them breathing a word to the other, not even daring to lock eyes in the mirror. After the last clippings were brushed away, his silent customer stood up and pressed some coins into Gotha's hand. When Gotha opened his palm, it contained a note.

Meet me at the corner.

From there, the barber told Inspector O'Brien, they'd gone into the nearest saloon and talked for three hours—and Thorn spilled everything. At the end of it, they'd arranged to meet again.

When?

The barber sat under his wife's gaze and looked down at his shoes, as he was prone to do. He didn't want to turn his friend in; the man had trusted him.

Well . . .

IT WAS QUARTER PAST NINE that night, getting toward closing time, and the soda fountain at Spear's Drug Store ruled the busy Harlem corner of 125th and Eighth Avenue. Theodore Spear himself was manning the till, and his clerk Maurice was working the fountain. Like any drugstore, the gleaming bottles and tins of nostrums along Mr. Spear's shelves—Dr. Worme's Gesundheit Bitters, Telephone Headache Tablets, Kinner's Corn Cure—were window-dressing for the real profits, which lay in the slot telephone, in alcohol elixirs that skirted the liquor laws, in sen-sen gum to cover up that elixir breath, and in petty luxuries like Cosmo Buttermilk Soap and Tilford cigars. But on a sweaty July evening, the only part of the store that truly mattered was the soda fountain, with its gleaming chromium faucets and beautifully tinted bottles of orange phosphate, strawberry syrup, and violet *presse*. Harlem swells and their ladies fanned themselves at the counter seats, and Maurice watched the street scene outside.

Everybody knew it was too hot to work that day; city after city on the East Coast was reporting relentless heat. Laborers in soiled overalls had been shiftlessly waiting around for hours, escaping the sun under store eaves, and now whiled away the gathering dusk in the light thrown out by the shop windows onto the busy street. A gentleman stylishly dressed for the evening walked down the sidewalk, ignoring the workmen, and exchanged greetings with a friend.

"Let's go take a drink," his friend suggested, which was a fine idea indeed.

The gentleman demurred. "No, I don't want a drink. You go along by yourself."

What happened next came in a flash: The tall and lanky friend sank back into the gathering dusk, and a workman—a tough in a blue flannel shirt—seized the gentleman's arm and shoved him into Spear's drugstore.

It's a holdup, Maurice frantically signaled to Mr. Spear at the till.

In a fluid motion, the thief yanked out the gentleman's coat lining, gathered up its contents, pushed him down into a chair by the cigar counter, and withdrew his own weapon. A crowd of roughneck laborers came barreling in behind him. But rather than break up the robbery, they *also* seized the gentleman in a silent, desperate scuffle. Before Maurice and Mr. Spear knew it, the victim was pinned down, yet the drugstore till remained completely unmolested.

Nothing was what it seemed; the workmen had pulled out revolvers and slapped a pair of handcuffs around the fellow's wrists.

"He's shaved his mustache," one of them muttered.

"What's your name?" demanded a gruff foreman framed by the dusk.

"I am Martin Thorn," the handcuffed gentleman announced defiantly to the astonished store patrons.

The grizzled lurker in the doorway now also appeared transformed. The plain clothes of a slouch cap and dirty overalls no longer disguised a man that the startled druggist and his shop clerk knew from all the newspapers.

"And I am Inspector O'Brien," he replied.

III.

THE
INDICTMENT

SOLVED BY THE JOURNAL.

MRS. NACK, MURDERESS!

She Bought the Oilcloth Found Around the Body of Her Mangled Lover, William Guldensuppe, the Turkish Bath Rubber.

11.

A CASE OF LIFE
AND DEATH

MARTIN THORN KNEW it was O'Brien all along—why, from the moment he'd walked into Harlem.

"I've thought so for five minutes," he said coolly.

The inspector was unimpressed. "Got anything else but your gun about you?"

"I've got a knife."

Thorn helpfully reached for an inner pocket before a detective seized his cuffed hands.

"Just keep it where it is," snapped Inspector O'Brien.

Along with the .32 revolver, a closer search of Thorn's pockets netted the knife and $6. Still in their plain clothes, the "laborers"—top detectives O'Brien, McCauley, and Price, along with the five beefiest backup officers from the precinct—whisked their suspect onto the 125th and Eighth El platform for the next train downtown.

Surrounded by police, Thorn sat stoically through more than a dozen stops on an elevated steam train that passed the second- and third-story apartments of Manhattan; he could glimpse the ordinary scenes of men and women settling in for the evening, washing dishes and hanging clothes for work. They reached Houston and Bowery just after ten p.m. As the El platform closest to HQ, the rowdy station was an honorary portal into the New York legal system. The lights of the Gaiety Theater and the towering Casperfeld & Cleveland jewelry billboard were among the last glimpses of everyday life a guilty man might ever have. Nightlife swirled below as newsboys clustered around the steel pillars of the station. AN ELECTRICAL EX-ECUTION, the *Evening Post* announced. It was not prescience, just the fate of a wife killer up in White Plains, but it abutted a front-pager of the day's latest news on Mrs. Nack.

A plainclothes scrum double-marched Thorn down Mulberry Street, so fast that the hindmost officer could barely keep pace. They hadn't gone unnoticed. Someone—from Spear's drugstore, or from an El platform on the way down—had called ahead to tip off the *New York Herald* to a big arrest; the *Herald* instantly relayed it to the round-the-clock watch post they kept across from the police HQ. A reporter and a sketch artist were waiting in the street to meet the grim-faced men.

Who'd you get?

Thorn, still unrecognizable in his new clothes and shaven face, was quickly hustled past them, through the heavy basement door and down a hallway. The reporter jumped up and shimmied his head into the transom, in time to see O'Brien and McCauley disappear with the prisoner up a stairway toward the inspector's office.

Who'd you get?

But he already knew.

"Pickpockets and *petit* larceny thieves are not hurried to Police headquarters at night, heavily shackled and guarded," he noted dryly. There was only one man it could be, and the lights burning brightly through the night in Inspector O'Brien's window were all the proof anyone needed.

THORN STARED OUT into the night, his fingers smarting from where they'd been scraped by forensics. Professor Witthaus himself had come in to collect the samples from under his nails; even though nearly two weeks had passed since the murder, they weren't taking any chance of losing evidence, and his scrapings were now en route to the Loomis Lab to be tested for blood or viscera. The rest of Thorn's body had been scrupulously measured, too; the station used a Bertillon card system, where each new arrest was mugged for the camera and then a card was filled in with the painstaking caliper measurements of M. Alphonse Bertillon's wondrous anthropometric system. Everything from the length of Thorn's ears and cheekbones to the length from the elbow to the tip of the finger was noted. All that was missing were Thorn's fingerprints: Bertillon did not approve of such dubious new notions. Just a few weeks earlier the royal governor in India had adopted a new system invented by one of his own administrators, one that annotated whorls and loops, but neither O'Brien nor anyone else in the United States was bothering with such exotic ideas.

Instead, the inspector worked quietly at his desk, saying nothing for hours, content to let his suspect stew in uncertainty. The clock ticked past eleven, then past midnight; Thorn's gaze fell upon the piles of letters on O'Brien's table, all rifled from Gussie's apartment. The useless tin heap of her washing boiler still lay in a corner of the room.

So, O'Brien began: Why had he shaved his mustache off?

Thorn glared back sullenly. He'd shaved it off the previous Wednesday—the same day, that is, that Gussie had been arrested—but he wouldn't explain why. Asked to account for his movements, he gave a carefully rehearsed story.

"I at present live in a furnished room at Number 235 East Twenty-Fifth Street. I have not seen William Guldensuppe since I was assaulted by him at the house of Mrs. Nack," he claimed. "I have been meeting with her two or three times a week ever since, up until Tuesday night. Mrs. Nack spoke to me about leaving Guldensuppe, and buying me a barber shop in the country. She told me that Guldensuppe had been using her badly the last six months, and that Guldensuppe wanted her to open a disorderly house. She agreed to leave Guldensuppe and live with me."

They'd still been planning for their future together, Thorn said, when he last saw her on June 29—the night before her arrest.

"We took an Eighth Avenue car at Forty-Third Street and went to Central Park," he recalled. "We sat on a bench in the park until

about eleven o'clock at night. I told her I had seen in the newspaper
that part of a human body had been found in the river, and that it
stated it was a part of Guldensuppe's body. I told her how it was also
mentioned in the newspapers that a part of the body found must have
been boiled before being thrown in the river."

O'Brien eyed him intently.

"She said," Thorn continued, "she did not believe it was Guldensuppe's body, because she did not believe Guldensuppe was dead.
She told me that he had not been home since Friday morning, and
that she did not know where he was. Mrs. Nack went home after
we made an appointment to meet the next day—Wednesday—but I
saw in the morning newspapers that detectives were at Mrs. Nack's
house, and I did not go there."

The inspector allowed one of his long, disconcerting silences to
fill the room. But he was quietly pleased by this alibi. The times were
wrong: They couldn't have discussed Guldensuppe's identification
on the park bench that evening, because that revelation hadn't hit
the streets until the following morning. And he had an even more
unpleasant surprise for his suspect.

"Do you deny," he pressed, "that you were at Frey's saloon on
East Thirty-Fourth Street on Tuesday morning, Tuesday afternoon,
and Tuesday night playing cards with 'Peanuts' and Federer?"

"I don't exactly deny it."

"Do you remember being in Frey's saloon on Tuesday, June 29,
when Federer was reading a newspaper in regard to the reward of one
thousand dollars, and how Federer said to you, 'I guess that's you,
barber,' and you said, 'Yes, that's right'?"

Thorn could see the darkened city out O'Brien's window; everyone was asleep but them.

"Yes," he admitted.

"Do you remember being in the saloon on Tuesday, June 29, and
going out and coming back with a woman, and having one glass of
beer each in this saloon?"

"Yes."

O'Brien paused, readying his knockout.

"Do you remember being in Frey's saloon on the night of Tuesday,

June 29, and telling Federer that you were going to meet a woman, and it was a case of life and death, and exhibiting to them a pistol?"

"I cannot say that I remember that," Thorn answered warily. "I had been drinking a good deal that day."

"Do you remember going back to Frey's saloon about eleven o'clock that same night, and playing pinochle with Federer and Gordon until nearly one o'clock in the morning?"

"Yes."

"Do you remember saying to them that by tomorrow night at this time you would be on the ocean?"

Thorn stared blankly at him. "I do not remember saying that."

He didn't need to; plenty of others at the saloon did.

The hours crawled onward until four in the morning, when O'Brien finally let his prisoner collapse onto a cot in his jail cell. Thorn had scarcely fallen asleep before he was awoken again, first to stand before a magistrate, then to drag himself back into O'Brien's office. The inspector was waiting for him, seemingly unaffected by the early hour, and invigorated by the fine day the Detective Bureau was having. And he wasn't alone.

That's him, said Mrs. Hafftner, looking the unshaven prisoner up and down. *That's who rented the house.*

Thorn kept a stony silence as another man was brought in.

That's him, said the undertaker's assistant. *That's who picked up the surrey.*

After they were led out, O'Brien turned his searching gaze back to Thorn. "Looks pretty bad, doesn't it?" the inspector remarked.

Martin Thorn fanned himself with his fedora, considering the situation.

"I don't fear death," he replied evenly.

"HIT HIM!" they roared down the cell block.

Thorn grabbed the bars of his jail cell and looked down the station's hallway; a man was being dragged in heavy shackles, shoved and smacked by jeering detectives.

It was John Gotha.

"I won't go in there!" he yelled. He looked exhausted and hollowed out. "I have done nothing, and you have no right to lock me up!"

"Go on, go on!" a detective yelled. "Hit him with your club!"

The mêlée continued down the hallway, and Thorn stared as his friend scuffled with the officers; he could hear yelling and the sounds of a solid police beating all the way into the next block of cells, until they finally disappeared.

The officers slung Gotha into an empty jail cell with a couple of final yells and dramatic groans, then waited a moment. And then, through Gotha's wan countenance, there flickered a sunny expression.

Thanks.

The detectives rolled their eyes. The whole ruse had been at Gotha's insistence; the lanky barber was still bitterly disappointed that he hadn't been arrested in Harlem alongside Thorn. *That was part of the deal*, he insisted. They'd been too busy with Thorn and had left Gotha there feeling like a fool. So now they were giving him the sham arrest that he'd wanted.

If they knew Thorn like he did, Gotha explained, they'd understand covering up his role as an informant. Gotha worried that their suspect could slip free or get turned loose, and he'd known Thorn too long to believe that any betrayal would go unpunished.

"I first met Thorn nine years ago," he recalled. "We were introduced in a saloon, where we played cards together."

They were a curious pair at the card table. Gotha was unmotivated and gawky, so tall that colleagues nicknamed him "Legs," and so unsuccessful in his barbershop trade that his wife had resorted to living in her parents' basement. Thorn was handsome and talented, and he always seemed lucky with women and money. Gotha couldn't help a sneaking admiration of his friend's life. But Thorn had a fierce temper when a card game didn't go his way, and Gotha was under no illusions about the murder charges against his old pinochle partner. Thorn, he admitted, "would be capable of such an act."

For now, his friend would stay in the dark about his betrayal; but as Gotha walked free from his untouched jail cell, he could no longer hide from the reporters.

JEFFERSON MARKET COURTHOUSE was less a municipal building than a misplaced Gothic castle, its bands of red and tan brick spiraling over the Sixth Avenue El and up into a great crenellated clock tower; far below, a heavy iron door swung open day and night to admit a ceaseless rabble that was, as one reporter put it, "old—prematurely old—and young—pitifully young." That Friday morning in a grand-jury hearing, the assistant district attorney led a procession of witnesses—Mrs. Riger, Frank Gartner, and a nephew of Guldensuppe's—through their statements, but then stopped short at John Gotha.

The terrible secrets entrusted to the man had kept him awake and unable to eat for days; reporters and jurors craned to watch the shaken man led to the stand. Martin Thorn was not present for this indictment, but that was of little comfort; John Gotha was clearly a haunted creature.

"He had the look of a man going to the electric chair," a *Herald* reporter marveled.

Laboring to keep his composure, the hapless barber spoke of drinking with Martin Thorn just three days earlier. "I met him at a saloon between 128th and 129th Streets, on the west side of Eighth Avenue. We had a couple drinks, and I said 'You made a botch job of that fellow.'"

Thorn had stared at him in terrible silence for a full minute.

"I know it," he finally said. "Have you read the newspapers? It is all the woman's fault."

Gotha struggled as he recalled his friend's next words. "I looked at him, and he said 'You are the only friend I've got, and I'll tell you all about it. I expect you to keep a closed mouth.'"

"Well, then," Gotha stammered, "he spoke about Guldensuppe, and said they wanted to get rid of him. He said: 'We talked the matter over, and decided to kill him. We looked about and rented the house at Woodside. We thought it was far enough out of the way and decided to do the thing on Friday. She bought the oilcloth at that place in Astoria, and bought the cheesecloth at Ehrich's.'"

"Thorn told me that he reached the house early and went upstairs and waited for Guldensuppe and Mrs. Nack to arrive, as she was to bring him. While waiting he took off all his clothing but his under-shirt and socks. He did not want to get them bloodstained. About eleven o'clock he said he saw Mrs. Nack and Guldensuppe come up to the front gate. They entered the house."

The witness paused; the packed courtroom was dead quiet. Then, Gotha recalled, clad in underclothes and with a revolver in his hand, Thorn had hidden himself behind a closet door in an upstairs bed-room. He could hear the two talking downstairs.

"Go and see the rooms upstairs," he heard Gussie tell her boy-friend. "I think you'll like them."

Thorn cocked his pistol.

Guldensuppe's heavy footfall came up the stairs, step by step, growing closer. He could hear his rival whistling, walking room to room, looking out windows. Then, as the slit in the ajar door dark-ened, the hinges on the closet moved.

He fired point-blank into the face. The masseur had a moment of recognition—his hands flew up—but they never made it. Gulden-suppe crashed to his knees, then slumped backward onto the floor.

Gotha swallowed hard, and what he said next made the jury gasp.

"*He was not dead*. Thorn dragged him into the bathroom and put him in the tub." Thorn slit his throat until a final breath came out of the hole he'd made. "*I heard a snore*," was how he put it.

The assistant DA stopped Gotha for a pregnant moment. "Are you *positive*"—he leaned forward—"that Thorn said Guldensuppe was 'snoring' or breathing when the razor was drawn across his throat?"

"Yes," Gotha said quietly. "He told me the man was 'snoring' when he cut his throat."

And Thorn kept cutting.

"He nearly severed the head from the body with the razor," Gotha told the jury. Then Thorn went downstairs to Mrs. Nack, who was waiting patiently for him.

"It's done," he said.

"I know," she replied. "I heard."

"He told her," Gotha continued, "to go away and come back at five that evening."

With hot water running at full blast, Thorn finished sawing off the head, then sliced away the chest tattoo. He sawed and bundled the legs, the midsection, and the chest—terribly strenuous work, really—then mixed up a basin full of quick-drying plaster and dropped the head in. When it was set into a smooth ball, he washed the tub and floor clean, lit his pipe, and waited for Mrs. Nack to return. They quickly carried their parcels out to the surrey and from there drove it onto the Tenth Street ferry.

"As the boat neared the slip the passengers walked to the front of the boat," Gotha explained. "Thorn remained behind with the bundle, and at a signal from Mrs. Nack that everything was all right, and as the boat was entering the slip, it was tossed from the stern."

The head went overboard as well. But ever the barber, Thorn now had second thoughts—not about the murder, but about his victim's *hair*. He fretted that he hadn't shaved off Guldensuppe's telltale mustache. But he wasn't really that worried, because the block of plaster sank instantly.

"They can't find it," he boasted to Gotha, adding dismissively, "I don't care."

But the bundled arms and chest were different: They *didn't* sink.

"I saw by newspaper reports that it was recovered fifteen minutes after I had dropped it from the boat," Gotha recounted Thorn saying. "Great God, what a fool I was! In the first place, we selected the house in which there was no sewer connection, and in the next place I permitted myself to be persuaded to hurry off to dispose of the bundles before having weighted them. If I had examined the house and seen where the drain led to, it never would have happened that way. I was a fool [in] every way. . . . I must have been blind, but the woman led me to do some things that I should not have done."

Among those things, Thorn didn't include the murder itself. No, Gotha's friend was angry at the *way* they'd murdered. "I should have weighted the bundles I threw into the river, but Mrs. Nack said no."

After disposing of the other portions uptown, Nack and Thorn parted. He pawned the dead man's clothes and watch for money to hide out, first in the Maloney Hotel, and then for $3 a week in an apartment on Twenty-Fifth Street.

The witness was spent, his story nearly told. The grand jury didn't need enough evidence to convict Thorn, just enough to determine that he could be tried—and now they'd heard plenty. They conferred while Gotha waited miserably on the stand.

"Mr. Gotha, I do not want to detain you, because I can see that you suffer," the jury foreman said in a kindly tone. "You should leave the city and take a long rest."

Gotha still looked terribly shaken, and he couldn't help it. His explanation before he was led away was simple and appalling: The murderer's parting words in the saloon still haunted him.

"Thorn said to me," he choked out, "*'I wish to God I had not told you all this.'*"

In that farewell in the saloon, a realization had crept over John Gotha—one that brought his anguished confessions to his wife, to Inspector O'Brien, and now to this grand jury. From the moment he became Thorn's sole confidant, he'd also become a marked man. Gotha had been horrified by his friend's insistence that they meet the next evening, because he'd instantly understood what it meant.

He was to have been Martin Thorn's next victim.

12.

HEADS OR TAILS

"GOING FISHING?" the small boy asked.

The crews swaggered past him and the swelling crowd along East Tenth Street, pulled their gear out from a tangled mass of ropes and hooks along the foot of the pier, then boarded the police launches gathered by the riverside. These were naphtha boats—steamboats that vaporized petroleum instead of water, which made for quick starts and fiery wrecks—and the men were grapplers, salvagers who worked the docks to drag the riverbed for dropped casks of wine, crates of oysters, and the occasional lost anchor.

This job was a little different. A couple of dozen grapplers had been rounded up, and policemen joined them on six launches. Rather than the usual draglines, they were deploying long rakes with splayed-out tines, and peculiar ice-tong implements that bristled with metal teeth. The riverside crowd knew exactly what these specialized tools were for.

"Three cheers for Guldensuppe!" yelled a spectator. "Rah! Rah! Rah!"

Captain Schultz of the harbor police ushered newsmen aboard his launch and maneuvered midstream to demonstrate his men at work. The imperturbable Schultz was in a droll mood. He liked reporters, and his grisly specialty in body dragging meant that he was always good for the darkest humor in town.

"Heads you win, tails you lose!" yelled a wag from onshore.

Schultz smiled and directed the reporters' attention to rivermen tossing lines into the water on the approach to the ferry slip. Finding a plaster-encased head would be no challenge for them.

"These men know how to find and pick up a gold watch," he boasted. "With their hooks down at the river's bottom, they can feel anything that they come in contact with as well as if they had their fingers on it."

A series of splashes echoed across the water; police looked up and shook their heads in exasperation. Street urchins were stripping off and swimming out from the riverbank, their gamine bodies diving among the rakes and hooks to try to touch bottom. The riverbed was a good twenty-five feet down, though, so all they were doing was getting in the way.

"Something's caught!" yelled a grappler. "I've got something!"

The mass of New Yorkers onshore whooped as the men on the launch swiftly and steadily pulled the line up to reveal . . . a waterlogged black overcoat.

"Try a fine tooth comb!" jeered an onlooker.

The hooks and rakes had no sooner splashed back into the murky waters of the East River when the *William E. Chapman*, a wrecker steamboat, came chugging up the channel and dropped anchor. A man could be seen emerging onto the deck in a comically outsized diving suit, climbing over the gunwales onto a ladder, then pausing while two crew members rigged up a massive brass helmet.

The *World* was now conducting its *own* search.

The *Journal* had already run an operation with hooks a week earlier, an expensive stunt that hadn't yielded them much copy. But on this morning the *Journal* was completely upstaged. In a flash of brilliance, Pulitzer's crew had gone beyond mere grappling hooks and hired veteran deep-sea diver Charles Olsen. He was a survivor of the generation that had discovered the bends while doing underwater work on the pilings of the Brooklyn Bridge. The bottom of the East River, the grizzled diver explained to a *World* reporter on board the steamer, remained a treacherous place for divers.

"Unless you catch the tides just right, it is impossible to keep on your feet," he warned. Still, he thought the search might be a short one. "In my opinion, the head, in its plaster of paris casing, would sink just the same as a big, round stone. I don't think the tide would change its position."

If they followed the route of the ferry, Olsen suggested, they'd get Guldensuppe's head. Two assistants then screwed his helmet on tightly, checked the rubber hose leading into his suit, and set to work operating the air pump on deck. Olsen waited until the red Diver Down flag had been raised atop the steamer. Then he clumped down the ladder in his weighted boots, paused, and disappeared below the surface with a mighty splash.

Over on the police launches, the dredging proceeded at a painstaking pace; they were combing each inch of the riverbed. The grapplers might well have had the talent to find a sunken gold watch, but so far all they were pulling up were stones and tin cans. Meanwhile, the steamer crew paid out more and more of the 130 feet of rubber hose to Olsen's diving suit, receiving nothing in return but an occasional bubble of air on the surface. The prospect of finishing in mere hours was now fading.

But what the police didn't see as they toiled away was the slightest of movements on a signal rope leading up the *World*'s steamboat—a wordless series of tugs. Quietly, the *World* crew began raising Olsen as he relayed his message up the length of rope.

He'd found something.

THE DOOR of the narrow three-story brick boardinghouse on 235 East Twenty-Fifth Street opened to two Manhattan detectives waiting on the steps.

Stolen property, they explained to Mrs. Hoven, the pretty young widow who ran the home. They'd come to examine the room of a gentleman who had checked in the week before; he was believed to have pawned some ill-gotten clothing and possibly a watch as well. She knew exactly who they meant—though, she confessed with some embarrassment, she did not actually know his *name*.

"A week ago yesterday at about ten o'clock," she recalled, leading the detectives upstairs, "a stranger rang my doorbell and asked me if I had any furnished rooms to rent. I told him that I had, and invited him into the house."

But curiously, he had another question as he came inside.

"Do you recognize me?" he'd inquired rather searchingly.

"No, I can't say that I do," she'd admitted after a long pause.

"Why," he claimed airily as he stepped inside, "I was a great friend of your husband's."

Her late husband had known many people in his job as a hotel cook, she explained to the detectives. After his death three years earlier, Mrs. Hoven had resorted to managing a residence house where she and her two young children lived. She hadn't attached much significance to the question; the boarder, however, seemed unperturbed that she didn't recognize him—relieved, even.

"I showed him first a hall bedroom," she recalled. "He was not satisfied with it. It was too small. Then I took him to the front room on the second floor. He liked that one very much, and immediately engaged it. He paid me three dollars in advance."

By the time she thought to ask his name, though, he'd already locked his valise and his walking stick—his only apparent possessions—in his new room and left for the day.

She opened up the room to the detectives. He was a peculiar boarder, she admitted. When she went to clean his room, she couldn't help noticing that he was neat—a little *too* neat. Everything was always left packed and ready to go at a moment's notice.

"He never left a scrap, not so much as a hair brush around," she marveled. "You could only tell he had been in the room by the condition of the bed."

Unlike a hotel, where a fellow was far too easy to trace through the register, this sort of room was a fine place for hiding in and leaving quickly. Here, at one of the thousands of residence houses in Manhattan, one could be safely obscure. Even the landlady herself never saw him again after their first meeting.

"He used to come in late at night after the rest of us had gone to bed." She shrugged. "He would leave the home early in the morning before we were out of bed."

As promised, there was nothing inside the room but the walking stick and the valise. The detectives opened the latter carefully, as if wary that they might find something more than just clothing inside. Yet at the top of the case was an entirely ordinary and spartan set of possessions: a brush, a comb, trousers, socks, and shoes. But then, from the mysterious boarder's bag, there tumbled out something else: copy after copy of murder coverage from the *World*, the *Journal*, and the *Herald*.

THE NEWSPAPERS RELISHED their continuing role in the drama. When Augusta Nack's lawyer visited her cell with a newspaper announcing Thorn's arrest, her startled exclamation of "My God!" was gleefully illustrated by a *Journal* artist who showed her dropping the evening edition in horror. Now the *Journal* approvingly noted its presence in Thorn's valise, claiming that he had done little in his hideout but pore over the "morning, afternoon, and evening" editions of their paper.

Thorn would have plenty to read in the latest issues. A reporter accompanying Professor Witthaus and the coroner for yet another examination of the Woodside cottage witnessed them discovering a bullet hole in a baseboard, and claimed to find a second bullet that had entered into the lath of a wall. To top it all off, the paper ran an illustration of "Blood Spots on Martin Thorn's Undershirt," drawn so that Thorn himself appeared to be coming straight at *Journal* readers, thrillingly ready to decapitate them. Thankfully, Hearst declared, "the *Evening Journal*'s pen and pencil" had stopped him in his tracks. "And the police," he generously allowed, "for once deserve unstinted praise for having made Sherlock Holmes and Inspector Bucket look tardy."

The *World* played the skeptic; it complained that "a nail made the bullet hole" found by the *Journal* and inconveniently noted that Inspector O'Brien denied the bloody undershirt even *existed*. Yet among its plentiful complaints—and even more plentiful ads for Cowperthwait's Reliable Carpets and Dr. Pierce's Pleasant Pellets, for business was rolling in now—the *World* also boasted the best coverage of

O'Brien's interrogations and Gotha's ruse. Following up a disquieting comment by Gotha that Thorn had secretly joined the crowds at
the morgue to admire his own handiwork, a *World* reporter discovered that Thorn did indeed resemble a man who'd walked up to Dr.
O'Hanlon during the first autopsy.

"Horrible case, isn't it?" the man had said. And then, to O'Hanlon's
surprise, the visitor had pointed out a collarbone stab wound—one so
well hidden in the lacerated flesh as to be invisible to the untrained
eye. But before the startled doctor could remark on this, the mysterious man had melted back into the crowd.

If Thorn couldn't help admiring his own handiwork in the morgue
and in the press, then it was no accident that the *Herald* was the third
newspaper found in his valise. A cut above the *Journal* and the *World*,
it was the one quality newspaper to throw serious resources at the
case. Before the arrival of Pulitzer, the *Herald* had been the city's
colossus, with a circulation of more than 190,000. Under the boisterous editorship of celebrated bon vivant "Commodore" Bennett, it
had cavorted with the best of them; along with a splendid 1874 hoax
claiming escaped circus tigers were roaming Manhattan, it had also
pulled off the greatest publicity coup in journalistic history when it
sent reporter Henry Stanley in search of Dr. David Livingstone.

Those glories were long past, and *Herald* circulation had fallen
to a distant third behind the yellow papers, but it could still land a
scoop or two. Gotha's fears of Thorn, they discovered, were fright-
eningly justified. Another acquaintance had heard Thorn pondering
aloud how one might lure, say, *some fellow* into Mount Morris Park,
shoot him in the head, and then arrange the body to make it look
like a suicide. Gotha was precisely the sort of depressive man whose
apparent suicide would have evaded suspicion—and the park was
just a few blocks from where Thorn had arranged to meet him. The
plot was a chilling coda to Guldensuppe's murder, and the *Herald* had
uncovered it before anyone else—including the police.

In fact, one could pretty well gauge a newspaper's health by how
well it was covering the case. Galloping to the top of the circulation
pile was Hearst's brash *Journal*, pulling ahead of Pulitzer's *World*;
behind them, with still solid coverage, were the *Herald*, the *Staats*

Zeitung, and the quietly industrious *Times.* Lagging with lackluster stories were the ailing *Tribune* and the once mighty *Sun,* as well as scrappy but outgunned titles like the *Evening Telegram* and the *Press*; while the *Telegram* tried to lure readers with a Free Trip to the Klondike promotion, the latter was reduced to profiling the Woodside duck who broke the case. ("It is an ordinary duck," their hapless writer concluded.) At the bottom of the heap were the has-beens that could scarcely plagiarize yesterday's newspapers—the *Mail and Express,* the *Commercial Advertiser,* and the scrawny *New York Post.*

But buzzing along Newspaper Row late on the night of July 8 was a rumor that the *World* was about to leap ahead of them all with the biggest of breaks—one that might instantly upend the investigation.

IT WAS ONE A.M. when detectives marched into the *World* offices.

Where is it?

The rewrite and layout men, finishing their final late shifts for the next morning's July 9 issue, were the picture of innocence. Why, they were busy preparing a story on Mr. Valentine's turnip giveaway, where the local merchant gave away 171 barrels of last year's crop— lovely, fine specimens they were, too—because the vegetables just weren't selling. There'd almost been a riot on North Moore among paupers coming to get them; one poor man plain fainted on the sidewalk while trying to roll his barrel of turnips home, and . . . Where was what?

Where's the head?

Someone had seen the *World* diving crew draw a slimy white mass out of the water late the afternoon before. The *Herald* believed the *World* had the scoop of the day—literally scooping William Guldensuppe's head off the bottom of the East River—and that Pulitzer's henchmen were now concealing the ghastly thing in their editorial offices. In a burst of righteous indignation, the *Herald* called in the police.

Where is it?

The diver had indeed brought up a white chunk of stone the size of a human head, a *World* staffer patiently explained; but rather than the plaster-encrusted remains of William Guldensuppe, it had proven to be nothing more than a clump of barnacles that had dislodged from the hull of some passing ship.

"To reassure the gentlemen in charge of the *Herald*," a night reporter replied tartly, "*The World* has not the head of Guldensuppe and would not keep it if it had."

Yet there was no denying the head's importance. Old-timers in the newsroom still recalled "the Kelsey Outrage" of more than twenty years back, when Long Island poet Charles G. Kelsey unwisely wooed a very engaged woman named Julia. She'd set a candle in the window as their sign to meet, but he was seized in her yard by locals armed with tar and feathers, most likely led by Julia's fiancé, Royal Sammis. After turning the lovelorn poet into a scalding mass of tar, they sent him screaming out into the night, never to be seen again. Julia and Royal married three months later, freed of the bothersome suitor, and everyone lived happily ever after—at least until ten months later, when fishermen pulled Kelsey's tarred body from Huntington Bay. Or rather, they pulled out the bottom half of it; the top was gone, and his genitals had been hacked off.

As with Guldensuppe, the facts of the Kelsey case seemed clear: The identity of the victim, the perpetrators, and the motive all appeared obvious. There was even the same shock of betrayal: The candle that lured Charles Kelsey was lit deliberately by Julia, who then allegedly watched his tarring. But without a complete body, and with stories floated by the defense of live Kelsey "sightings," no jury had been able to convict a single person involved. The whole grisly affair was crudely preserved for decades in a popular turn of phrase—"as dead as Kelsey's nuts"—but Royal and Julia Sammis still walked free.

The assistant DA had been busy insisting to newspapers all day that, history aside, he didn't particularly need Guldensuppe's head to secure a conviction. Suspicious that the *World* had beaten the police to the punch, rival papers were glad to repeat the assertion that finding the final piece of Guldensuppe's body was a mere formality. HEAD NOT NECESSARY, the next morning's *Herald* headline assured readers.

But the small fleet of hired grapplers that gathered at the riverside again that next morning hinted otherwise. Reporters could already see that not all the other evidence would hold up; Mr. Buala, for one, now claimed he couldn't recognize Nack and Thorn as the couple who rented his Woodside house—because, detectives grumbled, he feared a conviction would keep him from being able to rent it out again. These suspicions were not exactly mollified when the annoyed wine merchant stubbornly attempted to keep the coroner from touching his precious baseboards to retrieve a spent bullet.

The longer Guldensuppe's head stayed missing, the more the questions would grow around the unthinkable. Could Nack and Thorn really get away with murder?

13.

QUEEN OF THE TOMBS

THE CROWDS WERE ALREADY GATHERING outside of the Tombs that morning, milling below thick granite walls built to evoke the ancient Egyptian temple of Dendera but instead memorializing every form of corruption bred by modern Manhattan. There were always crowds here: bailsmen, lawyers, police, food hawkers, and fatherless urchins all lurking in and among massive columns carved to look like papyrus stalks.

It was hardly a welcoming spot to linger. Intended for a city of 300,000, the decrepit pile now served 1.8 million New Yorkers, with three and sometimes four men crammed into cells meant for one. But it had been a cursed place from the beginning, a heap on a swamp. The massive structure had instantly begun to settle, opening fissures from the roof to the foundation, throwing the stairways akimbo, and letting sewage ooze into the ground floor. Each of its cells measured only six by eight feet, with a single footlong slit facing outside; the darkness inside was perpetual, with gaslights left blazing at all hours, even on ferociously hot July days like this one. Each cell's narrow cot was shared by two inmates, sleeping head to foot, on sheets changed every six weeks. As prisoners lacked furniture, meals were eaten off tin plates perched on the rim of a malodorous toilet. Cold and rusty water dribbled from the single bathtub provided for each of its four floors. It was the largest jail in the country, and quite possibly the worst.

A prison commission had condemned the place as "a disgrace to the city of New York," which it certainly was, and recommended that "it ought to be immediately demolished"—which, to everyone's shock, it also was. Workmen were dismantling the fortresslike walls with derricks and tackles, even while the inmates still lived inside. Just a few days earlier a block of granite had tumbled into the streets below, nearly flattening a workman and two young boys. Not content with exerting its malevolence on those within its walls, the Tombs was now threatening those outside, too.

Inside the women's wing of the prison, amid the infernal clattering of demolition, a murmur passed among the inmates roaming the hallways and catwalks on their morning constitutionals.

"It's Mrs. Nack!"

The knots of prostitutes and shoplifters parted to gape as she passed by in a sort of regal procession. A blond-tressed inmate who had already befriended the midwife walked at her side. Carefully arranging the green ribbons atop her black hat, Mrs. Nack was led out by a side entrance and into a waiting streetcar, with reporters and citizenry in pursuit.

Across town, another carriage left police headquarters, followed down Mott Street by a second mass of hundreds of New Yorkers; they converged at the Jefferson Market Courthouse, where Martin Thorn was the first to stand before the crowded room for his arraignment. Dressed in a black coat and a straw boater, he didn't know quite where to put himself.

"Come on up the bridge, Thorn," the judge said, waving him over to the bar. "You can hear the proceedings better there."

The courtroom was sweltering and packed with the fan-flapping female curiosity seekers whom the case seemed to attract. With his back to the gallery as he ascended the platform, Thorn took no notice of them at all, or even of himself. The once-dapper barber now sported three days' stubble, the result of a suicide watch that barred him from shaving.

"Have you any counsel?" the judge asked.

"No sir," Thorn replied quietly.

"Do you wish for any counsel?"

"I don't know anybody."

It wasn't the usual response; most murder suspects had previous scrapes with the law to draw on. But Thorn was not a usual case.

"I will send for anyone you wish."

Thorn didn't know what to say. He twirled his hat on his finger and looked blankly at the floor.

The door at the back of the courtroom swung open, and the crowd turned to look—everyone, that is, except for Thorn himself. He heard a second prisoner led up to the table next to him, but he did not dare look to see who it was.

"We appear for Mrs. Thorn," her lawyer started before correcting himself. "I mean Mrs. *Nack*."

The courtroom tittered, and Thorn smiled quietly while still staring fixedly ahead. The two moved close together until few in the courtroom could see or hear what happened next: a quick squeeze of their hands. It was exactly two weeks since the alleged murder, and the first time they'd seen each other in more than a week. Mrs. Nack leaned in to her lover and whispered.

"*Shweige still,*" she murmured to him.

OR PERHAPS SHE DIDN'T. A reporter for the *New Yorker Staats Zeitung*, a paper eminently qualified to eavesdrop on a German defendant, heard this instead: "*Halt den Mund und Spricht nicht!*" But both messages were the same: Tell them nothing.

"Mrs. Nack and Martin Thorn refuse to talk," Hearst mused over the proceedings. "All of which is very strange, considering that she is a woman and he is a barber."

They had already said plenty, of course, as had their witnesses; the mythologizing of the case had begun. Within hours of the indictment, Hearst had a team assembling *Journal* clippings and reporters' notes into a 126-page illustrated book titled *The Guldensuppe Mystery*. The instant book hit the streets just days later, as the first title by the newly launched True Story Publishing Company. Naturally, it heaped praise on the *Journal* as a "great newspaper" while calling for the miscreants to be electrocuted.

The city followed that prospect so avidly that New Yorkers even attempted trying Thorn themselves. One Lower East Side summer-school teacher found that his charges only wanted to discuss Guldensuppe, and he allowed his bookkeeping course to be turned into a mock trial. The result was covered in the *Times*, which noted that "the bookkeeping lessons quickly dwindled in interest and the full details of the cutting up and hiding of Guldensuppe's body were gone over by the boys with the greatest relish." Amid the blackboards and inkwells, "Thorn" and his "attorney"—two eleven-year-old boys—wilted under the aggressive questioning of a roomful of street urchins. Despite an impassioned half-hour-long closing argument by the diminutive attorney, his client was found guilty and sent to the electric chair—which, this being a Manhattan classroom, was simply a *chair*. School trustees were none too pleased when they learned of this extracurricular jurisprudence. Children were sent back to their bookkeeping texts with a stern admonition from the principal: *"I shall permit no more murder trials."*

But it was only to be expected in a city where masseurs were now slyly referred to as "Gieldensuppers" and where even local vagrants took a wild-eyed interest in the case. One unhinged man, chasing telegram messengers around William Street while shouting obscenities, was dragged off to Bellevue yelling: "That's not Thorn the police got! I'm the only original Thorn! I sliced Guldensuppe! I'm a holy terror! All others are imitations!"

In fact, there *was* an imitation Martin Thorn.

THE MURDER OF WILLIAM GULDENSUPPE, announced signs at the Eden Musée on West Twenty-Third Street. The Eden was the most upscale—or perhaps just the least downscale—of Manhattan's fabled dime museums. It was one of the city's most popular tourist destinations, and its elaborate waxworks could hold its own with Madame Tussaud's of London. Boasting the world's largest wax tableaus, and airy recital spaces for visiting Hungarian musicians and Japanese acrobats, it maintained a top-floor workshop that could whip up a body within twenty-four hours from wax, papier-mâché, wig hair, and costumes. Just days after Gotha's revelations, New Yorkers were lining up on Twenty-Third Street to hasten past old Ajeeb the Chess Automaton and beyond the impressive new re-creation of a Klondike gold-rush mining camp. Instead, they ventured down into the famed Chamber of Horrors. Along with its usual exhibitions of the Spanish Inquisition and a "Hindoo Woman's Sacrifice," it now housed the Woodside Horror; the infamous bedroom and bathroom had been painstakingly re-created, complete with Guldensuppe's decapitated body draining into a bathtub, and a waxen Martin Thorn industriously plastering the severed head.

Over at the Tombs, the prison matron couldn't help noticing that Augusta Nack was becoming something of a tourist attraction herself. She received a bewildering number of admirers, some bearing bags of oranges and bunches of flowers for the woman who had done away with her beau. One man sent her a letter professing undying love: "Your face possesses a charm that entrances me," it rhapsodized. "I wish I could make your acquaintance. . . . I should long to take you in my arms and give you a thousand kisses."

The object of his affections snorted in disgust and crumpled the note into a ball. When a group of curiosity seekers arrived begging the prison matron to see a *real* Mrs. Nack, one not made of wax, she became even less amused.

"I'm no freak," Mrs. Nack snapped at the matron. "Tell them they can't come in here and look at me. I'm not on exhibition."

But then she paused to reconsider. If Eden Musée and the *Journal* made good money off the case, why couldn't she? The Musée charged fifty cents admission, and surely she could beat their likenesses and their price.

"Wait a moment," she called to the departing matron. "Tell them they may come in and look as much as they like—*if they'll pay twenty-five cents apiece.*"

Gussie was back in business.

MARTIN THORN PASSED the days in cells #29 and #30, a double unit he was crammed into with five other men—all petty offenders, and all chosen to watch the star inmate for suicide attempts. Deprived of that pastime, Thorn resigned himself to tutoring cell mates in pinochle, a pursuit occasionally interrupted to watch newly arrived drunks hauled down the stifling cell block. The most entertaining was Johnny Boylan, who was found collapsed on the Bowery, so weighted down with stolen silverware that he couldn't walk; when the police collared him, dozens of pieces came crashing out of his jacket. Once Thorn tired of watching these new inmates arrive, he read the newspapers. His own story had traveled across the country and the ocean; even the *Aberdeen Weekly* in Scotland was carrying the headline THE HORRIBLE MURDER IN NEW YORK next to yet another announcement of INTENSE HEAT IN AMERICA. But there was other news to follow here at home: whisperings that Japan and Spain were considering an alliance to wrest Hawaii and Cuba from America, rumors of President McKinley allying with England and France to finish the Panama Canal, and reports of massive strikes by coal miners in Ohio and Indiana. It bothered Thorn that his own starring role on the front pages meant he'd miss the city elections in the fall; with the five boroughs set to consolidate for the first time under a single mayor, it looked like an entertainingly dirty race.

He'd settled into his routine for a few days when a new cell mate appeared, a smoothly polished businessman named Horton. It was said that he had been a lawyer, or perhaps an estate agent—nobody was quite sure. In any case, the genial old gent wanted in on the pinochle game.

After a few rounds, Horton looked squarely at Thorn. "Where's the head?" he asked affably.

Thorn continued regarding his flushes and his next bid. "What head?" he answered coolly.

Another minute passed, and more cards were exchanged.

"Where's the head?" Horton cheerfully repeated.

The accused murderer gave his opponent a withering look. *"What head?"*

Another minute of card play crawled by. Then: "Where's the head?"

This continued all day long.

And it was, to be fair, a very good question. Captain Schultz's crews were doggedly working their way up the East River from Tenth to Ninety-Second Street in the largest dredging search operation the city had ever mounted. "The new industry of finding William

Guldensuppe's head," a *Herald* reporter cracked, "is developing rapidly." Readers in the daily papers lobbed suggestions for locating it—floating mystically body-homing loaves of black bread with a candle inside, for instance—but the river workers remained as busy and as empty-handed as ever.

A steady stream of bewildering leads poured in throughout the summer. Children proved especially fond of claiming severed head sightings. A boy found a plaster-caked head in Branchport, New Jersey, panicked, and threw it into a local stream. Despite a welter of news stories about "little Tommy Cooper" and his ghastly find, the police couldn't turn it up again. It took an intrepid *Herald* reporter to discover why.

"The main fault with the Branchport discovery," the reporter ventured, "is that there is no such person as Tommy Cooper."

Three more boys spotted a head floating by the 117th Street Boathouse, but to no avail. Yet another "decomposed mass" frightened passing ferry passengers and was indeed found to be a head—but of "a large fish." A grisly find made in an Upper West Side boardinghouse by a janitor—he ran into the local precinct station screaming, "A head! A head! My god, the head!"—proved to be a med school's well-polished learning skull. But when a seven-year-old girl from Woodside found an actual chunk of plaster from a local ditch, matters began to look more promising. The police wasted no time in busting the plaster chunk open.

And it really did contain a head—of cabbage.

Another Woodside child promptly discovered a brown derby hat with a bullet hole in it—evidence curiously unnoticed by the one thousand other children who had thrashed Woodside's undergrowth on July 4. Hearst's and Pulitzer's men both immediately fell under suspicion of manufacturing the relics.

"Woodside is undergoing a boom in the agricultural line. They plant plaster casts with cabbage in them, blood-stained clothing, and bullet-perforated hats, and within a day or two they raise a crop of fakes," jeered the *New York Sun*. "There is more money grubbing for plaster in Woodside than for gold in the Klondike nowadays."

Another bonanza of plaster fragments found at the scene only made matters worse.

"It is impossible to dig anywhere in Woodside, if one is to take as evidence the results of recent excavations, without striking this product," the *Sun* continued. "All the town needs to do in order to get good roads is to clear away the upper surface, and there, only two feet or so below, will be found a complete Plaster of Paris pavement."

Allegations emerged that *someone*—and only two good guesses were needed as to who—had paid a couple of local utility workers a dollar an hour to salt the neighborhood with bogus evidence. It was a brilliantly unscrupulous investment. By the end of August, *Evening Journal* coverage of the case helped vault Hearst's newly debuted paper to more than half a million in circulation. It was more than every other evening newspaper combined in New York, and nearly double its circulation from before the first parcel had been hauled onto the Eleventh Street pier.

Yet for all their plaster jokes and deep-sea divers, every newspaper seemed to come to a dead end when it came to finding Guldensuppe's head. Nor, alas, did pinochle games lull Thorn into giving any hints. His cell mate "Horton" was none other than Perrin H. Sumner, a colorful con known in newsrooms as "the Great American Identifier." In his three-decade career Sumner had nearly bankrupted an Indiana college, run Florida real estate swindles, fleeced would-be fiancées, passed off worthless mining stock, and—in his finest moment—descended on the Bellevue morgue to identify an unclaimed suicide as a mythical Englishman named Edgar. Sumner and two confederates buried the fellow and wept over the grave of their "friend," while producing documents to prove they'd inherited his fabulous estate; the promised riches would presumably lure greedy women and gullible investors. Instead, the whole affair earned Sumner nothing more than his immortal nickname. Jailed for yet another con job, he'd talked the DA into putting him in Thorn's cell to pry out the location of the head.

That hadn't worked either.

The grapplers and Professor Witthaus's lab were the two lagging investigations left; the professor spent July embarrassingly tied up in divorce proceedings, and the crews continued to toil thanklessly in the East River. Witthaus was the first to announce a result: The spots on the floorboards in Woodside were human blood, he declared, and the grisly sediment in the house's plumbing was a mix of blood and plaster of paris. As for the grapplers, they had nothing to announce, but they still expected to get paid. That August the city was hit with a whopping dredging bill—and while the incorruptible chief of the Detective Bureau had gambled that finding the head would justify the heavy cost, he hadn't built a network of cronies willing to overlook an expensive failure. Lacking Guldensuppe's head, Acting Inspector Stephen O'Brien lost his own: He was relieved of his post the following week.

"I HAVE BEEN DESCRIBED in a paper as a 'murderess,'" the prisoner mused. She shot a significant look toward the *World* reporter visiting her cell. "Do you, young man, think that I have that appearance?"

No, he quickly assured Augusta Nack—she didn't look like a murderess at all.

"It did not seem," the reporter assured readers, "that her facial expressions were those of a fiendish woman." To the contrary: Manhattan's most famous prisoner had "a sparkle in her eyes," not to mention a "finely modeled neck" and "very fine white teeth." He complimented the low collar on her black wrap, and well he might; Augusta Nack was granting the *World* the first full interview since her arrest.

"Wait a moment and I will get you a chair." She ushered the reporter into her cell. "We can sit in this corner."

She'd agreed to talk, she explained as they sat down, because the *World* was the one paper that had treated her fairly. The rivalry between Pulitzer and Hearst was such that now they'd even taken opposing prisoners; thanks to the early doubts that *World* reporters had thrown on the *Journal*'s accusations against Mrs. Nack, they were the closest thing she had to a friend in the press. The quiet and brooding Thorn, on the other hand, was a confirmed *Journal* reader, and when he talked much at all, it was generally to Hearst reporters.

"I will cheerfully tell my life story to the *World*," Mrs. Nack announced. "All the others have condemned me."

The reporter joined in her indignation as he looked around her quarters. Mrs. Nack had settled into the Tombs over the course of the summer. True, she'd complained about the bad food in her first days there, and was shocked by the sight of women smoking—"a most degrading habit," she complained—but then she wised up fast. She was the undisputed queen of the cell block by one simple strategy: The quarters she charged from curious visitors and female well-wishers went to buying coffee and cake for her fellow prisoners. Short of a good lawyer, a berth alongside Augusta Nack was the best luck a Tombs woman could hope for.

She felt for these women, Nack wanted the *World* reporter to know—for she too had suffered a hard lot in life. She was a deeply wronged woman. Herman Nack, she claimed, was a drunkard who had abused her terribly.

"Shortly after my baby was born he seemed to become more abusive." She shuddered. In the few spare moments when he wasn't ordering her around their home in Germany, she'd bettered herself by studying for a midwifery degree. "A short time after I received my diploma, we decided to come to New York." This had only made matters worse.

"I first made the discovery that, in addition to being cruel and neglectful, he was unfaithful to me." She sighed. "I caught him several times in our house with strange women." In lieu of contrition, Augusta recalled bitterly, Herman beat her and made her sleep in the cellar.

"I made up my mind to leave him. I considered that living the life of a slave was paradise compared to living with that man."

And that, she pleaded, was why *World* readers—especially women readers—had to understand that her story was not about a murdered man, but about a wronged woman. "I ask those women who are happy and who have good, true husbands and pleasant families and happy homes, not to judge me too harshly," she pleaded. Her concern wasn't with the murder—*there had been no murder*—but with how people viewed her leaving her brutish husband. She was drawn to Guldensuppe because of his tenderness. Was that so wrong?

"He was kind and indulgent of me in every way," she declared passionately, "and I do not feel that I am deserving of blame that I grew to love him."

She did not mention Martin Thorn.

Mrs. Nack stood up and excused herself—it was time, she explained, for her to crochet. Also, she'd have to make time for her devotions; she was a pious woman, she explained, and "never a day goes by that I do not pray to God." But she knew those prayers would soon be answered. As long as the police and the DA couldn't find a head for the body in the Bellevue morgue, she could insist that it didn't belong to her boyfriend. Even if they'd argued and fallen out, Willie would surely come back to save her.

"There is no doubt in my mind that William Guldensuppe is alive today." She smiled. "I know he will turn up soon and clear me of this horrible suspicion."

The story of Augusta Nack's life, it seemed, was not a sordid crime drama; it was a love story.

14.

THE HIGH ROLLER

WHEN THE DELIVERYMAN SHAMBLED unannounced into the district attorney's office on Centre Street, it wasn't to drop off a package.

I'm going to tell you everything, Herman Nack told the astounded prosecutor.

Assistant DA Ed Mitchell hastily sent for a stenographer as he guided the gruff bakery employee into his office. Clutching his battered homburg, Herman Nack was none too pleased at spending a day off on anything besides beer or bowling, but Gussie's *World* interview had been nagging at him.

"She said lots of bad things about me," he groused. "I wanted to tell what I knew about her just to get square."

Herman was a man ill used by the case: attacked in the street by *Journal* reporters, briefly jailed as the prime suspect, his failed marriage paraded before the nation. Now the *World* was calling him a vicious brute. He'd just wanted to be left alone, but after biting his tongue for two months, he could keep silent no more. Still, he insisted he didn't want to get into any trouble.

"If I say anything," he hesitated, "I will be as liable as she is."

He would be safe, the prosecutors assured him. They were joined by Detective Samuel Price, who leaned in with keen interest; he'd staked out and arrested Augusta Nack at her apartment and harbored deeper suspicions about her.

"There isn't much to tell," the deliveryman stalled. "But what I know and remember I will tell."

"My wife left me in 1896," he began. "We had a scrap. I had been giving her $10 a week, and she wanted the whole business, which was the $17 that I received. I told her I would only give her *five* dollars a week."

The stenographer calmly transcribed the events of that violent evening.

"She came at me with a knife. I seized her by the arms, and she threw the knife on the ground. . . . Two or three days after that she moved the furniture. She said she did not want anything to do with me but wanted to live with Guldensuppe."

What was galling to Herman wasn't so much that his wife was leaving him, but that she already *had* money from her own sideline: abortions.

"Do you know whether your wife attended women at your house?" Detective Price asked sharply.

"Yes." He nodded. She charged her customers $25 each. "She had no diploma, either. She failed her examination in Europe."

Not surprisingly, some of her customers hadn't fared so well.

"Did any of them die?" Price pressed.

"I know two, for sure," Herman admitted. "Another case was a girl who came from the country."

"Do you know if any of these women ever died in your house?"

"No, not in my house. My wife told me that one girl died in Bellevue Hospital. This was about five years ago."

Augusta was afraid of getting found out. Dr. Weiss of Tenth Avenue, as well as her current landlord and pharmacist, F. W. Werner, quietly assisted in taking care of the women after their botched abortions.

"How would she dispose of the bodies of the infants?"

"Any child would be buried by an undertaker—Alois Palm."

Mitchell and Detective Price sat amazed. They knew that some doctors and undertakers treated botch jobs and buried fetuses with no questions asked, but Nack wasn't just making wild allegations now. He was naming names. Palm still ran a thriving undertaking business, just down the street from Mrs. Nack.

In fact, Herman admitted, not all the children were buried.

"My wife placed dead children in jars containing spirits," he recalled with some distaste—because she'd stored them in *his* bedroom.

"How many dead children did you see in your room?" an astonished Price asked.

"About a dozen," Nack shrugged.

"Did you ever see her cut up any of the bodies?" the detective asked pointedly.

"She told me"—he paused to think back—"*that she had burned some of them in the stove.*"

The sounds of Centre Street filtered in from outside; the Criminal Courts Building stood just across the street from the Tombs, and they could almost see Augusta Nack's cell window. As the stenographer scratched away, Price finally broke the silence.

"How many?" he asked.

"A whole lot," the deliveryman ventured. "She burned them for eight or ten years, two or three a month."

Assistant DA Mitchell quietly did the math in his head: two, maybe three hundred infants had been cremated in the kitchen of Mrs. Nack's apartment on Ninth Avenue. Herman Nack sensed he'd already revealed too much. Maybe he wasn't going to tell *quite* everything—such as, say, just why his wife had to leave the old country back in 1886.

"There is something at the back of that," the burly driver hinted darkly. "If she says anything more about *me*, maybe I'll say something else. She knows what I could say."

"IT'S A LIE!" Mrs. Nack roared from her cell. "It's a lie, every word of it!"

The *Evening Journal* for September 2 had landed the story, but the *World* was the first to get a reporter to Augusta Nack's cell. She spun away from the Pulitzer reporter and raged at her ex-husband from inside her cell.

"Fool!" she spat. "*Fool!*"

Her lawyer was quick to show up and ward off the reporters.

"I am not going to let Mrs. Nack see anyone about her husband's charges," he insisted, though the story had already slipped from his grasp. On the way over to the jail he'd been confronted by *World* front pages with the damning headline:

SAYS THE ACCUSED MURDERESS OUT-HERODED HEROD

"It is only natural," chimed in the *Evening Journal,* "that Mrs. Nack, in view of her record of baby killing, should place so little value on human life."

The papers had already been seizing on any death they could pin to the case. When a Woodside neighbor died in July, it was said to be from shock over the crime; so was the death of John Gotha's ninety-five-year-old father-in-law that same month, though a better theory was that the man had died at the shock of being ninety-five years old. But now there was the dizzying prospect of *hundreds* of deaths connected to the case. The Tenth Avenue doctors and undertakers named by Herman Nack found their shops invaded by reporters. Dr. Weiss claimed to have no idea what Herman was talking about; nor did Mrs. Nack's landlord, F. G. Werner.

"I do not think that Nack means me," the pharmacist demurred. "Surely I never aided Mrs. Nack in any way."

Alois Palm tried rather unsportingly to pin it all on his own brother, a fellow undertaker. But for all the perfunctory denials, none of them threatened to take Herman Nack to court. For those familiar with the city's thriving abortion business, it wasn't hard to guess why they didn't relish the prospect of testifying under oath.

Discussing the case with reporters, Assistant DA Mitchell found that Herman's charges made a great deal of sense indeed. Even Mrs. Nack's friends faulted her as avaricious, and there certainly was quick money to be made in illicit abortions. What was more, she *needed* quick money.

"We have found out," Mitchell announced, "that she was a high roller."

"What was her object," asked a puzzled *Journal* reporter, "in preserving the bodies of infants in jars?"

"Why, to sell them," the assistant DA answered. "Medical colleges and students pay well for good specimens of the kind."

Herman's charges also explained one of the oddest testimonies from the early days of the investigation: that of Werner, Mrs. Nack's landlord and the proprietor of the pharmacy on the first floor of her building. When the *World* was still trying to undermine the Guldensuppe identification, Werner had been one of the few to claim that he didn't see a resemblance in the body. Now that peculiar denial had a motive. A pharmacist could make good money providing abortifacients on the sly; perhaps Werner was desperately trying to steer attention away from his shop.

More important, Herman's accusation gave Mrs. Nack a *motive*. Martin Thorn's motive for the murder—revenge—had been clear all along, and vehemently voiced in front of fellow barbers and pinochle partners. But what of Mrs. Nack? Why hadn't she just left William Guldensuppe and moved in with Thorn? The logical answer was: she couldn't. Mitchell believed that Guldensuppe had kept Gussie from leaving with his damning knowledge of her abortion operations— and of the mothers who had died at her hands.

"Guldensuppe knew this," the *World* reported, "and threatened to tell."

It wouldn't be the first time, either. Herman's charges unearthed still another bombshell. Right after Augusta left him, he'd paid some angry visits to her—and, perhaps, made a few unwise threats about what he knew. So, Mitchell revealed, Mrs. Nack had gone to one Ernest Moring—the brother of her friend Mrs. Miller, who ran Buck's Hotel—*and tried to hire him to kill her ex-husband*.

He'd turned her down, and nothing had come of Herman Nack's threat anyway. But when she was ready to leave her next beau, Mitchell reasoned, Mrs. Nack was threatened with exposure once again. This time she found the right man for the job: a jealous lover with enough anger to do the deed, and to do it for free. And that was how she kept Guldensuppe from talking—forever.

THE *WORLD* REPORTER ascended the rickety stairs of a Grand Street tenement, wandered down a dark hallway, and passed through a doorway into a modest ten-by-twelve room. Before him sat Dr. Giuseppe Lapenta, director, president, secretary, and treasurer of the Italian School of Midwifery. Its entire campus consisted of this modest room.

How much do your degrees cost? the reporter demanded from the startled gentleman.

It was the oldest and surest of headline grabbers. Within a day of Herman Nack's revelations, Coroner Tuthill announced that he would lobby for new legislation to restrain midwives. The *World* promptly pursued local midwives with gusto. Reporters pounced on nursing schools for poor immigrant women, where degrees could be had in fifteen days for $50, and marched out with indignant headlines like A SCHOOL FOR BARBARITY and DIPLOMA MILL FOR MIDWIVES.

"Out of 55,000 live births last year, 25,000 and over were reportedly attended by women of this class," the newspaper warned. "No one knows how many midwives there are in New York City."

That, alas, was due to the *previous* midwife murder scandal: the death of Mary Rogers, the beautiful shopgirl whom Edgar Allan Poe barely fictionalized in his "Mystery of Marie Roget." After her body was found in the Hudson River in July 1841, Mary's despondent fiancé committed suicide, and suspicions ran strong that "Madame Restell," the city's wealthiest abortionist, had dumped her body after a procedure gone awry. She promptly became the designated villainess both for moralizing *Herald* journalists and for the American Medical Association, who cast midwives as a meddling and undertrained menace. The state criminalized abortion soon afterward, and a later wave of obscenity laws made it illegal to even discuss the procedure.

This, naturally, merely ceded the procedure to opportunists and criminals. Unregulated midwives still readily pierced the amniotic sac and then induced contractions with abortifacients such as pennyroyal, tansy, and black hellebore. The better practitioners were often immigrants from Bohemia, where stringent training was still available; the worse ones included anybody walking in from Grand Street with $50 to hand over to Dr. Lapenta. But for those with plenty of nerve and few scruples, there was money to be made. And it was a consensual crime that no woman—from chambermaid to heiress—was eager to volunteer information about.

"Their methods are so hidden and their ignorance so dense that they have no conception of law to restrain them," the *World* thundered against midwives. "Most can hardly sign their own names." But another anxiety shadowed the genuine concern over their scattershot training: namely, that it was women taking business away from men. Even as the *World* was pursuing midwives, it was running the headline WOMEN FARM, MEN COOK—a story noting that "the New Woman" was moving into traditionally male jobs in farming and manufacturing, while more men were taking domestic employment. Hearst's *Journal*, though generally sympathetic to women's labor, still ran headlines such as SHE'S PRETTY, EVEN IF SHE IS A LAWYER.

Yet the reporters could hardly fault their own motives in pursuing Mrs. Nack. After all, for a case initially written off as a prank, the Guldensuppe affair was now becoming an open sewer of murder, dismemberment, adultery, contract killing, false identity, gambling, illicit abortion, and medical malpractice. And as *World* reporters swarmed local diploma mills, all of it would have been curiously familiar to the blustery old editors of New York during the Mary Rogers case more than fifty years earlier.

"Really," the *Herald*'s publisher had mused during the throes of that scandal, "the newspapers are becoming the only efficient police, the only efficient judges that we have."

ACTUAL POLICE AND JUDGES, though, were now moving swiftly. With Martin Thorn and Augusta Nack in attendance at the Criminal Court on the morning of September 17, their indictment was dismissed. That wasn't exactly a victory for the defense, because another indictment had just been handed down from Queens County.

Guldensuppe was lured from Manhattan, murdered in Queens, and then scattered in Brooklyn, Manhattan, and the Bronx. The consolidation of the city's five boroughs was just months away; had the crime happened a bit later, there wouldn't have been any question of jurisdiction. As it was, with Inspector O'Brien off the case and with the murder scene firmly fixed in Queens, the lawyers and the DA's office had agreed to a move. The two prisoners were handed over to Undersheriff Baker of Queens County and led to gather their meager belongings from their cells at the Tombs. Then they said their good-byes to cell mates and slipped out the Leonard Street exit.

One thousand New Yorkers were waiting for them outside.

Undersheriff Baker quickly bundled Mrs. Nack and Martin Thorn into a waiting carriage. A phalanx of black cabs slowly pursued them, all filled with reporters ready to cover the pair's every move and scrambling for hotel accommodations by the Queens courthouse. "The line of carriages looked like a funeral procession," a *Sun* reporter marveled.

The crowd surged, gawking at the prisoners as they headed toward the ferry slip by New Chambers Street. It was only as the boat finally pulled away from its moorings that, with the expanse of the East River stretching out before them, Nack and Thorn could feel some measure of solitude. Any solace in the quiet journey was brief; the undersheriff was staring quite fixedly at them, trying to read their faces. The ferry was passing the East Eleventh Street Pier, where the first gory parcel had been discovered.

Martin and Gussie remained expressionless, watching as their adopted island of Manhattan slipped away for what might be the last time.

Anything was a welcome change after the Tombs. The Queens County Jail was everything the Tombs was not: quiet, modern, and brightly lit. Thorn, though, was uneasy. He'd become used to the sound of pile drivers and hammers at the Tombs; in the eerie silence of the Queens jail, he could ponder the steady drip of evidence against him.

"I rented the Woodside cottage under the name of Braun," he finally blurted out to *Journal* reporter Lowe Shearon. It was a stunning admission, but Thorn insisted that it was perfectly innocent. Sure, he'd rented it under a false name—"What of it?"—but that was no capital offense. And a new claim by a clerk that he'd bought seven cents' worth of plaster on the day of the murder left him unimpressed.

"That is all rot. I never bought plaster of paris in my life. I never even had a pinch of it," he insisted.

And with that, he retreated into the darkness of his new cell.

WHILE THORN WAS ASSIGNED to Murderers Row, Mrs. Nack had pulled an upper-floor unit with a vista of Long Island. The landscape was still pleasant and green; in a few weeks she'd be able to watch the foliage turn color. If she looked carefully, she could even make out the infamous Woodside cottage from where she stood. Gussie didn't care; she was delighted with her new cell.

She'd said little, though, since Herman's disastrous retaliation for her last interview. So while the *Journal* worked over the sullen Thorn, the *World* sent to Mrs. Nack's cell their star women's columnist: Harriet Hubbard Ayer. Gussie instantly relented.

"Come in if you want to see me," she heard herself saying.

Mrs. Ayer was startled to be welcomed; Mrs. Nack was even more startled by who she was letting in. For the first time since being jailed, she was face-to-face with a bigger celebrity than herself. Harriet Hubbard Ayer was a household name, a glamorous riches-to-rags grand dame whose cosmetics empire had fallen apart in a messy divorce. After her ex-husband schemed, successfully, to commit her to an asylum, Mrs. Ayer made a sensational comeback as a beauty-and-manners columnist. Surely *she* would understand the terribly wronged Mrs. Nack.

"Must I be locked in?" Mrs. Ayer asked the jailer fearfully as she entered the cell. The memory of her own year in an asylum was never far away.

"Don't be afraid, you'll get out all right," Mrs. Nack assured her, clasping her hands in sudden sympathy. "I know just how you feel. *Ach, mein Gott!*"

Mrs. Nack's two cell mates fluttered about tidying the cell; they were so deeply in Gussie's thrall that they did all her washing and chores for her. As they fussed over the new arrival, Mrs. Nack led Harriet to a corner of the cell, where a table was festooned with one of the many bunches of flowers sent by admirers. She was, she

confided to the columnist, still angry at how newly overthrown Inspector O'Brien had interrogated her.

"Fifty times or more already Inspector O'Brien tells me he knows
just how the murder is committed. 'Ve know, *ve know*. Vill you tell or
not?'" She punched her palm as she slipped into her old accent. "I
say, screaming at him: 'Ven you know the story so well, vy in hell isn't
that enough for you?'"

Mrs. Nack regained her composure and gazed intently into the
columnist's face.

"Yes, I say just so," she continued. "Do you think if I have murder on my soul I could be as quiet as I have been? I sleep soundly all
night—ask the Warden."

"It's a fact," her jailer piped up from outside the cell.

And, Harriet asked tenderly, had she lost her friends since being
jailed?

"Yes." The midwife shook her head sadly. "My friends they all
say, so Augusta Nack is a murderer, or if she isn't we better not have
anything to do with her."

"Our friends want little to do with our troubles," Mrs. Ayer em-
pathized.

Instead, Mrs. Nack had her cell mates and her sewing for company.
Her dresses, already a sensation at her court appearances, would be
even better for the trial. And Mrs. Nack was, of course, a woman you
could trust with long needles.

"Have you seen in the papers that the Warden is afraid I am going
to kill myself?" she scoffed incredulously. "Well now, I am going to
show you how easily I could kill myself if I wanted to."

Nack crossed the room and pulled out a small basket from under
the sink; it was filled with silverware. To Ayer's amazement, she drew
five sharp steel knives and laid them out on the table before the columnist.

"You see"—the prisoner laughed—"if I want to cut my throat I
have every convenience. I could take a knife in each hand and have
some to spare. But I am not going to cut my throat. *I am going to be
acquitted*."

Every night before she went to bed, she admitted, she spun and twirled about her cell in anticipation: "When I think of how near the trial is, I dance around."

"If we had a piano," a cell mate chirped, "it would help so very much."

And then the heavy iron door was unlocked to Harriet once again, just as Mrs. Nack promised. But as she emerged, the beauty columnist was haunted by what she'd seen. Mrs. Nack's was a curious love story indeed, for the fates of Thorn and Guldensuppe had not even arisen once in the conversation.

"Augusta Nack knows nothing whatsoever about love," Harriet Ayer mused to her readers in the next morning's *World*. "That is to say, of the love which means self-abnegation. She loves herself." As for Martin Thorn, the columnist believed that to her he was merely a losing hand that she now wanted to fold—just as Herman Nack once was, just as William Guldensuppe had been.

"If she thinks of Martin Thorn at all," she wrote, "I believe she thinks of him to hate him."

15.

KLONDIKE WILLIE

BUT AUGUSTA NACK was thinking about Martin a great deal indeed. Even as Harriet prepared her article for the next day's October 3 edition of the *World*, Mrs. Nack motioned an inmate over to her cell.

Rockaway! came the summons as he strolled along the top floor of the jail. Rockaway Ed was a trusty, part of the peculiar prisoner hierarchy within Queens County Jail. Ascending to the rank of a trusty meant freedom: freedom to walk the halls and deliver messages and packages, freedom to walk the exercise yard, even the freedom to leave the prison when the sheriff wanted errands run. The trusty was second only to a "bum boss" in the underground ranking of prisoners, and when *Journal* men had first visited the jail, it was Ed who'd shown them around; he was considered the best guide. When, that is, he could be found there at all. He was on the last two months of a six-month sentence for pilfering some jewelry, and on a good streak he could stay clear of jail for the entire day, returning only to sleep on his hard pallet bed at night.

Ed came up close to the cell door.

"I believe I can trust you," Mrs. Nack whispered. "And if you will do what I tell you it's worth twenty-five dollars to you."

That sounded like escape money, and Ed's own sentence was going to end before Christmas. "Oh, that's all right," he assured her. "I'm not looking for pay."

"Well." Mrs. Nack hesitated. "I want to send a message to Thorn, and I want you to take it. I'll put it in a sandwich."

Food was a good medium of communication; Mrs. Nack was already known for securing cell-block friendships this way, so food handed through her cell door to a trusty wouldn't attract any notice.

Three days later when she'd saved up enough food and paper, the parcel passed through the barred door and into Rockaway Ed's hands. As he walked down the cell block, and then down the three flights of stairs to Murderers Row, he could see that there was more than just a sandwich in the parcel: Whether to hide the note, or simply out of a hostess's pride, Mrs. Nack had sent a side dish of potatoes as well.

At the bottom of the stairs, it was a straight shot through the iron cell-block door and to Thorn's room. But Ed bided his time; he knew that sooner or later he'd be wanted by the sheriff for an outside errand, and he was right. Sent out of the jail, he still held Mrs. Nack's parcel as he walked out through the locked doors, into the autumn sunlight, across the Court Square, and into the outpost of the *New York Journal*.

Whatever Augusta Nack could pay, William Randolph Hearst could pay better—much better.

I've got it, Rockaway Ed announced.

Journal staffers pounced. He'd slipped the lead to them days ago, and they'd been waiting with writers and artists at the ready to make a copy.

Rockaway Ed was hustled back out the door with the letter; he was to go immediately back to the jail and deliver it, they told him. If Thorn wrote a reply, they'd intercept that one, too.

A staffer who knew German quickly translated the note into the text that would appear in the next morning's paper:

Dear Martin
I send you a couple of potatoes. If you do not care to eat them, perhaps the others will. Dear child, send me a few lines how you feel. Dear child, I believe there is very little hope for us. I feel very bad this afternoon. Send me a letter by your sister or by your brother-in-law. I wish they could procure us something so that we could end our lives.

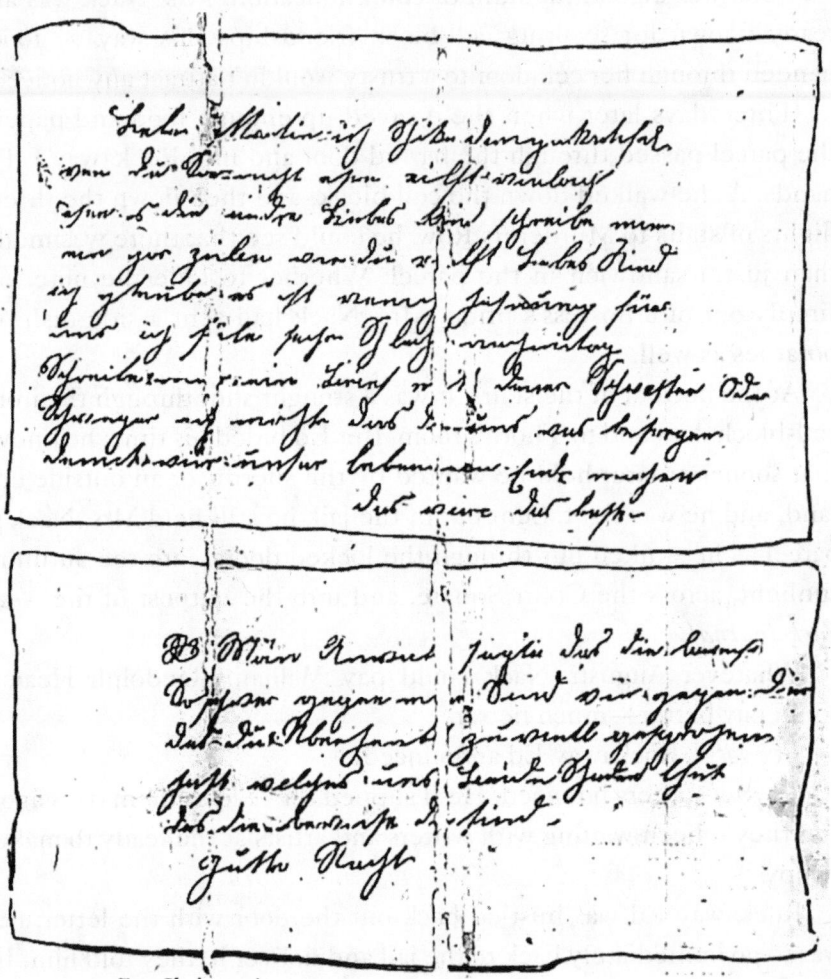

This would be best.

My attorney assures me the evidence against me is as strong as that against you, and that you have talked too much, which injures us, for the proofs are at hand.

Good night.

It was a puzzling note, because it was palpably false. The evidence was *not* as strong against her—she hadn't spoken publicly against Guldensuppe before his disappearance and hadn't unburdened herself to a friend about killing him. In fact, if it wasn't for

Thorn's presence, it might have been difficult to mount a murder case against Mrs. Nack at all.

It took a stunned moment to sink in: Mrs. Nack was trying to get her accomplice to kill himself.

"WHERE IS IT?" Sheriff Doht demanded as he burst into Thorn's gloomy cell. Jailer Jarvis barreled in behind him as Thorn grabbed for his clothing.

"Hand me the vest!" the sheriff yelled. Thorn yanked a sheet of paper out of a pocket and frantically tore it, stuffing pieces into his mouth.

"Don't let him, that's what I'm after!" the sheriff barked to the jail keeper. Jarvis closed his beefy hands around Thorn's neck, choking and rattling him as the writhing prisoner desperately tried to swallow the scraps.

"Give it up, Thorn!" they roared. "Open your mouth!"

The denizens of Murderers Row eagerly lined their cell doors, watching Thorn's eyes and face bulge; he was propelled backward over his cot until his head hung upside down, and Sheriff Doht pried his jaws open and reached into his mouth for the chewed scraps of paper. Jarvis at last released his grip on Thorn's throat, and the prisoner gasped in long drafts of air.

The fragments bearing Thorn's writing were reassembled on a table in District Attorney Youngs's office:

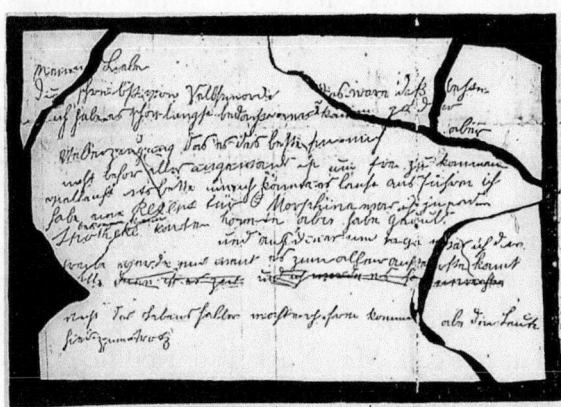

Some attending *Journal* reporters quickly translated it:

My dear—you wrote of self-destruction. That would be best. I had thought it over long ago and came to the conclusion that it would be best for me, but not before all is done to gain liberty. Perhaps it will be the better way, and I will, and it will be easy to accomplish it. I have a prescription for morphine that I can buy or get at any drug store. But have patience and endurance and say what I write to you. If it comes to extremes, then it is time, and I will arrange it so. It is not on account of living that I would like to get free, but to spite the people here.

The watch on Thorn's cell was instantly doubled, and his sister and brother-in-law were searched carefully whenever they entered the facility. As the only visitors Thorn deigned to see, they were almost certainly part of his plan for obtaining the morphine overdose.

"I am sorry," DA Youngs sighed. "The *Journal* did not give me Mrs. Nack's original letter. No scrap of her note has been found. He either threw the letter down a sink or tore it into fragments and swallowed it." The Hearst reporters shrugged it off; Doht's lousy security at the jail wasn't their problem.

"Bring the sheriff here," snapped the DA to a detective.

Sheriff Doht, led into the office, stammered out an excuse: Nack's letter was surely a fabrication by a German-speaking prisoner in the jail, or by the *Journal* itself.

"I don't blame you boys," he leered at the reporters. "I understand how you work."

The Hearst men scoffed at him; Doht just wanted to cover up his own missteps, which had been piling up. He had tried to induce vomiting in both prisoners by filling their soup with grease, with the ridiculous notion that he'd extract confessions out of them while they retched; then he'd hung a picture of a man's disembodied head over Mrs. Nack's cot while she slept. DA Youngs was unamused, and the sheriff quickly backed down.

Confronted at her cell, Mrs. Nack also tried denying the note—

"Oh, my God, I never write such a letter!"—before breaking apart in fury when the text was read back to her.

"To whom did you give the letter?" she was asked.

"Rockaway," she spat in disgust.

What kind of a world was it when you couldn't trust a jewel thief?

JOURNAL REPORTERS SWOOPED DOWN into Hell's Kitchen and up the block of brick tenements past the corner of Forty-Second and Tenth—past Stemmerman's grocery, past Mssr. Mauborgne's Mattress Renovating, past a stable and the neighboring blacksmith shop—and piled into the five-story walk-up at 521 West Forty-Second.

Where's Guldensuppe's head? they demanded.

Standing in the doorway was Paul Menker, a local butcher now better known to the world as Martin Thorn's brother-in-law. "I know nothing about this case at all," he said flatly to reporters.

Where's the head?

"Anybody who tries to drag me into it will get hurt," he said, his voice rising.

Come now, the reporters pressed—*we have his confession.*

Menker was enraged.

"I know nothing about the case," the mustachioed butcher sputtered, before reaching for a rather unfortunate turn of phrase. "Bring a man that says I do, and I'll knock his head off!"

Excellent; the *Journal* reporters made sure they got that quote down. They were on a roll, for their rivals at the *World* had fumbled yet another a priceless lead. The same day that the *Journal* revealed the lovers' suicide letters, Pulitzer's team had landed a tantalizing story: that one Frank Clark had heard a boozy confession back in late July. While laid up in the Tombs infirmary, Clark had been prescribed bitter quinine for his malaria, along with a ration of at least three shots of whiskey to wash it down. He wasn't a drinking man, though, and each day he gave his drams to the man in the next bed—Martin Thorn. Warmed by his first liquor in weeks, his neighbor talked about the mysterious fate of William Guldensuppe.

"He often boasted," Clark recalled, "that he was impossible to convict without the head."

And Thorn kept talking, lulled by the seeming nonchalance of his new friend. Clark was a talented forger—he could draw an exact replica of a dollar bill with nothing but a green pencil—but the man was no killer. What Thorn confessed next preyed on Clark's mind for months until he finally gave a 3,500-word affidavit to the district attorney.

"He told me that after he placed Guldensuppe's head in the plaster of paris, he threw it in a patch of woods," he testified. "He told me Gotha had erred when he said the head had been thrown into the East River. Thorn said he told Gotha it was his *intention* to so dispose of the head, but he was frightened off."

The attention being paid to the ferries and riverside in the days after the murder was discovered, not to mention the *Journal* hiring grapplers out on the river, simply made it too perilous for Thorn to come out of hiding to finish the job. Arrested with the head still on dry land, though, he'd found an even better solution.

"Two weeks after Thorn's arrest a man came to the Tombs to see him," Clark continued. "This was on July nineteenth."

It was on that visit, Clark said, that Thorn told his visitor exactly where to find the head. His accomplice promptly located it, packed the heavy chunk inside a tackle basket, and that very afternoon boarded a fishing excursion vessel, the *J. B. Schuyler*. With his rod and tackle, he didn't stand out from the other leisure fishermen on the side-wheel steamer. As the *Schuyler* floated among the fishing banks miles offshore, Thorn's accomplice simply tipped his basket's parcel into the water. Two days later, he returned to the Tombs to report the good news. "Thorn was very happy," Clark reported.

A visit to the ailing forger by the district attorney left prosecutors convinced of his story—but they refused to give the *World* the identity of Thorn's accomplice. And there things sat for the next six days, without much follow-up by Pulitzer's reporters—until the *Journal* came piling into Menker's hallway.

Is it true? Did you really do it?

Mrs. Menker, Thorn's sister, tried to fend off the reporters. Her husband was a good, hardworking man, she explained, and didn't know anything about the case.

Doesn't the prison record show he visited Thorn on the nineteenth and the twenty-first?

Paul Menker was a decent man, the wife insisted—and, she added, he will throw you down the stairs if you don't leave us alone. The *Journal* reporters quickly retreated, leaving the butcher quaking with anger.

"I tell you that Guldensuppe is alive!" he roared after them. "That Thorn is innocent! *That Guldensuppe will be found!*"

IN FACT, one official was wondering whether he just might be right. A letter had arrived in Coroner Hoeber's office back in early August, from a woman claiming to be the wife of an attendant at the Murray Hill Baths:

> *My dear sir:*
> *I cannot any longer keep quiet. Guldensuppe lives and keeps silent simply out of revenge against Thorn, of whom he is insanely jealous. He will only appear after Thorn has been sentenced to death. If the police would only look around Harlem they could easily find Guldensuppe. More I dare not say.*
>
> *Respectfully,*
> MRS. JOSEPHINE EMMA

Hoeber's staff was marveling over the newly arrived letter when they looked up to see an unannounced visitor peering at it: Mrs. Nack's lawyer, Manny Friend.

"I intended not"—the angry coroner slipped into his native German syntax—"that you should see that letter!"

They were old enemies, and Friend instantly accused the coroner of holding out evidence on him. Hoeber, the lawyer yelled, was "a dirty, insignificant little whelp." The two scuffled, and Hoeber's staff dragged them apart. Maybe the coroner wrote the letter *himself* to get attention from reporters, the lawyer yelled. "I believe," he jeered, "that he has resorted to this method to gain a little more advertisement for himself."

If so, then Hoeber was going through a lot of ink. A cascade of mysterious and often unsigned confidential letters now arrived at his office. One claimed that it was *Guldensuppe* who'd been hiding in the closet waiting to attack Thorn—and that he'd been killed in self-defense. At least two more claimed that Guldensuppe was alive and well, and seeking out his fortune prospecting in the Klondike.

The accused himself insisted that he'd be vindicated.

"I have always believed that he had gone to Europe," Thorn assured a *World* reporter about yet another Guldensuppe sighting in Syracuse, New York. "I am sure he will turn up in time to clear me of the charge of murdering him." Perhaps it was just as well that the reporter did not note that his own paper attributed the latest sighting to a Mr. "O. Christ."

Soon enough, another letter insisted that everyone else was wrong:

> *Kindly do not believe any of the cards being sent to you saying that Guldensuppe lives yet, as he does not. He was murdered at Woodside, L.I. and the head you can receive by looking sharp at the Astoria Ferry pier about near the point of the Ninety-first street dock. . . . Will let you know more. The party that killed him does not know that I saw this.*

Yet another missive, sent by Mrs. Lenora Merrifield of 106th Street, claimed that Guldensuppe was working under an alias in a Harlem barbershop. When confronted by detectives, a puzzled Mrs. Merrifield didn't even recognize the letter; her teenaged son, however, showed a peculiar interest in the commotion it created.

But the most haunting notes were the anonymous ones penned in German and sent to Coroner Hoeber: *Guldensuppe is alive, and taking revenge on Thorn by setting him up to die.* No stock could really be put in these wild and unsigned allegations. But if William Guldensuppe was plotting retribution, it seemed he was about to get it: Thorn's trial was now set for October 18.

"THE POLICE DO NOT EXPECT to see Guldensuppe in this world," William Randolph Hearst joked. "In fact, they would be content to see his head."

It had been a splendid season for news. Along with this swell murder here in the north, Hearst also had a huge promotion to send a team of *Journal* cyclists eastward to Italy, an exciting gold rush out west, and from the south a bubbling Cuban rebellion against the dastardly Spanish. The latter had acquired a fine new angle over the summer: Evangelina Cisneros, the pretty eighteen-year-old daughter of a revolutionary, had been imprisoned for . . . well, depending on whom you asked, either for trying to break her father out of jail or for fending off the advances of a diabolical Spanish military governor. Hearst preferred the latter explanation.

Even as he sent reporters to run the gauntlet of Paul Menker's stairs, he'd sent another *Journal* operative—the hotshot reporter Karl Decker—to Cuba, to bribe a jailer, break into the prison with a ladder and a hacksaw, and chop out the iron bars of the damsel's jail cell. Disguised with a sailor's outfit and a cigar, "the Cuban Joan of Arc" was whisked away on a steamer bound for America. EVANGELINA CISNEROS RESCUED BY THE JOURNAL, his newspaper trumpeted the next day.

The rescue was not exactly *legal*. But Hearst was always pushing for more: Why just cover news when you could make it?

A NEW IDEA IN JOURNALISM, the *Journal* blared across a full-page illustration of a knight slaying octopus-like beasts: WHILE OTHERS TALK, THE JOURNAL ACTS. The paper was already launching city offensives against a gas trust and crooked paving contractors; now it would also shake the columns of national policy. Hearst lined up testimonials from the mayors of cities from San Francisco to Boston lauding his juggernaut, and even Secretary of State John Sherman delicately acknowledged the paper's rather tactless achievement.

"Every one will sympathize with the *Journal*'s enterprise in releasing Miss Cisneros," he admitted. "She is a woman."

The prime minister of Spain was more direct.

"The newspapers of your country seem to be more powerful than your government," he snapped.

Hearst was inclined to agree: The Guldensuppe case had paved the way for his paper to take it upon itself to shove aside any government, local or national, that moved too slowly to satisfy a pressroom deadline. The Cisneros rescue simply confirmed what he'd been claiming all summer.

"It is epochal," he announced from his office overlooking the city. "It represents the final stage in the evolution of the modern newspaper. Action—*that* is the distinguishing mark of the new journalism. When the East River murder seemed an insoluble mystery to the police, the *Journal* organized a detective force of its own. A newspaper's duty is not confined to exhortation, but that when things are going wrong it should set them right if possible."

He could afford to feel expansive in his powers, for his powers *were* expanding. The old order was literally falling away: *Sun* publisher Charles Anderson Dana was now on his deathbed, and Pulitzer's *World* was getting clobbered in the Guldensuppe case and in Cuba coverage. *Journal* sales were rocketing; a reader snapping it open to the latest revelations from Woodside or Havana would find them alongside a fine profusion of ads for everything from the Bonwit Teller department store to Seven Sutherland Sisters Scalp-Cleaner, or perhaps the Lady Push Ball Players—lasses in short garments who fought gamely over a giant medicine ball.

All this was laced with Hearst's own grand promotions. Just a day after raiding Thorn's brother-in-law's premises, Hearst was issuing new marching orders: Pull out all the stops for the arrival of Evangelina Cisneros.

"Organize a great open-air reception in Madison Square. Have the two best military bands," he barked to his managing editor. "Secure orators, have a procession, arrange for plenty of fireworks and searchlights. *We must have 100,000 people together that night.*" Rooms were hired at the Waldorf, reservations made at Delmonico's, and launches arranged to greet the bewildered ingénue as she arrived in New York Harbor. The story would then be splashed across the October 18, 1897, *Journal*—on the very day, in fact, that Martin Thorn's jury selection would begin. The *New York Journal* would yet again own the biggest local, national, and international stories for that day.

The *World*, one industry newsletter marveled, was now simply "scooped every day of its existence."

The paper wasn't just getting scooped, it was also getting hollowed out. Its star editor, Arthur Brisbane, was nettled by ceaselessly hectoring telegrams that Pulitzer sent from health retreats. In one the publisher cabled, THE PAPER SUFFERS AN EXCESSIVE STATESMANSHIP, yet in another he demanded the firing of a reporter for using the word "pregnant." He was stingy about the expenses for art—MAKE SALARIED ARTISTS EARN THEIR SALARIES, he warned—yet he kept constant tabs on the editorial page, perhaps the least commercial section of the paper. Just about the only relief the absentee owner's daily cables offered was this one: I REALLY DON'T EXPECT TO BE IN NEW YORK AT ALL THIS FALL. In fact, the *World* was perfectly capable of running without Pulitzer; instead, it would have to run without Brisbane, who jumped ship for the *Journal*. All it had taken, as usual, was a wave of Hearst's checkbook.

But amid these triumphs, just three days ahead of Thorn's jury selection, it was the *Brooklyn Eagle*—not the *Journal*—that carried the first word of a curious development in Germany. The call for jurors, it seemed, would have to wait: Carl and Julius Peterson, two "reputable merchants of Hamburg," were departing for New York via the ocean steamer *Fürst Bismarck* to personally testify about an unexpected old acquaintance they'd just recently run into.

The *Eagle* headline said it all:

GULDENSUPPE ALIVE?

IV.

THE
TRIAL

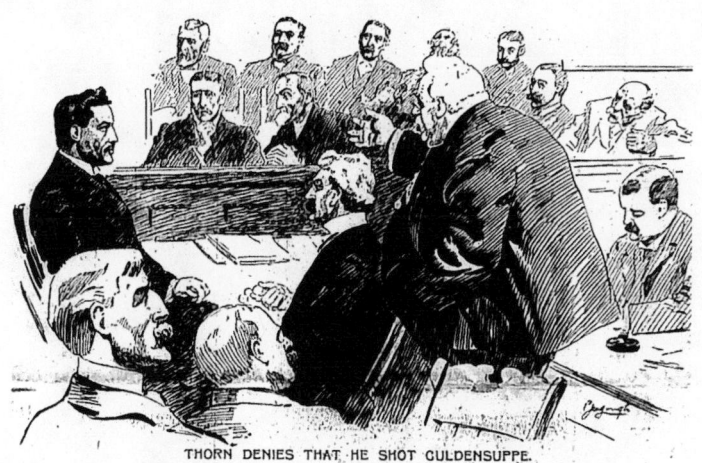

THORN DENIES THAT HE SHOT GULDENSUPPE.

16.

CORPUS DELICTI

A THICK FOG BLANKETED the Hudson, the cold seeping into the coats of the journalists huddling expectantly around the frigid Hamburg-American pier.

"The *Fürst Bismarck* has been sighted off Fire Island," confirmed a *Journal* reporter.

It wouldn't be long now; the *Bismarck* had broken transatlantic records more than once in its runs from Hamburg to New York. The November 5 arrival would boast the usual kingmakers and captains of industry, of course; Republican boss Hamilton Fish was on board for this voyage, as was a Pabst brewery scion. But that wasn't who the reporters were waiting for.

From the mist, the towering form of the *Bismarck* materialized on the river. It augured an entirely new identification in the case. Throughout the summer the coroner's office had turned away an array of disconcerting characters who wanted to view the body for no apparent good reason. The visitors who did have a reason were scarcely any better; one Josephine Vanderhoff had turned up, dressed in black and yelling at the top of her lungs that the body inside must be her husband, Marcus, a missing painter. It wasn't.

No, contended another helpful citizen. The body was surely the missing Virginia photographer William Edwards. When Edwards's minister visited to view the pickled body, he turned it into a family outing; reporters watched in undisguised fascination as the minister, his wife, and his thirteen-year-old daughter examined the hacked-up body and other clues. Remarkably, they immediately identified the abandoned valise found in the early days of the case; it had indeed belonged to Edwards. That made sense, as the clothes in it had been the wrong size for Guldensuppe. The minister could even explain the enigmatically marked-up slates found inside: Edwards was a spirit medium, and they were used for ghost writing. So perhaps he'd found a more direct line of communication with the dead—by joining them. But the minister's daughter examined the corpse's hands and shook her head; it wasn't him.

So the identification by the rubbers at Murray Hill Baths remained. But the problem of the missing head—the faint possibility that Guldensuppe was hiding abroad—remained a vexing one. And every journalist on the pier had another recent case in mind: Luetgert.

Just two weeks earlier, days after the Peterson brothers announced they'd be coming, a Chicago trial had concluded for the infamous sausage-maker Adolph Luetgert. Nobody had *seen* him kill his wife and throw her body into his factory's acid-rendering vat, and nothing but five bone fragments—some as little as a toe joint and a broken tooth—had been found in the vat, along with two incriminating gold rings. The defense claimed the police had planted the rings, though, and that the bone fragments were from pigs.

The jurors simply didn't know what to think.

The Luetgert trial ended in a hung jury, and Thorn eagerly read the wire reports that covered it. It was not hard to guess at the reason for his interest. And with the testimony of the Petersons—why, he might not even have to go to trial at all.

Slowly, carefully, the mighty S.S. *Fürst Bismarck* eased into its berth and the gangway was lowered. One by one, top-hatted gents and wives swathed in furs against the cold descended; reporters waited at the bottom, notebooks at the ready, and checked the manifest for the famous witnesses.

No Carl and Julius Peterson were listed.

SO SORRY, Thorn's lawyer explained. *We just received a cable, and it turns out the Petersons will be on the next transatlantic steamer.* It was an extraordinarily shameless excuse; but this was no ordinary case, and William F. Howe was no ordinary lawyer.

The office of Howe & Hummel was the best known in the city. Open twenty-four hours a day across the street from the Tombs, it was a cash-up-front operation that served as counsel for the Whyo Gang, the Sheeny Mob, the Valentine Gang, and every safecracker and pickpocket syndicate in Manhattan. When seventy-eight brothel madams were arrested in a one-night sweep, every one named William Howe as her attorney. He was a 300-pound whirlwind of indignation, a crusader in an endless array of loud green and violet waistcoats, checked pants, and diamond rings on every finger. In four decades Howe had personally defended 650 murder and manslaughter cases—and he was accustomed to winning.

"You cannot prove a *corpus delicti* by patchwork," he'd roar to anyone who listened. "And I shall prove that the body in the Morgue is *not* that of William Guldensuppe."

Publicly the DA's office laughed Howe off, but in private they feared their diamond-fingered foe. The Latin for "body of crime" meant the proof that a crime had actually occurred. The notion had originated with Lord Chief Justice Sir Matthew Hale, who pointed out that confessions alone were not trustworthy. It was powerfully revived in America in 1819 after the Boorn brothers case in Vermont, when a "victim" turned up alive shortly before a scheduled execution. But Howe was invoking a deliberate misreading—that a murder charge needed a *complete body*.

"They have not got the head," the lawyer needled. "And what is more, they can never find it."

Howe was enjoying the attention immensely. Reporters could come in and marvel at his Tombs office, a roughhouse operation where Howe cheekily kept the combination safe filled with coal for the furnace—actual money was hidden very quickly, and well away from the building—and where his staff amused themselves by serving one another with fake subpoenas. Beyond those, there was scarcely a scrap of incriminating paper in the place. Once, when his law offices were raided by police, they'd found nothing in the desks: no account books, no memoranda, no nothing. Howe and Hummel were the perfect gangsters' counsel, acting on nothing but their wits and a handshake.

Blessed with such a memory, Howe could reel off precedents for his defense of Thorn. "I cannot see how the District Attorney can get around the identification of the body," he insisted.

Take the case of the Danish preacher Soren Qvist, who smacked an insolent gardener with a spade and drove the fellow off his property— or so he said, until the man was found buried in his garden. At least, *someone* was found there, as the face was impossible to identify. The preacher professed amazement, but confessed after concluding that he must be guilty. It wasn't until two decades after his execution that a very alive vagrant was identified as the "victim"; the whole thing had been a revenge plot, he admitted, using a disinterred body seeded with suitably damning personal effects.

"Then there was the Ruloff case in this state," Howe noted, re-calling an infamous linguist suspected in at least eight murders in and around New York. "The prisoner was charged with having mur-dered his child. The body was missing altogether, and Ruloff was liberated."

True, he allowed, Ruloff was executed later—but only *after* he'd gone out again and murdered a store clerk.

Exasperated by such maneuvering, the police already had two hapless detectives on the next steamer to Hamburg to see whether Howe was up to his old tricks. This, after all, was the lawyer who had once scotched a murder case by secretly paying a witness to move to Japan. This was the lawyer who'd once gotten another murderer acquitted by blaming a stabbing on the man's four-year-old daughter.

"Well"—Howe smiled at any doubters—"when you see Gulden-suppe walk into the court room at Thorn's trial, you will all be might-ily surprised."

IF GULDENSUPPE *had* walked up to the Long Island City Courthouse that Saturday, he'd have had a hard time getting noticed; the place was abuzz with activity as carpenters added extra benches to the courtroom. More than 500 attendees were expected on Monday, and amid the lumber and dust, Sheriff Doht and DA Youngs were puzzling over how to rearrange the furniture.

Here.

They'd spent nearly two hours shifting tables and chairs around, trying to figure out how to cram everyone into the horseshoe-shaped courtroom. There'd be 200 people in the jury pool alone, not to mention reporters from every New York paper and national wire service, and witnesses, and legal teams, and officers of the court. Somewhere among all that, they'd have to fit in the accused, too.

No, over there.

William Howe's spot was a peculiar challenge; he had a table custom-built for the case, specially designed so he could be flanked by both his legal team and the mounds of evidence. At last, the sheriff and the DA had it worked out: The defense would be shoved up against the jury box, while the rest of the floor would be taken up by six tables accommodating seventy-two newsmen, including in the floor space directly in front of the judge. When the judge looked up from the bench, the first people he'd see would be the press; that would also be what he'd see when he gazed upward, as the first rows of the galleries were saved for sketch artists. The rest of the galleries would take the jury pool and a precious few spectator seats. Sheriff Doht was flooded with ticket requests—many of them, he noted, from women.

Pick your chairs! came the call to the news reps.

As the men scrambled for places, more sounds of construction filtered out from the courtroom's storage chamber. It was being converted into a newsroom bristling with telegraphs and typewriters; the prosecutor's thirty exhibits of clothing, oilcloth, and flesh that had been stored there were now instead overflowing from the desk and floors of Sheriff Doht's office.

There was scarcely any less commotion outside. Up and down Jackson Avenue housewives had cleared out guest rooms and hung Room for Rent signs for visiting reporters. Provision wagons were rumbling around the semicircular plaza in front of the courthouse, roasted-peanut vendors were staking out their territory, and sign painters were at hasty work: Four new saloons had opened across the street from the courthouse, including in the local butcher's shop.

"Preparations are being made as for a fair," mused a *Journal* reporter. "Everybody expects to make money."

Not least, naturally, was the *Journal* itself. Hearst had stolen a march on the *World* again by getting the courtroom wired. COURT TO PRINTING PRESS IN ONE MINUTE, crowed the *Journal* that weekend. For the first time ever, telephone wires from the courthouse plaza would instantly relay testimony—not just to the newsroom, but *directly into headsets worn by the Linotype operators*. Even if the *Journal*'s half million readers couldn't physically fit into the courtroom, they'd still be able to vicariously attend the trial.

"It is as though the words as they drop from the mouths of Gotha and other witnesses were by some magic instantaneously cast into type," the paper's front page promised rapturously. "It is as though some wizard had swept away the seven miles of tall houses and changed the course of the East River so as to bring the *Evening Journal* newsroom and the Long Island City Court House side by side." Testimony would hit the page, they boasted, before spectators could even tell their friends out on the courthouse steps.

Sharp-eyed saloon provisioners on the square could see another curious addition being made to the side of the courthouse: small cages. These, too, were a *Journal* idea. Hearst had hired three U.S.– record-holding racing pigeons—Aeolus, Flyaway, and Electra—so that courtroom sketches would arrive in minutes at the receiving cage set up in a *Journal* window on Newspaper Row. There a motion-detection circuit would ring a bell to alert editors and pressmen that the gallant birds had arrived with the latest cylinders.

There were, in fact, at least three other good trials scheduled for that same day: the prosecution of a recent Columbia graduate for highway robbery, the murder trial of a man who gunned down a police officer while raiding a church donation box, and the assault trial of a husband driven mad by his wife's incessant whistling of Sousa's "The Liberty Bell." Only Thorn's trial, though, would warrant the kind of attention that the *Journal* was paying.

"To the *Journal*," Hearst announced piously in a signed editorial, "Martin Thorn is the same as any other man brought to the bar of justice, presumably innocent until convicted. The *Journal* does not hound any man."

Observing Hearst's enthusiastic preparations for the trial, though, one sober *Times* reporter was feeling rather dour. "Every day there will be some fifty different pictures of scenes in the courtroom," he groused. "There is no lawful means of averting this disgusting visitation."

AS THE SUN ROSE that Monday, November 8, 1897, hundreds of potential jurors—nervous and excited, bleary-eyed and annoyed—waited on the courthouse steps, while newsboys, policemen, and journalists milled among them. The *World*'s fashionable Harriet Ayers was easy to spot, as was novelist Julian Hawthorne, fresh from reporting the grisly Luetgert trial for the *Journal*. At length a gray-haired janitor shuffled up and wrested open the courthouse doors; the great mass came coursing in, briskly shepherded by deputies into the galleries and onto the courtroom floor.

Sitting at the new defense table was William F. Howe, resplendent in a gray double-breasted suit, a yellow chrysanthemum in his lapel. He sported a cravat embroidered with a diamond medusa and doffed a yachting cap festooned with his initials in solid-gold buttons. His bejeweled fingers glittered under the gaslights as he waved to galleries filled with Long Island farmers. The attorney looked profoundly unworried, even as a police captain read that morning's newspaper with two-inch headlines proclaiming MURDERER over an engraving of his client.

Good morning! he boomed in his operatic baritone, startling DA Youngs. The district attorney was balding and bespectacled, wearing an off-the-rack suit; side by side, the barrel-chested defense lawyer and the knock-kneed prosecutor resembled a vaudevillian with his straight man.

Good morning, Youngs replied politely.

The defense attorney instantly decided he didn't trust the fellow.

"I rather fear Youngs, he's too infernally *polite*," he confided to a *Herald* reporter.

The courtroom quieted down as Judge Wilmot Smith took the bench, and his clerk called roll for the jury pool.

"William Hix," he began. There was a painful silence.

"*He's dead,*" someone yelled.

The court briefly broke into a tumult—but the explanation, alas, was true. The clerk stolidly moved on until he'd called roll for all two hundred citizens. *Present*, rang male voices of every age and accent from the galleries. When the last was called, the clerk turned expectantly to the district attorney.

"Mr. Sheriff," Youngs ordered. "Bring up the prisoner."

A murmur and then a hush fell over the room. After a few minutes had ticked by, the tramp of three pairs of shoes could be heard echoing through marble hallways outside. The door handle turned, and a man in a sober black suit walked in with Sheriff Doht and Undersheriff Baker by his side.

"He's not so bad looking," a spectator observed.

Doht unshackled the shiny new irons and sat Thorn down by an ebullient Howe, who beamed at his slightly bewildered client. Thorn fussed with his pomaded hair a bit—he'd swept his cowlick up into an insouciant curl—and then smiled hopefully, a little nervously, at the crowds around him. The district attorney, though, was all business.

"We are here to open the case of *The People versus Martin Thorn*," Youngs announced to the judge.

"We are ready to go on for the defendant," Howe thundered back.

From the two hundred men called, Howe and Youngs would have to settle on twelve; they'd excuse some by mutual agreement and could peremptively challenge others on their own. There was careful strategy involved in that maneuver, though; each side only got thirty peremptory dismissals. As the clerk filled a lottery wheel with slips of paper bearing jury-pool names, nobody was sure which side would have to come out swinging first.

The clerk drew a name.

"L. E. Blomquist, of Woodside."

Woodside?

THE SPECTATORS WERE EXCHANGING significant looks when a rather alarmed-looking man shambled in. A deputy grabbed him and immediately began leading him toward the witness box, much to the fellow's consternation.

"Hold on," Judge Smith said to the erring court officer. "*That* is not Mr. Blomquist."

It was a reporter running late, and he quickly fled into the amused press corps. After some confusion and jostling of chairs in the crowded room, a slightly wild-haired and bearded man made his way up to the witness stand instead. It was Mr. Blomquist, and he confirmed that he was a citizen, though a native of France.

"How long have you lived in this country?" Youngs asked him.

"Since 1870," he answered. Recently he'd been working as a housepainter—and yes, in Woodside.

"Do you know Martin Thorn?"

The painter turned a stony gaze onto Thorn.

"I think I do."

There was a rustle from the crowd as people leaned forward.

"When did you meet Thorn?"

"I think I have seen him in Woodside."

A murmur rose up. Reporters nudged one another in recognition— they *had* interviewed Blomquist. He really was one of the neighbors, though he hadn't talked all that much.

"Have you an opinion as to the guilt or innocence of the accused?"

"I have," Blomquist said evenly.

"Have you any special scruples against capital punishment?"

"No." His eyes bored into the defendant. "*Not in this case.*"

"What's that?" Howe asked sharply. "When was it you saw him in Woodside?"

"June twenty-sixth," the painter responded.

Good Lord, what were the odds? Blomquist had just gone from the jury pool to a possible witness. Howe had to use his first peremptory dismissal already; the man was quickly excused. So were the next two jurors, who stated bluntly that they believed Thorn had done the deed. "I think he's guilty," one of them blurted to guffaws. A fourth—an elderly Swede—didn't understand English, or indeed why he was there. A fifth sounded perfect until, as he was being sworn in, he made a confession.

"I think I ought to say this, just here," he stammered. "I'm rather of too nervous a disposition to serve on this case. I've got nervous trouble. I've got vertigo—dizzy spells."

"I won't make you dizzy," Howe promised in a kindly tone, but it was not to be. Another two men confessed that they were over seventy years old, which was an instant disqualification. So was being a firefighter.

The air in the packed courtroom grew rank, even pestilent, so bad that the judge had to empty the room out twice. When at last a bell rang out lunchtime from the courthouse's downstairs canteen, the judge and staff rushed from the stifling room with alacrity. The rest of the crowd poured into the street; all the local establishments were out of food within minutes, before many patrons could make it to the counter.

Back at the courthouse, Howe dined in peace; he'd done enough celebrity trials to know the value of packing his own sandwiches. The peremptory challenges, he admitted to reporters, were following a pattern: Youngs knocked out jurors opposed to capital punishment and circumstantial evidence, while Howe knocked out anyone from the pool—known as talesmen, in court parlance—who were already convinced of Thorn's guilt.

"I'm going at every talesman with extreme care to see whether he has formed an opinion—whether he has read anything of the scores of hats, the hundreds of coats, and the tons of plaster of paris," he mused. Howe wouldn't bother asking them if they'd already discussed the case, of course. Finding a man in New York who hadn't was impossible. Even so, demanding a change in venue was never Howe's style; his firm's reputation in the city was so fearsome that it was like a baseball team playing to a hometown crowd.

After lunch the courtroom filled again. As the afternoon passed, the jury numbers finally crawled upward. The first approved juror was a retired oysterman named Jacob Bumstead; the next was a farmer; and the third bore an uncanny resemblance to Uncle Sam.

"Do you know the duties of a juror?" he was asked.

"I had ought to," he replied, beaming through his patriotic whiskers.

Amid all this sat Thorn, who could be observed twiddling his thumbs between his knees, then leaning back to stare up at the ceiling; he appeared to be counting the gaslights. With each change in position and each new juror, artists leaning against the gallery railing whipped out new sheets of paper; *Journal* men could occasionally be observed slipping out to run them to the pigeon cages. Meanwhile, the *World*'s beauty columnist took stock of the defendant's features.

"Thorn is a very average specimen of the type known as the degenerate," she warned readers. "He is not well made. His arms are too long for his legs. Thorn has no back to his head. A pair of deceitful, grayish eyes—the ears of epileptics and mental incompetents—a square chin."

But that chin, she admitted, *was* rather fetching.

"Cheap Don Juans, third-rate actors of melodramas, and Martin Thorns are frequently found with these highly attractive chins," she wrote.

By five o'clock, Thorn had the peers who would hear his case. They had run through sixty-four candidates to select a jury of twelve. *Journal* artists could be seen dashing out again—a *New York Press* journalist had wickedly spread the rumor that one of the paper's champion racing birds had fried itself on a power line—and William F. Howe strolled out onto the courthouse steps. He pronounced himself delighted with his case and with the jury.

"This," Howe bellowed expansively, "is magnificent."

17

COVERED IN BLOOD

THE MEN WHO STEPPED OFF the Long Island Rail Road's special jury car the next morning held ordinary jobs; there were three farmers, three oystermen, a grocer, a saloon keeper, a janitor, a street contractor, a real estate agent, and a floor waxer. They weren't used to this sort of fuss, or to the courthouse crowds that parted before them and their escort of deputies. The twelve men trudged down a long marble hallway punctuated by a warning sign from the sheriff:

LOUD TALKING IN THESE HALLS

IS FORBIDDEN

While Court Is in Session

by order

HENRY DOHT, Sheriff

Led by their genially rotund foreman, Jacob Bumstead, the jurors were dutifully silent, if still a bit groggy. The farmers had stayed up until midnight talking crop forecasts and fretting over their livestock—"I'm afraid something'll happen to the brindle cow while I'm away," one said with a sigh. "Best milker for miles around, that cow." The others had warded off thoughts of the case by playing cards over cigars and cider, then puzzling over the newfangled electrical switches in their hotel rooms.

But now it was time.

The deputies pushed open the door, and twelve men filed into their jury box, their footsteps echoing in the nearly empty room. Bumstead settled in heavily against one front corner of the box; Magnus Larsen, a rather pained-looking road builder from Norway, took the other. The silence around them did not last for long: A janitor was still sweeping out clouds of dust when the first spectators poured through the gallery doors, clutching precious white slips that read "PASS ONE." The upper galleries filled with men and women talking excitedly, while down in the arena entered DA Youngs and Counsel Howe, along with their scores of accompanying journalists. Youngs was still looking a bit uncomfortable in his skin—he'd only just gotten over a neck rash—but Howe, in his yachting cap, helmed his custom-built table as if he were setting sail for the West Indies. The reporters duly noted the flower in Howe's lapel that day—a pink rose—and sat, as if at a county fair, guessing at the volume of gems on his person. "About a half-pint of diamonds," one *Times* reporter hazarded.

There was other guesswork going on, too: A *Herald* man was keeping track of the betting pools on whether or not Thorn would get the chair. But Howe wasn't having any of it. "Just you watch. Martin Thorn will be a free man," he grandly assured reporters, slapping his client on the shoulder. He wasn't worried at all, not even by an anonymous note that warned: *The yellow journals have a plant on the jury.* Well, just looking at the jury box quickly dismissed that theory. These were not exactly men of the world: One of them dealt with courtroom drafts by sitting with a handkerchief atop his bald head.

"*Hear ye! Hear ye!*" cried the court clerk. The old-fashioned formalities, it seemed, were still used in Queens. Howe and Youngs shook hands, and the DA promptly began his attack.

"This is one of the most remarkable crimes of the century," Youngs announced to the hushed room. "One of the most widely advertised in the world."

But now, he said, it was time to examine the facts.

"*Somewhere*, at *some* time, by *somebody* a most terrible tragedy has been enacted," he began. "Was this a crime? And if so, who were the actors in it?" Youngs paced the floor of the courthouse, looking searchingly at the jurors.

"The person alleged to have been murdered is William Guldensuppe, the place a cottage in Woodside, the time June 25, 1897, and the man accused of the murder sits there." He swung out his arm and pointed at the prisoner, sitting just a few feet away. *"Martin Thorn."*

The accused returned his gaze coolly, with scarcely a flicker of his eyes.

"The evidence will be mainly circumstantial," Youngs continued. "A murderer of this kind does not seek the broad highway for the place of his crime, but we shall show you link after link of evidence that will bind Thorn in a fatal embrace.

"Mind you," he added, "the head is still missing."

Youngs gave the jury a quick recounting of the case—the love triangle, the fatal cottage in Woodside, the body cut in four, the head forever hidden in plaster—and he turned to the jury box.

"Where is Guldensuppe?" he asked warmly. "He was well known to many. The great newspapers of the country have published his pictures." The roomful of reporters basked in his momentary attention. "There are few people in the East that have not seen a picture of the missing man. If he were alive, hundreds of witnesses would be produced by the defense to prove it. *He has never been seen since he entered that cottage with Mrs. Nack."*

And they, the jury, would not be fooled.

"You have been selected with great care," the DA assured them, at last returning to the prosecution team's table. All eyes turned to Howe and Thorn.

"I shall also prove"—here Youngs suddenly leapt back up from his seat like a billy goat—"that Guldensuppe 'snored' in the bathtub *even after Thorn had begun to turn the knife."*

The men visibly shuddered. The trial of Martin Thorn had truly begun.

WHEN YOUNGS CALLED his first witness, the air in the room had already grown foul again, and it was about to get worse. Youngs slipped on black rubber gloves and produced a piece of red oilcloth. He hesitated before passing it to a court officer. The officer, he suggested, should wear gloves, too.

"It is *covered in blood*," Youngs explained, "and if you have a cut on your hand, it might be dangerous."

John McGuire was called to the stand; the fifteen-year-old boy had picked out some friends of his in the gallery and was grinning broadly at them. He'd already been signing autographs at just fifty cents a pop on their new copies of the latest Old Cap. Collier dime novel: *The Headless Body Murder Mystery*.

The prosecutor briskly turned the boy's attention to more serious matters.

"Where were you shortly after one o'clock last June twenty-sixth?" he asked.

"I was at the foot of Eleventh Street," the teenager replied. "East River."

"Did you see anything?"

"I seen a bundle a block away from there in the water," McGuire answered earnestly. "I showed it to Jack McKenna. He swam out and got it and brought it in. There was a wrapping of brown paper, and then a wrapping of oilcloth, and then a wrapping of cheesecloth with a bloodstain on it."

An attendant held a creased and fetid piece of red-and-gold oilcloth up to the boy.

"Was this the oilcloth?"

"Yes."

His friend Jack McKenna proved to be a saucer-eyed twelve-year-old with none of Johnny's bravado, and unsure whether Judge Smith or Counsel Howe was in charge of the courtroom.

"What was in the bundle?" the prosecutor asked him gently.

"The upper part of a human body, with arms and hands on it," the boy stammered. "There was no head."

The prosecution team shuffled through a stack of morgue photographs that lay on the exhibit table, one observer marveled, "like a ghastly pack of cards," and plucked out a grisly shot of the severed thorax.

"Is this the part of the body found by you?"

"Yes, sir."

His turn over, the boy gratefully bounded away, and Howe stood up to cross-examine Officer James Moore, the first policeman on the scene.

"Some portion of the breast was removed. How deep was the incision?"

"I can't say, exactly," the policeman replied modestly.

"Were any bones splintered?" Howe pressed.

"I can't say."

"How was the head severed?"

"I don't know."

"How was the lower part severed?"

"I can't tell that, either."

Wasn't it possible, Howe reasoned, that the head might have been eaten off by fish? There was surely a reasonable explanation for everything the boys found. The prosecution team was rather more skeptical; fish, after all, did not know how to bundle parcels and tie knots.

"A piece of rope was found by the oilcloth in the dock?" the DA asked.

"Yes," the officer replied.

"I object!" Howe pounced. "That's immaterial. There's plenty of rope around the docks, isn't there, Officer?"

"*I* object," the prosecutor snapped back.

"*Please* don't," Howe sighed theatrically, and his audience guffawed.

The witnesses proceeded at a brisk pace, with Herbert Meyer and his little brother, Edgar, called up to recount finding the second package in the woods by the Harlem River. One *Telegram* writer dryly observed that the younger child, a towheaded boy still in knickerbocker pants, possessed "a voice entirely out of proportion to his size."

"He is a good little boy," Howe said, smiling indulgently at the bemused jury.

"Was there any one else there but your brother and your father?" the prosecutor dutifully went on to ask the older brother.

"*Yes,*" Edgar replied.

The defense and prosecution alike looked up, startled; nobody had heard *this* before. In the youthful logic of the two Meyer children, it may simply have been that nobody had ever asked them that precise question. Martin Thorn, whose foot had been swinging impatiently under his chair, suddenly froze.

"A man jumped out of the bushes," Edgar prattled on diligently, "and asked me about the blackberries, saying they weren't ripe. I told him they were *raspberries*, and—"

"Do you see that man in the court?" the prosecutor interrupted.

Edgar looked all around the room, sweeping his gaze back and forth several times as the crowd held its breath.

"No, sir," he said finally.

Martin Thorn exhaled and allowed his foot to fidget again.

Officer Collins of the Brooklyn Navy Yard stepped up to identify the legs, but the rows of newspapermen paid particular attention when a more familiar officer took to the stand: newly promoted Detective Sergeant Arthur Carey, the very first to track the oilcloth in the case. Carey was a sharp dresser: In his silk-faced Prince Albert jacket, left rakishly unbuttoned, he might have been the only witness to risk outshining Counsel Howe.

Carey nonchalantly handled the dirty piece of oilcloth. He'd carried another swatch all over the city while looking for fabric dealers and was unfazed by the grisly evidence.

"What did you subsequently do with the piece you retained?" the prosecutor asked.

I matched it to the other one at the morgue, Carey explained, waving the oilcloth about. A deathly stench wafted from the bloody scrap.

"Please, don't move it any more than you *have* to," Howe winced from the defense table. "You ought to have more consideration for our health."

Judge Smith agreed; the air was so bad that he adjourned for lunch. Or, at least, what lunch they still had an appetite for: Magnus Larsen, whose corner seat in the jury box was right next to the exhibit table, looked like he was about to turn green.

THE AFTERNOON'S FIRST WITNESS was a morgue keeper named Isaac Newton—a gaunt, severe fellow who failed to see anything funny about his name. He'd been in the job for more than a year and had handled some 7,000 bodies in that time. The DA's office, though, was only interested in one.

"Did you see these three portions together and take any measurements?" he was asked on the stand.

"Yes."

"Did the pieces fit?"

"*I object!*" Howe bellowed.

"This would seem to be a question for an expert, and this witness is hardly qualified," Judge Smith agreed.

"We intend, Your Honor, to show that this is a misfit," Howe explained, and Thorn nodded his vigorous agreement. The beaming defense counsel, his thick watch chain swinging around and his eyes alight, turned to Newton for cross-examination. "Have you these pieces of a body in your possession?" he asked.

"Yes."

"As I understand"—Howe leaned in—"they have been pickled, or whatever the process is, and are as yet intact?"

"Yes, sir."

"They could be *brought* here?" the lawyer asked with unfeigned delight.

"Oh yes, sir," the morgue keeper agreed, a little puzzled. "I suppose so."

"There!" Howe crowed. "I shall object to *any* evidence by this witness, or *any* identification of photographs, on the ground that the body itself is available and is the best possible evidence."

The crowd, packed into the airless courthouse, wasn't sure whether to be delighted or horrified by this prospect—or both. And, Howe reminded them, there had been false identifications at the morgue before; indeed, just recently a woman had identified her husband at the Bellevue morgue, only to have him turn up very much alive at home the next day.

"Many visitors have called at the morgue since you were there. . . .

Were you there when some persons from Virginia said the body was that of Edwards, a photographer?"

"*Object!*" Youngs cried.

"Overruled." The judge waved it off. "Proceed."

"I don't remember the circumstance," Newton replied.

"You see Mr. Moss here?" Howe pointed to another lawyer at the defense table. "You don't *remember* him coming with an order to show the body?"

"Yes," the morgue keeper admitted slowly.

"I see in this photograph—I don't know whether it is the *original*," Howe muttered contemptuously as he shuffled through the gory stack on the exhibit table, "that the great toe overlaps the next. Have you seen that condition in others?"

"Yes."

"How many?" Howe demanded.

"I don't *know*," Newton snapped.

"Fifty?"

"I never kept count."

"Then forty-nine? Thirty?"

"Well, very likely."

And then there were, Howe mused, the other famed distinguishing characteristics of the body—five in all, including a mole and a small scar from a finger infection, or a "felon."

"Now it is claimed"—Howe lifted his fingers—"that on the first finger of the left hand there is a scar left by a felon. You have seen it?"

"Yes."

Howe considered this for a moment. "By the way," he said offhandedly, "have *you* ever had a felon?"

"Yes," the morgue keeper replied innocently.

"Show it to me," Howe commanded.

Newton held out his hand from the witness stand, and the towering defense counsel took it in a curiously courtly gesture.

"Now, isn't that strange!" Howe eyed the morgue keeper's hand and turned triumphantly to the jury. "*Your felon was on the same finger of the same hand!*"

There was a gasp in the courtroom, then incredulous laughter as spectators considered their own hands. Why, some of them also had those scars on their fingers!

"No doubt," Howe boomed delightedly, "there are thousands of cases *precisely* similar."

The district attorney jumped up quickly to stem the courtroom's laughter. "You have other bodies with such strange features as twisted toes, or moles in certain spots or scars in other spots, or possibly one of the five peculiarities you mention. But did you"—Youngs paused dramatically—"did you ever see a body *bearing all five marks?*"

"No," Newton said plainly.

"That's all." Youngs smirked at Howe.

"One moment!" Howe bellowed as Newton stood up. The morgue keeper sank back down dejectedly. The defense counsel leveled his gaze at the official, and took his most serious tone. "Do you remember the case of . . . Aimee Smith?"

Newton recoiled slightly, as if struck. "Yes," he said, and swallowed hard.

It was an infamous local scandal: Back in March, a young woman had been left to die of a sudden illness in a Third Avenue hotel, but the "Mr. Everett" who signed the hotel register as her husband was nowhere to be found. After days passed, "Mrs. Everett" proved to be the pretty young Hackensack Sunday-school teacher Aimee Smith— and "Mr. Everett" was identified by a porter as her married Sunday-school headmaster, Nelson Weeks. Fearing scandal, he'd fled the hotel and left her to become a Jane Doe in the Bellevue morgue.

"How often was *she* falsely identified?"

"Not at all." The morgue keeper bristled. "I identified her as soon as I saw her."

Bring back Isaac Newton tomorrow, Howe demanded as the court let out for the day. He wasn't finished with him just yet.

AS THE COURTHOUSE EMPTIED OUT, *Journal* pigeon posts fluttered past the windows—the first four pages of tonight's issue would be devoted to the case, shoving aside every other national and international story, including a Spanish overture to President McKinley, a nearly unanimous vote by the Georgia legislature to ban the "brutal" sport of football, and word that infamous outlaw "Dynamite Dick" had been gunned down by lawmen in the wilds of the Indian Territory. With tomorrow's witnesses slated to be a parade of doctors and professors, the capital circumstantial case was turning historic.

"Interest in the case is not wholly that of a passing sensation," a *Brooklyn Eagle* reporter admitted. "The legal aspects of it are scientific and important, and may be cited for precedents in many trials of the future."

Howe, sparkling at the defense table, was quick to assure everyone that it would also be a historic *victory*. "We will disprove nearly all of the prosecutor's testimony," he announced flatly.

It wasn't just bluster, either: A *Herald* reporter had good word that betting on Thorn now ran at roughly even odds. Sure, the evidence looked bad for him, but Howe had an impeccable reputation for beating the rap. Yet as they left the courtroom, there was another presence—up in the gallery—that was altogether more surprising.

Maria Barberi?

The ranks of reporters crowded around her. Barberi had been the first woman ever sentenced to die in the electric chair—and just a year ago, she'd been at the defense table herself, appealing a murder conviction. But she'd been freed by reason of insanity, since Maria slit her lover's throat with a straight razor in what her lawyer argued was a "psychic epileptic fit"—a curiously selective fit, it must be said. The case was so sensational that it had already been turned into a Broadway play. And now Barberi was a free woman, sitting in the gallery right beside the lawyer who had saved her from the chair: none other than Manny Friend, who was now representing Mrs. Nack.

In her round spectacles and a white floral hat tied under her chin with a wide bow, Maria looked for all the world like a schoolmistress. "I did not see the use of showing those awful pieces of cloth so many times," she complained to the *Evening Journal*. It made her feel especially sorry for Thorn. "Every time they were held up my heart thumped, and I know that his did."

Sitting in the courtroom with Barberi was cheap advertising for

Manny, and the message about Mrs. Nack's case was clear: *If I got Barberi off the hook, I can get Nack off, too.* William F. Howe was less impressed as he walked over and, towering over his fellow lawyer, sized up Manny Friend.

"What are you *doing* here, anyway?" he asked.

It was a good question—and when the answer came later that night, the case would be turned upside down.

18

CAUGHT IN THE
HEADLIGHT

MANNY FRIEND SIMPLY HAD no time for drama that night.

He'd tried. Shadowed on the Long Island Rail Road by reporters, Mrs. Nack's lawyer was followed into the city and to the Harlem Opera House. As rain and wind whipped outside the theater, Mr. Friend and his pursuers strode down 125th Street, past Hurtig & Seamon's music hall, and then disappeared under a marquee reading THE FIRST BORN.

It was a melodrama set in Chinatown—a tragedy of honor and revenge—but as the houselights dimmed, Friend fretted about the real revenge tragedy that had just played out before him back at the jail. The reporters out in the ornate lobby were surprised to see Friend walking purposefully away, leaving before the show had even really started; his face was flushed, his movements nervous, his affect that of a man who simply couldn't stay still.

Is it true? they yelled as they ran after him. *Has she confessed?*

Friend stopped in the lobby, stunned; but on second thought, it shouldn't have been any surprise at all. Of course the jail staff couldn't keep their mouths shut.

"She has made a full confession," Friend stammered, looking deeply ill at ease. "I shall go home, disconnect my phone, and refuse to see any one or answer any questions. She has made a full confession. That's all I can say."

Within minutes on Newspaper Row, reporters from the *Times*, the *Herald*, the *Journal*, and the *World* were jumping onto streetcars to wake up everyone from Captain O'Brien to Sheriff Doht for reaction quotes. When reporters descended on William Howe's house on Boston Avenue, though, they found it darkened and quiet; he wasn't home.

But the *Herald* knew where to find him. Howe was still in his pajamas and nightcap when the *Herald* arrived at the lawyer's room in the Park Avenue Hotel. Howe had allies at the paper—including, it was said, a reporter secretly on his payroll—and they knew that during big cases he worked out of the Park Avenue. The luxury hotel off Thirty-Third was an immense cast-iron castle painted a blinding white and lit up at night—precisely where one would expect William F. Howe to hold court. The imperial-sized lawyer waved the reporters into his suite, then paused to draw out a metal flask from his luggage.

"Yes, I've heard the news," he sighed. "We got the message from Friend. I was in bed and asleep—dreaming of the ultimate acquittal of Thorn—when I was awakened by a boy pounding on the door. There is no doubt about it. Look at this." He passed a *Herald* reporter a note sent up by the hotel's phone operator: *Mrs. Nack has confessed and will be a witness for the state.*

Another knock came at the door—this time it was a *World* reporter, scarcely seconds behind his rivals. Stirred by his growing audience, Howe passed around the flask, lit a cigar, and soliloquized to the reporters.

"I had the *most perfect case* that was ever worked up for a jury. Only today I had Dr. Huebner, a medical expert, go to the Woodside cottage and take the measurements of that bathtub. The doctor found that the tub was only two-thirds as long as the body of the murdered man—*if* he was murdered. Had he been placed there, only an expert in anatomy could have cut up the body."

And there was his coup de grâce: Howe had quietly been serving, it just so happened, as counsel . . . *for Nelson Weeks*. The disgraced Sunday-school supervisor was up on a manslaughter charge, and Howe happened to know that morgue keeper Isaac Newton was a *friend* of Weeks's. The body in the Aimee Smith case had *not* been quickly identified by Newton; it was identified by two detectives based on a notebook in the body's possession. It was assumed to be stolen until they visited Smith's family, found the daughter absent, and matched the family's photos to the unclaimed body at Bellevue. So when the morgue keeper said that he immediately identified Aimee Smith—his fugitive friend's dead mistress—Howe knew the man was lying under oath. And if he could discredit Newton, then Howe could discredit *all* the physical evidence in the morgue keeper's possession, for he had cannily established during cross-examination that Newton was in direct charge of the Thorn case's body parts.

Tomorrow, at one swipe, he'd have knocked the legs right out from under the prosecution—*if only Manny Friend had been patient.*

"I cannot understand one thing." Howe shook his head, after a long pause. "And that is how a lawyer who has a client with so little against her could permit his client to make a confession."

"Were you surprised when you received the news?" a *Herald* reporter asked.

"I had a suspicion she might tell a pack of lies to save her own neck," Howe replied grimly.

There was a stir at the door, and in staggered Howe's assistant, Frank Moss, disheveled from a nighttime sprint to the hotel; he'd been bowling down on Seventeenth Street when he got the news. A glance at the reporters in the room told him everything.

"Well," Moss panted, "I suppose you have heard."

"Yes." Howe regarded his cigar thoughtfully. "What are we going to do?"

But it seemed a mere formality to even ask. Even as the sounds of the night ebbed away outside, the old lawyer was already working out his next move.

HOWE AND HIS TEAM arrived at the courthouse the next morning amid a mad rush for seats; the confession was all over the papers. The wire services had picked it up, so that Californians and even Londoners woke that morning to the news about Mrs. Nack. Spectators were pressing to get in, and when the doors were finally thrown open, the men in the crowd sprinted for the best seats, in the Right Gallery; fashionably attired women, slowed by their long skirts, took the Left Gallery. Reporters and artists gawked at these "specimens of womanhood"—many of them being, a reporter noted dryly, "young . . . and not ill-looking." Some had brought their opera glasses, and one beaming pair of beauties wore identical plaid frocks for the occasion. Their gallery bloomed with so many fancy hats that a *World* reporter dubbed it the Flower Garden.

Whispers flew around the women's gallery that a heartbroken Thorn had committed suicide overnight, but this romantic rumor was dashed when the young barber was led in. Only Martin Thorn, in all the courtroom, had not yet heard the news; as he sat down at the defense table, Howe wordlessly handed him the *World*, opened to that morning's front-page headline:

MRS. NACK HAS CONFESSED THE MURDER

Thorn went pale and stiffly passed the newspaper back.

"Augusta Nack," announced the court clerk.

A roar rose over the courtroom as the side door opened.

"Augusta Nack!" the clerk yelled over the commotion, and the star witness was guided through the packed room's maze of chairs and tables. Mrs. Nack swept by Thorn without a glance, smoothing her skirt as she sat down in the witness chair. She was clad in black— black dress, black lace, black straw hat, black ostrich feather—with sleek apple-green banding and silk gloves. Her appearance, the *Times* sniffed, was "cheap and tawdry"—and yet, it confessed, "strong and sensual."

"State your name," the prosecutor began.

"My name is Augusta Nack," she said in accented English, and verified that she was a German immigrant married to one Herman Nack.

"Were you living with Herman Nack in June?"

"No." Mrs. Nack flushed slightly.

"With whom?"

Thorn stared at her from the defense table, his gaze as fixed as hers was averted.

"With William Guldensuppe," she answered.

"When did you become acquainted with Martin Thorn?"

"I advertised a furnished room, and he came and took it in June 1896—I think until January of this year."

It had ended badly, of course; Guldensuppe had landed Thorn in the hospital for four days. Then, she said, Thorn began visiting when Guldensuppe was away at work.

"What passed between you and Thorn?"

A hint of a smile began to cross Martin Thorn's face, but Mrs. Nack continued looking away from him.

"He always told me to leave Guldensuppe and live with him. I refused."

"Why?"

"I told him from the first night I was a married woman," Mrs. Nack replied earnestly. There were titters in the courtroom, and she added, "He said, 'It is not so. I know your husband lives in Astoria.'"

The prosecutor quickly stepped in. "Now in March, what did Mr. Thorn say to you about Guldensuppe?"

"I told Thorn I couldn't live with him, and I gave him twenty dollars. A couple of days later he wanted more, but I said I could not give it to him. Then . . ." She paused, and her words echoed out over the horrified crowd. "He said—*I don't want money. I want Guldensuppe's head.*"

There was a commotion in the gallery; a transfixed spectator leaned so far past the railing that she nearly toppled over. The courtroom fell silent again as the prosecutor led Mrs. Nack's recollections forward.

"Wanted his head?"

"He wanted his head," Nack nodded. She was becoming animated; the ostrich feather atop her hat bobbed with each motion. "I got scared. Then he says he will kill Guldensuppe and put his body in a trunk and lock it, and I should send it express to where he is going to hire a room. I say—*I won't do it.*"

"Go on."

"I said, *Kill me.* He said, *That will give me no satisfaction.*"

Her face darkened as she kept it turned away from Thorn.

"He came one evening in my house, and said *Do you love me?* And

I said, I told you I can't love nobody, and he took me on my neck, here," she pointed at her throat. "He strangled me till I was half dead and the blood come out of my mouth."

By Nack's telling, her role was curiously passive: *She* had been the victim, too.

"I want to say that I always did what the man wanted me to because I was afraid," she added. "When the house was hired, Thorn told me that I should bring Guldensuppe over and he will kill him. I had to do everything that man told me."

"What did you say to William Guldensuppe?"

"I told Guldensuppe that he should come with me, I got the house where I am going to open a baby farm."

As if to protest this very notion, an infant briefly squalled from the women's gallery.

"A baby farm?"

"Well, he always told me I should do something," she shrugged.

At about nine on Friday morning, June 25, they took the Thirty-Fourth Street ferry and then a streetcar out to the cottage.

"I had the key, and I went inside and I was so excited I went out into the back yard," Mrs. Nack told the courtroom. There was not another sound in the room save for the furious *scritch scritch* of reporters' pencils. "Guldensuppe went upstairs, and when I was in the yard I heard a shot. After a while Thorn came out and called me. He said—*I shot Guldensuppe. He's dead.*"

She'd never hurt Guldensuppe, she explained, never even saw his body; she left for the afternoon, and when she returned, Thorn had wrapped him up in parcels.

"Was there anything bought for the purpose of wrapping up parcels?"

"I bought oilcloth."

"Look at that." The prosecutor held up a foul swatch of the red-and-gold cloth.

"Yes." Mrs. Nack nodded. "That is it."

They'd thrown the plaster-encased head off the ferry on the way back, and she disembarked with another package under her arm—Guldensuppe's clothes—and burnt them that night in her apartment's stove. The next day they hired the undertaker's carriage to dispose of the larger parcels.

"Now, state what happened on Saturday the twenty-sixth, when you went over there with the wagon."

"He had a bottle of ammonia," she explained, the better to clean the blood spots. "I cleaned the bathtub. There was some white stuff in it, I suppose."

"Don't *suppose*," Howe snapped from the defense table.

"It was the plaster of paris," Nack added apologetically. After dumping the parcels and meeting again Monday night, she said, they parted until their arraignment.

"Here is a photograph." The prosecutor held up a portrait. "Who does it represent?"

"William Guldensuppe," her voice trembled.

"Here is another photograph—do you recognize it?"

"Yes," Nack said quietly. "It is the cottage in Woodside."

The prosecutor paused thoughtfully, then leaned in. "Mrs. Nack," he asked softly. "Why do you make this confession?"

Her eyes began to well up.

"I make it to make my peace with the people." She began to sob and reached for her handkerchief. "And with God."

Augusta Nack burst into tears, and for a moment everyone in the courthouse was speechless—everyone, that is, but the counsel sitting by Martin Thorn.

"*God?*" Howe's incredulous voice rang out in disbelief.

THE DEFENSE COUNSEL drew himself up to his full height and towered before the witness box. Across William F. Howe's chest hung his favorite diamond pendant, a massive creation known among court reporters as "the Headlight"—and Mrs. Nack began blinking nervously, as if blinded by its rays. But then, Howe's sartorial splendor was always more than mere vanity: It was a warning, a proof of enemies bested before.

"Mrs. Nack," he said gravely. "You have told us that on June twenty-fifth, after Guldensuppe was killed, you took his clothes to your home. Is that true?"

"Yes."

"And the clothing was saturated with blood?" Howe asked.

"Y-yes."

"This was the day you say Guldensuppe was killed?"

"Yes."

"And you knew it?"

"Yes, I knew." Her voice grew quieter.

Howe lowered his own voice to a stage whisper. "Did you cry, Mrs. Nack? When you burned Guldensuppe's clothes?"

"No." She appeared confused. "I didn't."

"You cried today, didn't you?" Howe asked in mock surprise.

"I have often cried . . . ," she began.

"*Today!* In the court room!" Howe yelled. "Yes or no?"

"Yes?"

"You bought the oilcloth?" Howe continued briskly.

"Yes."

"And you bought it for purposes of wrapping his body in it, didn't you?"

"Yes." Augusta blinked nervously.

"Did you cry then?"

"No."

"Did you cry when you heard the shot that killed him?"

Mrs. Nack was catching on.

"Yes," she now replied.

Howe looked at her queerly, his face a mask of puzzlement. "You knew *perfectly well* that Guldensuppe was taken to Woodside to be killed, didn't you?"

"Yes," she stammered.

The lawyer mused on this, looking at the jury to share his confusion.

"Did you *love* Guldensuppe?" he finally asked.

"No," she insisted stoutly. "I didn't love anybody but my husband."

The silence was broken by a bitter laugh of disbelief—Thorn's. It was nearly his first utterance of the trial.

"You still loved your husband while you lived with Guldensuppe?"

"I stopped loving my husband then and began to love Guldensuppe," she stammered.

Howe smiled; he'd caught the witness in her first contradiction.

"You plotted to kill the man you loved?"

"No," she shot back. "I did not."

"But you paid the money for the rent?"

"Yes."

"And bought the oilcloth?"

"Yes," she snapped.

"And the house was rented for the purpose of killing Guldensuppe?"

"Yes." Mrs. Nack's eyes teared up again. "You must excuse me."

"No, *I won't*!" Howe roared, and leaned into the witness box as the crowd laughed nervously. "When did you begin to love *Thorn*?"

"I don't know."

"How long before the killing?"

"I never loved him until he choked me. Then I had to."

"*He choked you into loving him?*" Howe asked incredulously.

"Yes," she insisted. "I was afraid of him."

"How long did this frightful love continue?"

"Always." Nack reached quickly for an explanation. "Thorn told me if I didn't leave Guldensuppe, he'd buy some stuff and a syringe and squirt it into Guldensuppe's eyes and into my eyes—and that then we wouldn't be able to see each other. And that *then* I could have Guldensuppe."

Acid attacks were not unknown among jilted lovers, yet Howe looked puzzled.

"It was fear of this syringe," he intoned, "that made you buy oilcloth before this man was dead, and fear of this syringe after he was dead made you burn his clothes?"

"Yes," she insisted.

"Why, Mrs. Nack, did you go back to the house again?"

"Thorn told me so."

"Ah—fear of the syringe again?"

"Yes," she nodded earnestly.

The courthouse was stifling; more spectators had crept in past the guards, and they were now spilling out into the aisles and sitting on the steps.

"You prepared to go to Europe, didn't you?" he asked after a long pause.

"No," she said loudly. "I did not."

"Did you not intend to go to Europe?"

"I did not know what to do," she said blandly.

Howe smiled broadly, amiably.

"No, of course you did not know what to do. I know that. I understand that very well." Howe spun around and roared: *"Did you not intend to go to Europe?"*

"Well, er—yes."

"Were you going away or were you not?"

"No," she now said. She was reversing herself on one question after another, and Manny Friend watched helplessly as the rival lawyer enmeshed his client.

"What do you mean by saying that you *did not know what to do?*" Howe demanded.

"I did not want to remain," Nack said, struggling to explain her testimony. "I could not pay the rent."

"Didn't you have $300 in your corset when you were arrested?"

"Yes."

"Yet you couldn't pay your rent?"

"Well . . ." Mrs. Nack hesitated and decided to try a new story. "Thorn told me I should skip," she began brightly, and added piously, "I said no. Truth is truth and—"

"Mrs. Nack," Howe interrupted to guffaws, "we don't want any homilies on truth from *you*."

The defense counsel paused to have his team search for an old copy of the *New York Journal*, then turned back to his witness. "Mrs. Nack, when you were before Judge Newberger in New York, did you say to Thorn, 'Hold your mouth, keep quiet'?"

"No," she insisted. Now it was the reporters' turn to look astonished: They had *heard* her. "Nothing of the sort."

An old copy of the *Journal* was passed forward, bearing the facsimile of her intercepted jailhouse letter to Thorn. Howe read the English translation out loud: *"Dear Martin—I send you a couple of potatoes. If you do not care to eat them, perhaps the others will. Dear child, send me a few lines how you feel . . ."*

He then passed the newspaper to her.

"That your writing?"

"Yes."

"You call him 'Dear child' and 'Dear Martin.' What do you mean by that?"

"I never loved him," she sputtered. "But I did . . . *show* him I loved him. Since he choked me."

"You only *pretended* to love him?" Howe gasped in understanding. "Make believe?"

"Yes."

"And that letter was only a *make-believe letter*?"

"Yes," she insisted as laughter bubbled from the courtroom.

"Did your fear continue while you were in jail?" Howe pressed.

"No."

"Then why did you write the letter?"

Nack kept her eyes averted from Thorn, even as he broke into a quiet grin.

"Because I thought he was hungry?" she ventured.

"Then it was for sweet charity's sake?" Howe swept his arms grandly.

"Yes," she eagerly agreed, to a new blast of laughter from the court. Howe beamed at the crowd, the gems glittering from his fingers.

"Now regarding the potatoes . . ." He turned back to his witness. *"—Is it not true that you shot Guldensuppe!"*

"No!" she cried, starting from her chair.

"Is it not true that you cut the body in pieces?"

"No!"

"Didn't *somebody*," Howe thundered, "tell you to deny that you shot Guldensuppe and cut up his body?"

"No," Mrs. Nack laughed in disbelief.

"Don't *laugh*, Mrs. Nack," Howe shook his finger. "This is an awful matter."

But Mrs. Nack could not stop laughing; her testimony was falling apart, and she was becoming hysterical.

"Answer me!" he demanded.

"No!" she yelled.

Howe handed her photographs of her lover's mutilated body. *Not your handiwork, then?* But he wasn't finished—he'd also had a little talk with her ex-husband about her business as a midwife. Didn't she also help women . . . *avoid* birth?

"How many *children* did you kill?" he crowed.

"None," she shot back, then wavered. "So far as I know."

Didn't she have a chute in her old apartment for disposing of fetuses straight from the stove grate into the sewer? No? And hadn't she tried hiring Thorn to kill her husband?

"No," Mrs. Nack replied, her expression hardening. Howe narrowed his eyes back at her and tapped a table impressively.

"This is too important a case to mince matters, and I'm going to ask some direct questions. I want you to think before you answer. Mrs. Nack, don't you remember a place in New York in which you lived with Thorn for two entire weeks before the killing?"

"Lived with Thorn?" she stalled.

"You heard the question!" Howe bellowed. "Answer it."

"No, I did not."

"I call your attention now to a house on East Twenty-First Street. . . . Didn't you visit Thorn again and again at this place?"

"I did."

"Did you not remain in the house with Thorn at night several times?"

"No, I was there a couple of hours."

"Yes, when he wanted you to be as a wife to him."

"No, never," she stated primly. "I never was a wife to him. That was the reason I loved him. He was always a gentleman."

Howe exulted, buoyed by the rising tide of incredulity from the crowd. Now she loved Thorn, and called him a gentleman?

"Hasn't Thorn been as a husband to you?"

"No," she insisted.

But Howe had one question prepared for her like a dagger.

"Is this as true as any other answer you've given?"

"Yes," she declared.

The packed courtroom erupted into laughter and whoops; her testimony ended, a *Commercial Advertiser* reporter marveled, in "a scene of disorder in the court room which, in all probability, has seldom if ever been equaled in this state." DA Youngs and Manny Friend stared on miserably through the chaos as the judge gaveled the room to order; their star witness was pinned between lying to beat the rap and lying to stay respectable. Howe knew this, and he'd destroyed her on the stand with it.

Yet one man scarcely paid attention to Howe and Nack at all; he was collapsed in a far corner of the jury box, doubled over and in pain.

Magnus Larsen?

Judge Wilmot Smith quickly called a halt to the proceedings, and reporters and the crowd had a sudden shock of realization: In the middle of their murder trial, another man was dying before their very eyes.

19.

SCYTHE AND SAW

THE JURORS SPENT the night disconsolately gathered around the Garden City Hotel billiard table, not even bothering to pick up the cues, just aimlessly rolling the balls. They couldn't focus while Magnus Larsen was at death's door; he was doubled over with appendicitis by the time the train pulled up, and had to be carried to the hotel, where doctors decided to operate on the spot. Injected full of morphine, Larsen was now laid out on his bed upstairs in room 27, slipping miserably in and out of consciousness.

At the empty courthouse the next day, disappointed crowds scoured the floors for souvenirs, and locals pointed out the chairs in which Nack and Thorn had sat. When the trial reconvened two days later, the matter of life and death was not Thorn's but Magnus Larsen's. A scrum of reporters ran after Howe on the way in, cutting one another off with overlapping questions: *Will you—? Can you—? Have you—?*

"Yes, yes, yes—no, no, no," Howe joked from atop the courthouse steps, then marched inside. The artists were already after him, sketching his rose-and-scarlet scarf; fastened across his chest by a weighty gold cable shone a diamond-encircled moonstone pendant. It was the size of an egg, and carved with the figure of a young maiden.

"The gallery was nearly full of Long Island folks," one *Times* reporter smirked, "who, as this blazing, scintillating apparition flashed up, leaned forward and gasped and gazed."

Thorn soon followed him in, looking rather reinvigorated himself.

Howe jokingly shook a fist under his client's nose: *Bah, look at all the trouble you've caused this week!* The prosecutor and Judge Smith, though, had a more pressing concern to attend to: When, exactly, could their missing twelfth juror report back to the courthouse?

"Larsen had a very narrow escape," an attending physician explained. Upon opening the juror's abdominal cavity, they'd discovered that it was already filling with pus. "We found a perforation of the appendix. It is certain that he will be unable to leave his bed for three weeks, and I am not prepared to say that he will recover— though the indications are that he will."

Continuing without Larsen was mulled, but to Howe it was out of the question.

"No!" he said sharply. "Such a proceeding would be against all legal precedent." In the Cancini case of 1857, he noted, a man accused of killing a policeman had agreed under similar conditions to continuing on with a jury of eleven. After he was sentenced to the gallows, though, his conviction was thrown out: Even Cancini himself hadn't the right to waive his guarantee under the state constitution to trial by a jury of twelve peers.

"The judge would censure me if I consented to any such arrangement and I would deserve to be censured," Howe added stiffly. "The court would very properly ask me if I had ever read the law." Restarting the trial from the beginning, but with the eleven remaining jurors and one newly selected one, was a slightly less shaky idea—but only slightly.

Prepare for a brand-new trial, Judge Smith decided, in ten days' time, on Monday, November 22. *Journal* reporters dashed for their telephones and their pigeons; and on his way out of the courthouse, Howe suddenly cut in as Manny Friend chatted with a cluster of men from the *World* and the *Times*.

"*You!* You insignificant little imp!" Howe roared at Mrs. Nack's counsel on the courthouse stairs. "You *insect*! I ought not to notice you! You are not worthy of being considered a respectable rival of Howe & Hummel!"

It was more, perhaps, than just his usual grandstanding. The master of legal escapes, William F. Howe knew there was one final rap that he couldn't beat—and that at seventy-one, his career was already longer than his famed appetites augured. Falling quiet as he walked away, he turned suddenly to a *Times* reporter.

"This," Howe said plainly, "is the case of my life."

HOWE ARRIVED at his office on Centre Street to cheers and congratulations from his staff, with a coterie of reporters following as he settled back into his lair. The usual huddle of gangsters and madams awaited appointments, but Thorn was still on Howe's mind. The lawyer had instantly—without the least discomfort—abandoned his theory about Guldensuppe being alive and was now instead pouring all his effort into pinning the murder on Mrs. Nack. The black-clad femme fatale, Howe added, was "a damnable spider" sinking her fangs into the love-struck Martin Thorn.

"From my first interview I found him *saturated* with chivalry," he rhapsodized, "ready, if necessary, to yield his life to this Delilah who has placed him in this present position."

Yes, Thorn was chivalrous—"too chivalrous for his own good," the lawyer lamented. For William F. Howe himself was the city's great defender of virtue; he and Abe Hummel ran a million-dollar operation in breach-of-promise cases, where comely showgirls settled with wealthy men who'd wooed them without intent of marriage. A private communication from Howe & Hummel was all that was needed for the firm and the showgirl to evenly split five or ten thousand in hush money. It was extraordinarily lucrative, and extraordinarily *moral*, and just about the only man it hadn't worked on was the actor John Barrymore, because he didn't give a damn about his reputation. But Martin Thorn was no Broadway rake, Howe insisted. The humble immigrant barber was the victim of "this modern Borgia" and her venomous lawyer.

"She is the biggest liar unhung," Howe snapped. "And I want to say, for publication, that the conduct of Mr. Friend is the dirtiest piece of unprofessional work I have heard of in all my experience."

All that dirt would stick to her, Howe promised—for his firm had dug up plenty more. They now had the names, he declared, of the two women she'd killed with botched abortions—and he'd have Herman Nack himself on the witness stand to back it all up.

"Mrs. Nack admitted that she herself had cremated Guldensuppe's clothes—she must have been skilled at the art of cremation," Howe mused aloud. "Apropos of all this cremating, it is just possible—mind you, I say possible—that Guldensuppe's head was cremated instead of having been dropped overboard."

And if that wasn't damning enough, sitting in Howe's office was a brand-new witness: a stern, bespectacled Bronx landlady named Ida Ziegler. A full three months before Mrs. Nack claimed the plot had begun, Ziegler had received a curious response to her home-rental ad for 1671 Eastburn Avenue.

"On one Sunday," she began, "I believe it was prior to the fifteenth of March, a woman in the company of a man called upon me and wanted to see the room that I was advertising. The gentleman, after examining the rooms, said they were all very comfortable, and suited him just fine; but to the lady they were not at all suitable." Mrs. Ziegler, a little wounded, enumerated all the alleged faults of her lovely home. "Because there was not any *sewer conduit* leading from the house; the neighborhood was *too lively*; the house was *somewhat conspicuous*; because the bathtub was *too small*, although an average man could bathe himself with ease. She also became displeased with the rooms upon learning that I was not in the habit of going out during the day."

The prospective tenant, the landlady recalled, also had a very peculiar question. "We had a garden in the back of the house. She asked me whether I would *strike water* if I were to dig three feet down."

The woman, she said, was a midwife who had given her name as Mrs. Braun. Ziegler was shown a photograph of Augusta Nack.

That's her, she said.

THORN READ THE NEWSPAPERS that Howe sent him, played pinochle, and tried to lose himself in a volume of Emerson's essays left in the jail. He was not feeling very high-minded, though: For days the accused barber had been left unshaven, much to his professional disgust. When his jailers finally deigned to break out his shaving cup, the undersheriff and a barber showed up at Thorn's cell with manacles.

"What are you going to do with those things?" the prisoner asked.

"Just put them on, that's all," the undersheriff replied.

"I never put handcuffs on a customer when I shaved him," Thorn shot back.

"Look here, Martin," his jailer said, pulling Thorn's arms behind the chair back and slapping the cuffs shut, "we are going to run no chances."

Thorn fumed as he was shaved—they kept missing the stubble over his lip. It only took a look in the mirror after he was unshackled to see why. DA Youngs had directed the jail to bring back Thorn's mustache for the trial—to grow it in, inexorably, against his will—so that soon he would look precisely like the man their witnesses had seen entering the Woodside cottage.

And yet his days were not without some strange rewards. As Thorn sulked over his treatment at the jail, a Howe associate led a short impresario and a willowy actress through the heavy clanging door to the Flats, up to the bars of Martin's cell. Florenz Ziegfeld, Broadway's showgirl master, was not particularly used to visiting jails. But even stranger was the presence of his star talent and personal mistress, newly acquired from the Folies of Paris—Miss Anna Held, whose famed dark eyes stared out from promotional posters all over town.

Thorn greeted Howe's assistant warmly, while eyeing the actress with caution. He'd seen her soak up publicity by sitting in on some of the trial, but she was strangely out of place here on Murderers Row. Still, the sympathy of a famous starlet was not a bad thing for an accused man to have, especially with *World* reporters watching nearby.

What do you think of Mrs. Nack's confession? she asked breathlessly.

"She lies!" He shrugged. "All lies."

Anna watched as Martin Thorn sat in his cell, nuzzling the stray dog he'd adopted; a brindle-and-black bulldog-pug mix, it had recently wandered into the jail and unaccountably attached itself to him, refusing to leaving his side. Thorn cheekily dubbed it "Bill Baker," after the jailer who'd shackled him. The mutt, he mused aloud, was his only real friend anymore—since Mrs. Nack certainly wasn't.

"Would you have died for her?" the actress asked.

"Yes, I would," he replied evenly. "But she has killed my faith in all women. She killed Guldensuppe herself. I have loved that woman, and she has ruined me."

Miss Anna Held leaned dramatically against the cell door; she felt so dreadfully sorry for him. *New York World* artists frantically sketched her mooning through the cold bars of the prison cell.

"Were you . . . happy with her?" She lowered her voice.

"Yes," he paused. "I was, once."

The *World* artist tore off his sheet; it was a minor publicity coup for Howe and a fine morning front-pager, with the glamorous starlet providing an appropriately dramatic quote to accompany it: "Thorn is a man of impulse, a man of passionate temper," she explained to readers, "and such men are but easy prey in the hands of women they love." It was good copy, and—taking a page from the *Journal*'s favorite strategy for humiliating them—*World* editors even put together an accompanying montage of competitor's pages, to show how the *World* had been the first to discover that Mrs. Nack was about to make her treacherous confession on the stand.

But the *World* had already blown the scoop.

Blurted out in Thorn's conversation with Held were four startling words about Mrs. Nack—*She killed Guldensuppe herself*"—his first public acknowledgment that there *was* a murder, and that it was of Guldensuppe. Not one of Pulitzer's editors recognized its importance, but Hearst's men did. As the *World* fussed over its showgirl-in-prison illustrations for the next morning, the *Evening Journal* trumped them with a late-edition headline: THORN CONFESSES HIS PART IN THE MURDER.

The *World* just couldn't get it quite right. It still managed innovations, such as running women's fashion plates with actual photographed faces superimposed on the pen-and-ink dress drawings; the result looked comical, but reproducing an entire photo in the newspaper was quite difficult. Still, it hinted at the future. Soon all nineteenth-century news would be distinguishable from that of the looming twentieth century at a glance: The old was monochromatic and engraved, the new, color and photographic. And while Hearst hadn't sprung his attack with photography yet, he was busy opening up a widening lead on color printing. Pulitzer anxiously telegraphed from Maine about the headlines he was seeing in Hearst's paper: not about Nack and Thorn, but about the *Journal* itself—or, as he called it in a coded cablegram, "Geranium":

> I AM EXTREMELY INTERESTED TO KNOW WHETHER THAT STORY ABOUT GERANIUM ORDERING TWO MORE COLOR SEXTUPLES IS TRUE—ABSOLUTELY TRUE.

It was. Hearst had ordered up more color presses, and his *Evening Journal* was punishing other competitors so badly that for one precarious night, until it got its finances in order, the *Evening Telegram* ceased publication altogether. The *New York Times*, itself barely recovered from bankruptcy, was trying to beat back at the tide of yellow journalism by running a pointed new motto on its front page: "All the News That's Fit to Print." But other papers were inexorably drifting with Hearst's powerful current. On the same day that the *Evening Journal* boasted such edifying stories as COCAINE PHANTOMS HAUNT HIM and HYPNOTISM NEARLY KILLS, one could also find all these headlines on a single page of the more respectable *New York Herald*:

> ABSINTHE HIS BANE
> ITALIAN FATALLY STABBED
> INQUIRY ABOUT POISON GAS
> FEROCIOUS DOG MANGLES A BOY
> SINGER ENDS LIFE
> THEY TRIED TO DIE TOGETHER

New York papers now ran far more column inches on crime and accidents than other cities did, and the *Journal* ran so much "bleed" copy in combination with women's-interest stories and comics that business, labor, and religion were nearly crowded out altogether.

Hearst knew his readers, and he knew what they liked.

"The two stories of Nack and Thorn have reached an equilibrium of contradiction," he announced to readers in a column. The real question, his paper now asked, was *Which one's more guilty?* They tallied some 1,147 letters from readers: 713 found Augusta Nack the guiltier party, 329 blamed both equally, and just 105 laid the blame on Thorn.

"He is no more guilty of the murder of Guldensuppe than a babe," a hypnotist wrote in. "Mrs. Nack forced him to do it by the power she exerted over him." Another reader begged to differ, offering up the novel theory that Thorn *and* Guldensuppe were the real conspirators: "It was a plot of Guldensuppe and Thorn to convict Mrs. Nack of murder," he wrote. "Guldensuppe got out of the way, and Thorn cut up a body that he palmed off on Mrs. Nack as Guldensuppe's." Nine-year-old Helen Weiss of Princeton, on the other hand, was ready to wholeheartedly condemn Nack and Thorn alike: "I think they are both guilty."

But an even more telling sign was tucked away in the latest ad for the Eden Musée waxworks, where the scene of Thorn cutting up Guldensuppe was no longer the main attraction. It had been replaced by a slightly different pair of deadly combatants: *Augusta Nack and Martin Thorn.*

ON SUNDAY MORNING BEFORE DAWN, newsboys hauled off fat bundles of the *Journal.* They were going to be sure sellers. The paper had produced an alarming scenario headlined THE INVASION OF NEW YORK, complete with "a thrilling description by an expert of what would happen with the Spanish Fleet in New York Harbor." But even that took a backseat to what they'd used to headline the entire front page: THE STORY OF MY LIFE—BY AUGUSTA NACK. Along with a sober-looking portrait of Mrs. Nack taking pen to paper in her prison cell, Hearst's front page was given over to her melancholy and remorseful account of life before she became New York's most notorious woman, back when she was still young Augusta Pusat. "I was born in the little village of Oskarweischen, in Posen, Germany," she wrote, remembering the poverty of her family there. "When I was a girl I used to tend the geese and drive them down to the water in the morning. . . . In Germany idleness is considered not the right thing for either girls or women, and when I was tending my geese and looking after the kettles to make sure that they did not boil over, I made my lace."

After moving to the United States, she was soon earning more money than the rest of her family in the old country—"I had everything—and they had nothing," she marveled—but after she begged her mother to save the family's prayers for their own needs, she received a stern response. *"My daughter,"* the elder Mrs. Pusat wrote back, *"you don't know. Everything you have may be taken from you in a twinkling of an eye."*

Mrs. Nack often thought upon that letter.

Her confession in the case, she told *Journal* readers, was inspired by the visits of the Reverend Robert Miles to her cell. At first she'd spurned him and his Bible, but then one day the minister had brought his four-year-old son, little Parker Miles, and as he prattled on and jumped up into her lap, asking her to tell him a story, her steely reserve cracked. She broke down in sobs and confessed to the loving God of Reverend Miles. The *Journal* had a fine portrait of the clergyman too, and of his angelic son on Mrs. Nack's lap; it was a heartwarming story for a Sunday paper, and it would fly off the stands.

But one person wasn't buying her story yet: the DA.

As the newsboys fanned out into the still-darkened streets of the city, Augusta Nack was quietly let out of her cell and joined the district attorney, Detective Sullivan, and Captain Methven in a waiting carriage outside the Queens County Jail. It was a private hire, with the passenger veiled so that nobody on the street could spot her. She arranged a shawl around herself in the bitter predawn air, and they headed up Jackson Avenue.

"Can you point out the place?" Youngs asked her again.

"Yes," she promised.

"If you do," he said significantly, *"then* we shall be prepared to believe what you say."

Youngs eyed her carefully as they made their way along the muddy avenue. His star witness had already been terribly undermined on the stand—it wasn't for nothing that William Howe was considered the best trial lawyer in the city. Youngs still hadn't offered her a plea deal, and before he did, he wanted more from Mrs. Nack, some solid evidence that Howe wouldn't be able to bully and balderdash his way out of.

Woodside, announced their driver.

The trio of lawmen stepped out of the carriage, and as the sun rose they watched Mrs. Nack wander aimlessly in the garden of the Woodside cottage—hesitating here, stopping there. She hadn't been back in five months, since just after the murder, and the gardens that had been lush in that dangerous time were now barren and frosted.

Well? Youngs demanded.

She couldn't remember . . . but . . . perhaps she *could* remember. Yes, what they were looking for was surely in an entirely different place.

Youngs snorted in disgust and sat heavily back in the carriage. He kept a peeved silence as they made their way through Flushing toward College Point, past a series of scrubby, empty lots.

"That's the place!" yelled Mrs. Nack.

The carriage stopped by a crumbling stone wall on a vacant lot; it was an African American neighborhood, and the party's presence was becoming uncomfortably conspicuous to passersby. The veiled prisoner pottered in the weeds a bit—Was it here? Perhaps it was there?—until the DA finally lost all patience. The carriage promptly left with a jolt, hauling the humiliated prisoner back to Queens County Jail.

"Did you find the saw?" Detective Sullivan was asked as he returned from the jaunt.

"No," he snapped. "We didn't."

The rest of Augusta Nack's story wasn't holding up much better. Within hours after she and Manny Friend paraded her newfound piety to the papers, a familiar figure turned up at the *World*'s editorial offices: Herman Nack. The bakery driver was upset—deeply upset. He'd already lost his job at the Astoria Model Bakery from the bad publicity, couldn't sleep at night from the worry it had caused. He appeared, one reporter remarked, like nothing so much as a sleepwalker.

"I can only think of her," he sighed.

With the *Journal* getting Augusta's childhood, the *World* ventured into Herman's.

"Where did you first meet Mrs. Nack?" the paper asked.

"In Kiel, in Germany. She was a servant girl then. The family she worked for was a very fine family. I was working in a pottery. I loved her, and that's all." He paused, then admitted thoughtfully: "By and by Guldensuppe, he loved her. He was not a bad man either. I always liked him, but he loved her—that was the matter with him."

"What do you think of the strange course the trial has taken?"

"What do I think about it?" he mused, and fell silent. "I think so much that I do not know what to think. It is with me think, think, all the time. Maybe she killed that fellow, maybe Thorn did. I do not know. If she did, I hope they will"—he stumbled over the language, and then over the emotion—"how do you call it? Put her in the chair of electricity."

He was growing animated. There was something else, he said, that had truly made him upset: her confession.

"I am sure of one thing: it was not from religion or fear of God that she tells about the death of Guldensuppe. She was *not* religious. She was *not* good. Sometimes she used to go with one of her customers to church—but when she comes home she laughs at such things." Herman Nack's expression was becoming anguished. "I want to tell you, sir, that woman will not go to heaven. She is bad—*she is bad*."

And a bad liar as well, by the look of it. The newspapers gloated after word of her failed carriage trip leaked out. But two days later, as laborers worked with scythes to clear a salt-hay field in College Point, a call came in to the DA's office. Just by the spot Mrs. Nack had pointed out, they'd discovered a rusting eighteen-inch surgeon's saw—a Richardson & Sons model for slicing through bone. It was found jammed blade first into the ground, as if someone had tried to murder the dirt itself.

20.

A WONDERFUL MURDER

MALWINE BRANDEL CLUTCHED a bouquet of red roses. Barely eighteen years old, with lustrous blond hair and blue eyes highlighted by her most stylish high-collared velvet jacket, she was begging Sheriff Doht to let her inside to that morning's retrial. *I want to give these to Martin Thorn*, she pleaded.

The sheriff regarded her with sheer disbelief. "No, I can't do that," he finally managed. "As long as I am in charge of these proceedings, Thorn will never receive any flowers in the courthouse."

But I must, she begged. Mrs. Brandel had recently lost her husband, and already had her heart stolen by the newspaper pictures of Thorn.

"Thorn is a fearfully *interesting* fellow," she said breathlessly. "I cannot believe him guilty of such a fiendish crime. The more I look at him and his honest eyes, the more I like him."

The sheriff shook his head.

"Don't you know," he mocked gently, "that you are subject to imprisonment if you send flowers to Thorn? He might *poison* himself with them."

"Then I'll give them to Mr. Howe," she insisted. "He'll give them to Thorn."

Sheriff Doht held out his hand; if she was going inside, she'd have to give up the roses. The heartsick young widow reluctantly parted with the bouquet, and he tossed it aside as she pressed past.

"I wish women with these sort of ideas would stay in New York," he muttered.

But they wouldn't. The ferries and streetcars coming over from Manhattan that morning were crowded with wave after wave of spectators. Women poured into the galleries, chatting and carrying the de rigueur accessory of the trial—opera glasses. "I came here out of curiosity—woman's curiosity, if you want to call it that," one devotee explained. Her name was Tessie, and she'd come up from Greenpoint early that morning to get the best front-row gallery seat. "I think that every woman that has heard of this case is interested in it."

"It is a woman's case, a story of a woman's troubles," another agreed.

"It's a wonderful murder," Tessie enthused. "Oh, but Mrs. Nack is an awful creature."

"I came here just to see Mrs. Nack," a neighbor chimed in.

"So did I," another offered. "I'd have given my last $5 and gone without breakfast to see that woman."

But on this day Mrs. Nack was nowhere to be seen; there were only platoons of journalists, newly installed justice Samuel Maddox on the bench—the last judge having excused himself on account of malaria—and, at the center of it all, the famed defense table. Howe was dressed in his usual splendiferous manner, and Thorn presented a fine sight, with his mustache now grown to full luxuriousness. One woman in the gallery admitted that she'd actually *sung* to him.

"I go to the Tombs to sing to the prisoners," she explained. "It was there that I became interested in Thorn and Mrs. Nack. I go to nearly *all* of the big trials."

And this one promised to be the biggest yet. A swift jury selection—LOOK MORE INTELLIGENT THAN THE FORMER LOT, ran one headline—drew together a group made up of two farmers, a florist, a property agent, an oyster dealer, and fully seven builders, for the November frost had left construction crews free to fill the jury box.

After quickly recalling the children and police witnesses of the first trial, they soon came to the first of the new witnesses: Mrs. Clara Nunnheimer, a Woodside neighbor. A fresh-faced and beaming young woman, she seemed to brighten the gaslit room as she took the stand.

"Do you recall the 25th of June?" the prosecutor asked her.

"Yes, sir." She nodded cheerily. Fridays, she explained, were her day for chopping wood. At around eleven she'd seen Mrs. Nack and a man in a light suit step out of a trolley car, then go inside the house next door. She never saw him come back out—but she did soon see a different man in an upstairs window—one in blue shirtsleeves.

"The fellow between the two officers there?" the prosecutor asked, pointing at a poker-faced Martin Thorn.

"Yes, sir."

Howe wasn't having any of it. "From where you were standing chopping wood in your back yard, you could see the features of a man who got off the trolley car?"

Mrs. Nunnheimer broke into a dazzling smile.

"Well," the Woodside neighbor explained, "I *watched* them."

The courtroom broke into laughter, and no amount of interrogation by Howe could dim the woman's sunny disposition. Nor could he rattle a thirteen-year-old girl who'd seen Thorn buying plaster at the local shop, the undertaker who'd rented out the carriage, or the neighbor who explained that he lived "kind of diagonally across from Mr. Buala's property."

"Are you the man who owned the ducks?" Howe asked dubiously.

"Yes, sir," Henry Wahle nodded from the stand.

"That ditch was a little slimy—that which you call blood, you say you saw it on top of the slime?"

"I suppose if I had a quart can I could have filled it up," Wahle said.

Howe looked triumphantly out at the crowd. "How can you say that the drainpipe from *that* cottage drained into *that* ditch?"

"Because," the witness said, instantly deflating him, "I was there when the plumbing was put in."

But Wahle wasn't the only one privy to a hidden clue. And as the women in the galleries focused their opera glasses on the stand, the truth of how the case was cracked—one that no newspaper had dared to reveal—now came to light.

THE DA HAD the same question for each of the victim's colleagues: "Did you ever see William Guldensuppe naked?" he demanded.

"I have," masseur Philip Krantz answered warily.

"Frequently?"

"Yes, sir." They'd worked in the Murray Hill Baths, after all.

"Did you notice any particular distinguishing marks upon the body of William Guldensuppe during his lifetime?"

Why, yes, Krantz replied—a tattoo of a girl on his chest, a mole on his right arm . . .

"Any *other* mark?" Youngs pressed.

"The scar on the left finger?" the coworker ventured.

"Anything *else*?"

Philip Krantz shifted uncomfortably in his chair.

"There was his . . . " And then he mumbled something.

"What?" Youngs called out.

Krantz mumbled again and looked down.

"Speak so the jury can hear," Youngs demanded, as courtroom spectators leaned forward.

"*His penis,*" Krantz said.

Guldensuppe, it seemed, was a memorable fellow.

"He had very *peculiar* privates," another coworker, Herman Specht, struggled to explain.

"This peculiarity of the penis," the DA went on, turning to the crowd and then back to the masseur, "was that so noticeable as to attract the attention of the other bath rubbers?"

"Yes," Specht admitted. "*Many* times."

"What can you say"—here Youngs drew out one of the morgue photographs—"as to the penis of Exhibit Number Five?"

That's the one, he replied.

"The most peculiar thing *was* his penis," a third coworker reminisced. "Like where he was circumcised on the head of the penis, underneath from the head he had a lump of skin hanging. Which he could *stretch.*"

Ladies in the gallery gasped, but the masseur had only just started.

"I saw him stretch it at least *two and a half inches,*" he added brightly.

All this was just too much for the defense attorney's dignity.

"Yes, a circumcision," Howe scoffed dismissively, and tried steering the testimony back to the mole and the tattoo.

"Mr. Howe dropped the subject of the penis very quickly," the district attorney jeered. But he wasn't about to let go so easily. As

Coroner Tuthill took the stand and held forth on the mole—"a warty growth under the right arm, just at the lower border of the axilla"— the prosecutor cut in impatiently.

"Did you notice the penis?" he demanded.

"Yes," the coroner sighed. "I am coming to that. A *very* peculiar penis. The peculiarity consisted in the fact that the upper portion of the foreskin was absolutely denuded down to the body of the organ, leaving no foreskin on top, but a long pendulous foreskin beneath it." He produced a drawing that he'd made and held it out. "I have a piece of paper here to illustrate that with—"

"I object!" bellowed Howe.

The galleries burst out into laughter, and Judge Maddox gaveled the crowd to order; he'd expel them *all* from the courthouse if he had to. Put the penis schematic away, he told the coroner.

"*Describe* it," the judge said wearily.

"The under portion of the foreskin," Tuthill replied, a little hurt, "extended down very long, an inch and three-quarters in length."

"Now, what was done with this body after your examination?"

"It was placed in formalin to preserve it," Tuthill said, indicating a container on the exhibit table. It was a small one-quart fruit jar, sealed with red wax; inside an alcohol solution suspended, one *Times* reporter recounted, "something looking much like small sections of tripe."

"Has that changed its appearance?"

"Very much so." Tuthill nodded. "The action of formalin is to harden and practically tan the skin. The penis has practically shrunken up and is as hard as a bone now."

Reporters were almost snapping their pencils. They couldn't print *this*. What the courtroom ladies now knew—and what the rest of the world would not hear a word of—was that back in July, the papers fibbed about how Murray Hill Baths employees so conclusively identified Guldensuppe. The papers claimed, rather metaphorically, that it was by his peculiar finger. But bathhouse attendants and morgue staff alike, when asked, agreed that of the thousands of naked men they'd seen, this one was *special*.

The judge wisely called a recess.

"CHURCH—OR GOLF?" demanded the jury foreman over breakfast the next morning. They'd all been sequestered from their families for the Thanksgiving holiday in the Garden City Hotel; when Judge Maddox had broken the news back at the courthouse, the crowd visibly pitied the twelve crestfallen men.

But perhaps Thanksgiving at the hotel wouldn't be so bad: the Garden City had been designed by Stanford White, and it was the most luxurious hotel for miles around. They came downstairs that morning to find preparations already being made for an impressive spread of turkey and roast duck. One juror promptly hit the breakfast table and stuffed buckwheat pancakes into his pockets.

"I wish there were *more* murders in this county," another cracked between mouthfuls.

But, alas, they were already a hung jury. *Church*, a stout minority of five argued. *Golf*, responded the other seven, noting that as they were sequestered, and many sermons of late referred to the Thorn case, it was their civic duty to stay far from baleful public influences. Such isolation could only be guaranteed by standing in the middle of an open field . . . with a caddy.

It was fortunate that the men were nowhere near the jail that day, for the inquisitive public had turned out in battalions. Just as when children flooded Woodside on Independence Day, the enforced idleness of Thanksgiving seemed to bring out the amateur detective in New Yorkers. Hundreds milled about, hoping to gain an audience with Nack or Thorn, only to have Sheriff Doht turn them away.

For Thorn, the day inside at first passed much like any other, with a marathon session of pinochle, albeit with the happy interruption of turkey and potatoes. His faithful dog, Bill Baker, fared well, and the jailers presented Thorn with a precious commodity indeed: a Havana cigar. As Thorn watched the smoke curl away through the bars of his cell, only a *Journal* correspondent managed to dampen his holiday spirits. What, the reporter asked, did he think of Adolph Luetgert's comments on the trial?

Luetgert? Thorn had avidly followed the Chicago sausage maker's retrial—it had begun the same day as his own, even—but he didn't know Luetgert had been following *his* retrial as well.

A newspaper was handed to the prisoner with a headline blaring across the front page: LUETGERT PREDICTS THORN'S CONVICTION. "I believe the jury will convict them both," the accused acid-vat killer told the press. "Nothing, I believe, can save them, unless the state has made an agreement with Mrs. Nack to let her off with imprisonment."

"Luetgert is guilty, *I* think, and ought to be hanged," Thorn snapped back. But the comment aggravated him. Picking up the *Evening Journal* later that day didn't help. After a day of reading religious books, his co-conspirator had issued a statement that a suspicious mind might read all sorts of deal making and betrayal into.

"I can say," Mrs. Nack announced to the press, "that I really knew what Thanksgiving is today."

BY FRIDAY the crowds had turned ruthless.

"Show your passes!" the courthouse deputies barked. Forged tickets had been showing up among those trying to get in. Bickering women seized seats in the courthouse galleries, refusing to go even when caught with bad and expired papers. "Out!" one guard yelled across a row, while another collared a spectator—"*He means you!*"

"It's a disgrace to have women in attendance," the DA complained bitterly from the courthouse floor, appalled that he'd had to present testimonies about Guldensuppe's foreskin in front of so many women.

Hearst, though, was unrepentant: "To show crime in its vulgarest and most revolting aspects," he announced piously to his readers, "is to perform a service."

Reporters eagerly telegraphed across the river what lurid details they could: BRAZEN WOMEN AND BAD AIR, one headline announced. For the courthouse was indeed suffocating again; the malodorous atmosphere, a *New York Press* reporter complained, was now "more offensive than ever, if possible." The district attorney himself was demanding an investigation into the courthouse's ventilation, and more than a few suspected that the first judge's malaria attack had been brought on by the evil-smelling miasma.

And yet the crowd pressed forward into the seats, nearly bowling one another over the railings, arguing and gossiping in equal measure—then breaking into a low murmur as the suspects were led in. Nearly lost in the commotion was the strangely familiar face of a rather dapper gentleman; the guards almost hadn't even let him in until he produced a subpoena from his soft camel-hair overcoat.

Herman Nack?

The subpoena was courtesy of Mr. Howe—and so, the press pool surmised, was Herman's new wardrobe. Before calling in the delivery driver as a battering ram against Mrs. Nack, the lawyer had first bought him a good shave and a fitting at his tailor. And so here it was, then: Herman, Gussie, and Martin glowering at each other from across the courtroom floor, along with some remnants of Willie floating in an old alcohol-filled fruit jar. The four principals of the tragedy were together in one room at last.

The bakery driver remained bewildered by it all.

"Just a crazy barber," Herman muttered to a reporter as he sized up Thorn. He peered over at his wife, whom he'd last seen the morning they were both arrested. "She looks pale," he said with a hint of concern, before quickly adding, "I don't know whether to feel sorry for her or not. She is nothing to me now."

With everyone finally seated, the testimony proceeded through a cross section of New York life: the newsboy who recognized Thorn at the ferry; the saloon keeper who saw Gotha and Thorn together; a pinochle player who spotted a pistol in Thorn's vest. Detective Sullivan identified the bullets from Woodside's walls, and an NYPD pistol instructor noted that their caliber matched Thorn's blue nickel-plated .32. Detective O'Donnell, the former plumber, identified a vial of the foul-smelling plaster he'd found in the Woodside sink trap. Thorn watched with mild interest, occasionally narrowing his eyes at Mrs. Nack; she refused to return his glances. But the man they all awaited was John Gotha.

As the tall and jittery witness was led in, Thorn smiled at the sight of his old friend. Gotha, though, locked his eyes on the floor. Thorn's informant looked puffy and tired, like a man who had been gaining weight but losing sleep.

"State your name."

"John Gotha."

The prosecutor walked him through Thorn's affair with Nack and the fight with Guldensuppe. Thorn listened with a faintly indulgent smile, as if his hapless friend was confused yet again. But Gotha's recollection of Thorn's confession sounded all too precise.

"I asked him if he done the murder, and first he denied it," Gotha recounted steadily. "And then he said yes, he did it. Told me how he went into the house about half past nine, and while he was waiting for Mrs. Nack and Guldensuppe he took out his pistol and tried it out. He said it didn't work at first. He snapped it several times before it discharged, and fired it off a couple times to make sure it was all right."

It made sense now. Thorn's first brawl with Guldensuppe was lost by a misfire; these test shots explained why two bullets were found buried in the plaster lath of the Woodside cottage.

Gotha made sense to Howe, too—but not quite in the same way.

"Were you not," the lawyer demanded, rising up, "a confirmed inebriate?"

"No, sir," Gotha replied indignantly.

"Were you not taken to the Inebriates' Home at Fort Hamilton?"

"No," the barber insisted.

Howe eyed his prey for a long moment, his gold-fretted scarf glimmering under the gaslights.

"How much *money*," he rang his words out slowly, "had you in your pocket at the time of the arrest of Thorn?"

"Well," Gotha said, shifting uncomfortably. "I didn't have much money."

"How—much—*money*?"

"About twenty dollars," Gotha admitted.

"Where have you been since Thorn's arrest?" Howe pressed.

"Been up in the country."

"Paid your board there?"

"I did."

"With what money?"

"My wife's money."

"Do you know the *police* paid your board there? Yes or no?"

Gotha looked over at the prosecutor helplessly, then back at Howe.

"Yes," he said in a small voice.

Howe directed the crowd's attention to Gotha's next residence, on West 122nd.

"Who paid for *that*?" he demanded.

"I paid for that," Gotha insisted.

"Where did you get the money? From Mr. Sullivan?"

"Yes, sir."

"The district-attorney's officer, is he not?"

"Yes, sir," Gotha mumbled.

"Yes or no!" Howe bellowed.

Gotha was perspiring freely now.

"Yes."

"How much did Sullivan give you?"

"Well," the barber stuttered, "he gave me enough to—"

"How much?" Howe roared. *"You understand the English language?"*

"I couldn't get no work!" Gotha blurted.

"One hundred dollars?" Howe pressed mercilessly.

"Couldn't tell you."

"You mean that, do you Gotha?" Howe yelled. He was towering over the barber now, quaking with indignation.

"If Mr. Howe wants to save time, I will put in the records of—" the prosecutor interrupted.

"Allow me to conduct my cross-examination!" Howe belted, and turned back to his cowering witness. "Sullivan has given you the money on which you have lived?"

"Not *all*," Gotha protested.

"Nearly all?"

Gotha sank down farther in his seat. "Nearly all," he replied quietly.

"Have you earned *one penny*"—Howe banged his fist down— "from the time you went to the police headquarters? Yes or no?"

"I have not *earned* it," Gotha stumbled, "but I got it from my wife's people . . ."

"Haven't done a day's work, have you?"

"No," he mumbled.

"You know"—Howe motioned at the teeming press tables—"there

was one thousand dollars offered by the *New York Journal* for the discovery of the perpetrator of this murder, do you not?"

"Yes, sir."

Howe turned back to him. "Is it not true that Thorn told you that it was *Mrs. Nack* who shot Guldensuppe?"

"No," Gotha insisted.

No further questions, Howe scoffed.

The whole thing, Howe declared, was a flimsy farrago to get a reward when the real murderer was already under arrest. With Gotha reduced to rubble, the lawyer now had Herman Nack at the ready to demolish his ex-wife's credibility. "I'll tear her apart," Howe assured a reporter.

But the district attorney had a surprise for him.

"The people rest," Youngs announced.

What?

The crowd was stunned. No Mrs. Nack? A capital case without the star witness? But they were hardly as amazed as the glimmering figure who stood before them on the courtroom floor. Howe was thunderstruck for what seemed the first time in his life, as the realization dawned on him.

In a single instant, the prosecution had just outflanked his entire defense.

CROWD MAY BREAK RECORDS, the headlines warned that Monday. Over the weekend Sheriff Doht's office had been flooded with thousands of applications, including a bar association's worth of lawyers; attorneys were making a pilgrimage to see how the Great Howe would magically free his client. But another constituency was not admitted.

"No women," Sheriff Doht told an uproarious crowd gathered outside. He was taking no chances; the mistake of allowing women to hear about Guldensuppe's anatomy would not be repeated this week. Newspapers couldn't even hint at the reason; they had to settle for informing their readers that the testimony was simply too shocking even for modern-minded ladies. Scores of women promptly laid siege to the sheriff's office and overflowed into hallways, all hoping to glimpse either Nack or Thorn.

But behind the courtroom's heavy oak doors, Martin Thorn was staring too—at the jury.

"I have been watching them pretty closely, though some think I take little interest in the trial," Thorn confided to a *Herald* reporter as the room filled up. He nodded toward the ever-smiling Valentine Waits, a perpetually cheerful farmer who had become a favorite of courtroom cartoonists. He appeared particularly well fed and jolly that morning. "I notice many of them are getting rosy cheeks."

The rest of the jury filed into the jury box, with the out-of-season builders looking almost as crisply groomed that morning as Thorn himself.

"Some of them have had a hair cut," he observed quietly. "I suppose I notice that because I'm a barber."

Thorn's voice, the *Herald* reporter mused, retained the same calm register of the barbershop—as "if he had been discussing freaks of weather with favored customers." His lawyer, though, was more boisterous: Howe slapped his client's back, prepared his papers, and then stood up before the quieted courthouse.

Gentlemen—his voice rang out. For they were indeed gentlemen, save for seven or eight canny women who had gotten in under the pretense of being newspaper artists; their sketch pads sat unused on their laps. "Gentlemen of the jury," he began impressively. *"Martin Thorn is innocent of the murder of William Guldensuppe."*

He strode up to the jury box, looking with great meaning at each man sitting in it.

"The killing of Guldensuppe germinated in the mind of the assassin—Mrs. Nack. She is a perjurer as well as a murderess. It was *she* who hired the cottage for the purpose of converting it to a slaughterhouse in which to take the life of her lover. Guldensuppe had been pestering this woman and she wanted him no longer—she wanted Martin Thorn. And so this Lady Macbeth of modern times came to Woodside and hired a cottage. *She* bought the oilcloth, while Guldensuppe was yet alive. *She* took him there to have him killed. *She* was the murderer. This anatomist who could carve a body as well as you could carve a turkey—this Lady Macbeth and all the Borgias rolled into one—then proceeded to cut that body up. After his butchery *she* put his clothes in a cooking stove, gentlemen, and watched the fire do its work. That's the creature that talks of confessing through God and her conscience."

Howe paused and turned pensive. His white hair glowed against the somber black of his suit, and now he spoke in a low, tremulous voice.

"In a long career in the court, I am in—*yellow* leaf," he confided. After days of vigorous bluster, Howe was turning old and kindly. "But I believe that justice will be done."

Summoning his strength, Howe turned to the packed house. "Martin Thorn!"

Captain Methven loosened Thorn's handcuffs and then led the prisoner behind the jury box, through the narrow passage, to the stand.

"Will Your Honor pardon me if I sit down during this examination?" the old lawyer asked, turning to Judge Maddox. "Out of respect to the court I prefer to stand, very much—but I ask that I may sit down."

"Yes," the judge nodded.

The effect was curiously intimate: Howe and Thorn were two men now, sitting and talking.

"Thorn," Howe asked genially, "what is your proper name?"

"Martin Thorzewsky."

"When did you first meet Mrs. Nack?"

"A year and a half ago."

A glance around the courtroom showed that she had not been brought in by the prosecution; their feint had already succeeded. He was on his own, even if their entire defense relied on attacking her.

"Did Mrs. Nack make love to you—or you to her?" Howe asked delicately.

"She made love to me."

"And did you love her in return?"

"I did," he smiled.

"Very fondly?"

"Very," Thorn replied quietly.

Soon, Thorn explained earnestly, she talked of leaving Guldensuppe, so they could run off together to start a lucrative orphanage in Woodside. But on the morning of June 25, when he visited the house they'd secretly rented, he had the shock of his life.

"I came there a little after eleven, and soon as I came up the stoop, the door came open and Mrs. Nack stood inside, a little excited. I asked her—'What is the matter?' She said, 'Oh, I just left Guldensuppe upstairs.' I said, 'What's he doing up there?' She said, 'I just shot him, and I am glad of it; I am rid of all my trouble now.'"

Thorn shook his head in disbelief: The woman had immediately tried pinning it all on *him*. "She said, 'We'll have to get rid of the body now—*you* have to. If you don't suspicion will fall on you because you had a fight with him, and you got the receipt in your name for the cottage.' So we proceeded to take the body, undressed him and put him in the bath tub, and I went out and bought the plaster of paris."

"Where did you go?"

"Fourth Street—I don't know, the corner." He shrugged. "When I got back Mrs. Nack had her hat and dress off, and I got hold of the body. Mrs. Nack took a big knife and cut his throat. When she came to the back of the neck she took a saw and cut it, and then she commenced to count his ribs. I said, 'What are you doing that for?' She said, 'So I won't cut the body too far down, so as not to open any of the bowels.'"

The crowd squirmed a little, but the detail rang true: The fairly expert carving of the body attested to great deliberation in the cut lines, and to someone with a knowledge of anatomy.

The courtroom was dead quiet as Howe rose and walked to the jury box. "Thorn," he inquired gravely, "were you ever convicted of any offense?"

"Never."

"Look at that jury, Thorn." Howe swept his arm out. *"Did you shoot William Guldensuppe?"*

Martin Thorn looked up from the chair: out over the courthouse, at scores of men scribbling in steno pads, at errand boys sliding telegraph dispatches under the door, at disheveled artists scrolling pictures into pigeon tubes, at hundreds of New Yorkers staring fixedly upon him from the galleries.

Then the defendant leveled his gaze squarely at the twelve men who would decide his fate.

"I did not," he said.

V.

THE
VERDICT

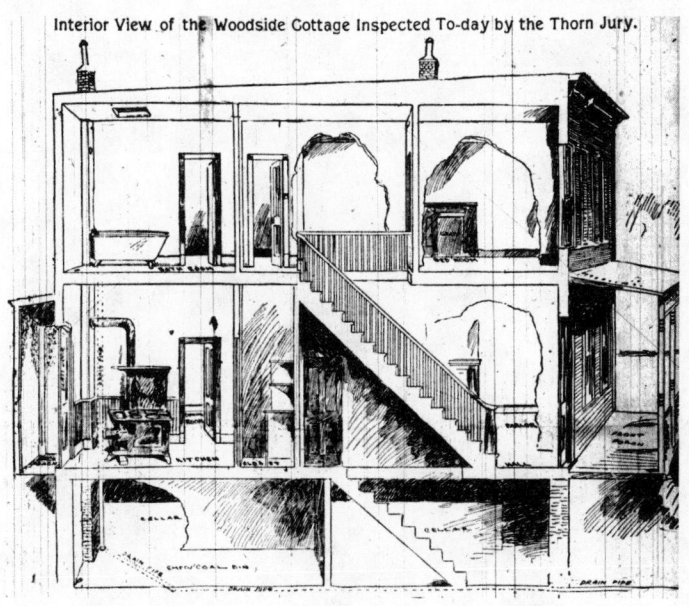

Interior View of the Woodside Cottage Inspected To-day by the Thorn Jury.

21.

MRS. NACK'S OFFICE

NOT EVERYONE WAS TRANSFIXED by Martin Thorn's stare. True, there were newspaper reports of his "evil eye"; Hearst even joked that its baleful power had caused that week's unraveling of Paddy Gleason, the Long Island City mayor caught trying to use the Woodside Water Company to scoop up a $60,000 windfall for himself. But the evil-eye rumor was taken seriously enough by District Attorney Youngs's daughter that she loaned him her lucky piece of coral; this, she told her father, was to be carried in his pocket for protection against Thorn. In his other pocket William Youngs dutifully carried a rabbit's foot—a present from his wife. But he knew Thorn had no unearthly power now, and scarcely even earthly power; why, the man could be undone by a schoolgirl.

"Clara Pierce," Youngs called out into the packed courthouse.

The prosecution, allowed a final rebuttal to Thorn's testimony, had tantalized the press with the lure of an appearance by Mrs. Nack; but alas, they would not give Howe the satisfaction of attacking her. "The case for the people was complete without her," one of Youngs's team insisted. Instead, wending past the jury box and up to the stand was a slender and neatly attired girl, her eyes wide before the murmuring crowd.

Who is that? the whisper ran.

"Where do you live?" Youngs asked her after she was sworn in.

"439 Ninth Avenue."

"Do you go to school?"

"Yes, sir." Clara nodded earnestly.

"How old are you?"

"Thirteen."

Her manner was a curious contrast to Thorn's or indeed nearly every adult who had taken the stand—her voice small and precise, free of artifice.

"Do you remember"—Youngs measured his words carefully—"Friday, the twenty-fifth of June?"

"Yes," she nodded. "I got home at two o'clock."

"How do you know it was Friday?"

"Because I got home early."

"Friday is the only day you get home early?"

"Yes, sir," she explained, adding that it was her time to visit Mrs. Stewart, a neighbor in the building, to babysit the woman's infant.

"What did you do with it?"

"I was bringing it down in its carriage."

"Did you take it to see Mrs. Nack?"

"Yes," the girl said plainly.

"You know Mrs. Nack?"

"I didn't just know her," the schoolgirl smiled. "She *lived* in 439 Ninth Avenue."

"Did you see her that day?" the prosecutor asked.

"Yes—between half past two and three o'clock."

"What was Mrs. Nack *doing* at that time?" he asked significantly.

"Trimming her hat," Clara replied.

A murmur arose in the courtroom. The girl was with Mrs. Nack—at a sewing table, calmly banding ribbons around a brown hat—at the precise moment Thorn claimed she was miles away cutting up a body.

No further questions, Youngs said as he walked back past Howe. It was a child on an East River pier who had begun the case one balmy June day; now, five months later and in the winter darkness of a courtroom, another child had ended it.

"IS THAT ALL YOUR EVIDENCE?" Howe scoffed.

"I believe it is," Youngs replied with a slight bow.

Pacing before the bench the next morning, the defense counsel had one last request for Judge Maddox.

"I ask"—Howe leaned forward—"that the jury be permitted to view the bath tub in which it is claimed the body was cut up—with a view to showing that no one person alone could have put that body in the bathtub without indentation of the tin."

"These premises are now in the same condition that they were at or about the twenty-fifth of June?" Judge Maddox asked.

"Practically the same," the DA cut in. "There are certain marks on the walls and things of that kind, but the premises are practically in the same condition."

"The district attorney cut out little pieces to have it analyzed with respect to the blood," Howe added. "Our point is that the bath tub should be viewed."

The judge did not look entirely convinced. "What say you, Mr. Youngs?"

"We have nothing to conceal at all," the DA shrugged. "The key is in the custody of Detective Sullivan."

"How long will it take to go from here to the cottage?"

"About twenty minutes."

After nearly thinking better of it, the judge decided to let them go ahead; Martin Thorn, not surprisingly, wasn't interested in joining them.

"Gentlemen of the jury"—Judge Maddox turned to the twelve men—"you will be conducted to this house."

With that, he sent them to fetch their hats and overcoats. Captain Methven and the rest of their police escort cut a path through the crowd as the jurors filed out into the cold air of the courthouse steps and down to the streetcar stop. While a private trolley was requisitioned for the jurors, reporters jockeyed to hire their own. An *Evening Journal* artist stood nearby and hurriedly sketched the scene in pen and ink.

It won't fit, a colleague informed him. *One bird can't carry a sheet that size.* The chagrined artist, realizing his mistake, promptly sliced the drawing down the middle. The two halves were sent across the river by different pigeons.

The jurors themselves wouldn't see the drawings; Captain Methven made sure of that. He hadn't allowed his charges to read anything in their off-hours—"nothing but hotel menu cards," he declared. But the twelve men climbing aboard the trolley had taken it all good-naturedly, and had even amused themselves the day before by forming a fraternity. After considering calling it the Thorny Club, they settled upon the Good Thing Club—good things, of course, coming to those who wait. They'd passed around cigars to make it official, made an appointment for a group photograph, and genially hazed their police escort by loading his rifle with blanks on the hotel's trap-shooting range. *Same time next year,* the jurors promised the officers after dissolving into hilarity. *We'll treat you to dinner.*

But now, it was all business.

The procession—the jurors and police sequestered in their one drafty streetcar, and a parade of reporters and spectators following them—rolled at a stately pace, beyond the saloons selling hot rum, past cart horses shaking off the cold, by greenhouses fogged with winter. When the convoy reached the sleepy corner of Second Street, a crowd was already gathered around the house that locals jovially referred to as Mrs. Nack's Office.

"All off here for Woodside cottage!" the conductor called back to his passengers, and the twelve men stepped out of their streetcar and into the scene of the crime.

THE PLACE had hardly changed at all.

The trees were bare now, the grass in the backyard high and un-mown, but otherwise it remained recognizable from last summer's front pages. The house's windows slumbered under closed wooden shutters, heedless of the men treading through the mud and ice up to the creaking wooden front porch. There the jurors paused while Detective Sullivan fished out a key and slid it into the lock.

Back, back, they could hear the police yelling behind them, shoo-ing gawkers to a perimeter around the property line.

The door groaned awake on its hinges, and they quietly filed into the darkened parlor. The air in the unheated house was frigid, leaving their breath visible in white clouds; with the power long shut off, Detective Sullivan busily threw open the shutters to let in the subdued light of the winter morning. *This way*, he motioned them downstairs. He'd been one of the first in the house back in the summer, and he knew it well. Down in the cellar lay the smashed remains of a chimney, a hole still gaping where detectives in search of Guldensuppe's head had attacked the brickwork with sledgehammers. A peek inside the hole revealed why that search had failed: The aperture inside was scarcely four inches wide.

Back upstairs and through the parlor, they paused in the kitchen to peer into the black iron stove that had held the ashes of the dead man's shoes, then trod up the steep flight of stairs to the house's second story. Their footsteps echoed loud and hollow through the hallways. It was a modest home, cheaply made and of small proportions, with just two bedrooms and a bathroom upstairs. The jurors barely fit into the front bedroom. Its walls still bore neatly penciled forensics notations and small scars down to the wooden lathing—specimens pried away by detectives extracting the two bullets that Gotha said Thorn had test-fired from his revolver.

At the next room, the men paused.

The second bedroom remained as it had been—without a hint of trouble, save for subtle shavings planed off sections of the floorboards for blood analysis. The closet was empty, its door ajar, waiting. With a rug over the nicked-up floor, one could imagine a tidy little boarder's room being made of such a space. Yet the murder had been perpetrated in *one* of these two bedrooms, for according to Nack and Gotha, Thorn had fired from this very closet, while Thorn contended that Mrs. Nack had done the deed herself in the front room.

The bathroom's back here. Sullivan waved them along.

The jurors inspected the metal bathtub, leaning down one by one to examine its surface. As Howe had promised, there was neither a dent nor a saw mark to be found. It would indeed have been difficult for one person to do the dismembering alone. But if both hands had grasped that terrible saw, which one had leveled the revolver or grasped the dagger—and in which bedroom?

Walking back downstairs, Foreman Morse led his jury into the weedy backyard, the ground furrowed with the diggings of detectives and treasure hunters. Then they strolled out front to the roadside ditch, where ducks cavorted in half-frozen water. It was the same flock that had turned pink with Guldensuppe's draining blood, and the jurors watched the ducks waddle past them and across the yard of the emptied house.

In a few hours, the jurors would have to decide just what had happened inside that cottage.

JUDGE MADDOX HADN'T YET finished his cigar when the jurors returned; the justice was gazing out over the packed room with a thoughtful look. It was too bad they hadn't taken a bit longer; cigars were just about the only way to make the room's air fit to breathe.

Quiet! He gaveled the tumultuous crowd, and he motioned for Howe to come up. The defense had elected to give the first closing argument, and it was time for him to make his last stand. The old lawyer tugged down on his pin-striped vest—a favorite gesture of his—and then turned to the hushed room with great seriousness.

"May it please Your Honor and gentlemen of the jury," Howe began quietly. "I firmly believe that the woman with a pistol taken from her apartment and brought here into this court is the one who shot William Guldensuppe. Mrs. Nack, the vile thing that left her husband, tells Thorn that she loves *him* dearly: '*I love Thorn and would die for him.*' Instead she made another man die—Guldensuppe."

Howe's voice climbed in indignation as he paced before the jury box.

"Yet you're asked to place the blame on this man! He was no more the murderer of Guldensuppe than you were. The District Attorney was too astute to have dared a second ordeal of that woman on the stand. He was afraid to have her confronted. He feared she would go to pieces on the rack of truth, and you would see into the recesses of her murderous heart. Thorn is on trial for what *she* did—and I say, God forbid that murderess should go free, and Thorn pay the penalty."

Howe paused before one juror and then the next—hovering,

one reporter mused, like an immense bee before each blossom in a flower box.

"Gotha is the *only one* who testified that Thorn confessed. *Gotha*. Judas was a saint compared to this *Gotha*."

Howe turned and swung out his arm.

"Who is *Gotha*?" he barked. "Thorn was a hard-working barber until he fell in with this vile creature, this harridan. *Gotha* left his wife and lived alone. And then he came here, with blood money in his pocket, to swear away the life of this *man*."

The courtroom was electric with silence, the crowd almost holding its breath.

"He had read about the one thousand dollar reward. He had Detective Price's one hundred dollars. But we don't stop with Sam Price's one hundred dollars. We have him going to the New York District Attorney's office. This barber, who from his looks couldn't earn ten dollars a week by shaving, gets one hundred dollars in a lump and then *lies* to you. He was acting a lie from the time he put on the handcuffs until he went on the stand."

Howe glanced between the jury box and the prosecution team.

"Suppose the evidence of Gotha were out of the case. What evidence is there that Thorn fired the shot or did any killing? Can they find anything besides that? No—and I can't conceive of your believing *Gotha*."

As for the innocent schoolgirl from Mrs. Nack's building, well—surely she told the truth, Howe admitted, but she or Thorn merely had their times confused. No, he declared, the schoolgirl's testimony made the case against Nack even worse.

"Trimming a ha-aat!" He banged down his fist. "Trimming a hat, *just after she trimmed her lover's body*!" Howe's voice, marveled a reporter, roared so loud that the chandeliers jangled. In the startled silence that followed, he stopped and mopped the perspiration from his brow.

"Now, as to your visit to the cottage just now—you didn't find a single indentation in that tub, did you? The body could not have been cut unless *two* people had helped with it. Under this indictment it is perfectly reasonable that you could find a verdict of murder in

the second degree—punishment worse than death itself. Imprisonment for life in a tomb of stone! Never leaving that tomb until the
dead body is carried out. Some of you"—he motioned to the jurors—
"may have been sick in your comfortable houses, and the very paper
on the wall begins to punish you with weariness. But picture *twenty
years* in a cell."

His voice dropped low, and he pulled up close to the jury-box
railing.

"To take the life which God has given—unjustly—is an awful
thing. Remember that the scenes of this day will never, ever leave
you. They will follow you to your farm"—he eyed Valentine Waits,
and then the builders—"to your carpenter's shop. These scenes will
sleep by you on your pillow. If it should transpire that this man is
innocent after you have judged him guilty, this man will haunt you
through your lives. If you find him guilty, at the final accounting *that
man's spirit will rise to condemn you before the judgment seat of God.*"

Youngs's summation was plodding and methodical: Thorn had the
weapons, had the motive, had been placed at the scene, and confessed to a friend. They had unprecedented circumstantial evidence,
and testimony by detectives and a firearms expert allowed the jury
to draw its own conclusion. "Put these things together in a mosaic,
gentlemen," he invited. "And see the picture they form."

The defense, Youngs noted tartly, changed its story with each
passing day—first it was Guldensuppe's body, then it wasn't; Thorn
hadn't been at the scene, then he had.

"Gentlemen of the jury"—the district attorney smiled faintly—
"the eloquence of Mr. Howe is world-wide in its reputation, standing
as he does at the head of the criminal bar of the city of New York. The
eloquence you have listened to today has been thrilling. And"—he
glanced at Howe—"through its exertion, no doubt more than one
guilty man has escaped."

Thorn stared ahead stonily, while Howe glared back in fine indignation.

"We lay no claim to any greatness of oratory," Youngs continued.
Balding and bespectacled, the very diminutiveness of the DA now

turned against the defense counsel. "He has given you that, but we have given you something stronger than oratory, more powerful than eloquence: *evidence*."

The district attorney paused before the jury box. He wanted them to also consider their solemn duty as Long Islanders—as the bulwark that honest tradesmen like them kept up against the depredations of the big city across the river.

"Gentlemen of the jury, he has appealed to your heart, your passions. I appeal to your common sense, to your heads. Don't let it go out that men and women can come over *here* from neighboring cities and conspire to commit crimes."

The crowd of reporters rolled their eyes; they'd be going back to that great corrupting city tonight—and be glad of it, too. But it was not the reporters that Youngs had turned toward.

"I know," the DA concluded as he gazed earnestly at the carpenters and farmers, "that I can leave the matter in *your* hands."

THE COURTROOM WAS RAVENOUS; closing arguments had taken so long that it was 2:25 p.m. by the time the twelve men left for the jury room. Judge Maddox had lunch sent in to the jurors, while the courtroom itself broke out sandwiches and bottles of ginger ale in a flurry of wax paper and napkins; the spectators, not wanting to lose their seats, had packed their own lunches. It was a masculine affair, with women still hopelessly crowded out on the courthouse steps and in hallways. Their only representative inside was a single black-veiled woman nearly hidden behind one of the spectator gallery pillars. *It's Thorn's sister*, the murmur went.

Thorn himself was led downstairs to a holding cell for lunch, while at his defense table Howe assumed a philosophical look. He was delighted with their case, he declared, but then his expression darkened. He'd torn down every major witness on the stand as an inebriate, a busybody, or an outright criminal—all of them, that is, except one.

"The *one thing* is the testimony of little Clara Pierce," he confided quietly to his associates. The schoolgirl's placement of Mrs. Nack in the city could undermine Thorn's entire alibi. "It may turn the jury against us."

Howe's sheer oratory, reporters and spectators agreed, had expertly maneuvered around the prosecution. "So long as Mr. Howe kept in a sphere above the actual evidence, he soared triumphant," the crime novelist Julian Hawthorne telegraphed from his post at the *Journal* table. Along the way, Howe had deftly rolled back his defense from brashly denying Guldensuppe's death to admitting that someone had caused the fellow to never be seen reemerging from that Woodside cottage.

But who?

"It is not believed that he cut *himself* up," a *Brooklyn Eagle* reporter wrote tartly. "It is not supposed that he took a saw with him into the cottage for the purpose of separating himself from his arms and his legs and incidentally his head."

And yet many clues to who *had* done the deed were not used. Gotha's testimony was a necessary gamble, but every other marginal witness had been ruthlessly excluded. Youngs saw in the first trial that Howe's specialty was in demolishing any witness with an ulterior motive or the least vulnerability in character. Mrs. Nack's testimony was left out, of course; but so was Mrs. Riger's account of the oilcloth purchase. It was said that the poor woman had suffered a breakdown over all the publicity. Frank Clark's old allegation from the Tombs of an infirmary confession was also left untouched; Youngs had planned to use it in the first trial, but now a con like Clark was clearly easy prey to Howe. But so, remarkably, was the analysis of blood spots on the floors. With poisoning charges and money troubles now hanging over Professor Witthaus's divorce, the forensics expert's character would have been mauled by the defense—and in any case, while forensics evidence might have worked in Manhattan, Long Island farmers and carpenters had no truck with chemistry professors.

How quickly would such a jury weigh a secondhand confession to an unemployed barber and a series of circumstantial clues from friends and neighbors? Not too quickly, it seemed. As the cigars and flasks were swapped among the denizens of the galleries, the courtroom's pendulum clock ticked slowly forward to three o'clock, and then to four. Passing by the guarded jury-room door a half hour later, reporters could make out raised voices.

Sitting at the jury room's table, among the picked-over remains of their lunches, one builder was demanding that the jury vote remain by secret ballot. And after six votes in a row, the foreman had opened the slips of paper, counted them, and hit the same result each time.

Eleven to one.

One hour later—after demanding and then poring over the intercepted jailhouse correspondence between Nack and Thorn—the twelve men filed back into the courtroom through the side door, and drowsy spectators scrambled to their feet.

"Remove your hats!" deputies bellowed up into the galleries as Judge Maddox returned from his chambers and then as Martin Thorn was led back in. Actually, it was Thorn doing the leading: He was so nervously eager that he was nearly dragging in Captain Methven with his handcuffed arm.

The twelve solemn men looked to the judge and waited.

"Gentlemen of the jury, have you agreed upon a verdict?"

"We have," their foreman replied.

"Defendant, rise," the court clerk commanded Martin Thorn. "Jurors, look upon the defendant. Defendant, look upon the jurors. What say you?"

The men locked eyes, and Thorn knew his fate.

"We find the defendant guilty," the foreman announced—"of murder in the first degree."

22.

THE SMOKER
TO SING SING

MARTIN THORN KNEW they were out to kill him.

"I suppose Howe will get a new trial, but it won't do any good in this county," he snorted to the *Herald* reporter waiting back at his cell. "You can't get a jury in this county who wouldn't hang you for stealing a loaf of bread."

There wasn't much left to cheer Thorn up other than wrestling with his adopted mutt—the only creature on earth uninterested in judging him.

So, did you do it?

Thorn sat down and looked pensively around his cell; the room had been freshly whitewashed the day before in anticipation of the press, and it still smelled of paint.

"I had no motive to kill Guldensuppe," Thorn said quietly, and then eyed the *Herald* reporter. "He did *exactly* what I would have done under the circumstances. What could he have done? I never had any ill will against the man for striking me."

So then . . .

"Mrs. Nack had a motive," he snapped. "I didn't."

But when Thorn's sister Pauline and her husband came to visit, his defiance was to no avail: They both looked thunderstruck.

"Martin!" his sister sobbed, and grasped his hand. "Martin!"

The husband stood by, eyes welling up, also unable to speak. Thorn sat his sister in a corner of the tiny cell, a rather melancholy gesture toward privacy.

"Martin!" she wept.

"Well," he motioned cheerfully outside. "Pretty cold out today, ain't it?"

She was not fooled by his nonchalance.

"Poor fellow!" Pauline dabbed her eyes and finally composed herself a little. Her expression turned indignant. "It's a shame that they should make a deal with Mrs. Nack. It's a shame. She—"

"Hush, hush." Thorn held his hand up. "I don't want you to say anything about her. I wouldn't care if she were turned loose tomorrow. I don't care what becomes of her."

His sister looked astounded—as did everyone else in the cell.

"Yes, I mean it," the prisoner insisted. "I do mean it."

His sister and brother-in-law left the cell as distraught as when they'd arrived, unsure whether they'd ever see him alive again.

Do *you mean it?* a *Herald* reporter asked.

"It doesn't make any difference to me what they do with her." Thorn shrugged. But he was struggling with his feelings, because it wasn't just the jury or the State of New York that he knew was out to kill him. "I am convinced," he said slowly, "that these letters that Mrs. Nack sent to me are part of a scheme—to commit *suicide*. She thought I would carry out my part of the contract, and then she'd change her mind. Then I would be out of the way, and she would have nothing to fear."

It's true, one of the jailers admitted quietly—they hadn't told the press at the time, but before the trial they found a smuggled dose of morphine in Thorn's vest—enough for an overdose. They'd had an extra guard on him ever since.

"You needn't trouble yourself about me trying to commit suicide," Thorn laughed. He wasn't going to die for Mrs. Nack—not *now*. And he wouldn't die for the people of New York, either. "I'm not going to do anything to save the county or the state the expense of killing me."

The prisoner's expression darkened.

"I'll make the state pay," he said.

HOWE WASN'T WORRIED about their case at all.

"I am smoking a cigar in contentment," he informed reporters the next morning. He'd file an appeal, and he expected to win it. "My mind is in a state of peace and tranquility. I shall take lunch in a dress suit and drink a quart of white."

"On what ground will you base your appeal?" asked a reporter for the *Eagle*.

"I do not wish"—Howe smiled enigmatically—"to unmask any battery."

His first salvo came just one day later, and from an utterly unexpected source: the jury's hotel bill. The Garden City Hotel dutifully filed an itemized list with Queens County's board of supervisors: $2,049.90 for both juries. It was steep, but it was a long trial and retrial, after all, and it included hundreds in private jury streetcars and in attending physician's bills for Magnus Larsen's appendicitis. The supervisors were relieved: Some had feared that, along with misadventures like Detective Sullivan's fruitless trip to Hamburg to find Guldensuppe, the entire cost of the case might balloon to $40,000 or $50,000. Instead, it was looking like everything might come in at less than $20,000.

But they hadn't anticipated William Howe.

Much of the hotel bill consisted of the usual pettiness—a tencent charge marked "Listerine," a twenty-five-cent charge when a juror borrowed a quarter for a poker game—and a few luxuries as well. Thorn's trained eye had also been right about the jury's newfound grooming; they'd run up an impressive $30 barber bill. But it was something else that caught his defense counsel's eye. The jurors had mown down more than $80 worth of booze and cigars in a single night—and many other evenings as well. The Good Thing Club, it seemed, was a little too much of a good thing.

Intoxication! Howe bellowed. The jury was incompetent to render a verdict, he declared, on account of their disgraceful state of inebriation. District Attorney Youngs, flabbergasted, quickly rounded up the jurors and their guards in his office and demanded affidavits.

"I saw no wine drunk," insisted Captain Methven. "They were allowed to have a bottle of beer or ale and cigars for dinner, but that's all."

One juror allowed that maybe they *did* have wine—but just a single glass.

"I saw only *one* glass of wine while I was there, and that was when I was sick," a much-recovered Magnus Larsen said primly before quickly adding, "I don't care for it anyway." The other jurors admitted to a little more. Maybe there were some other drinks, too—a glass or two—some Bass beer, a blackberry cordial, maybe Jamaican ginger for a bad stomach. But they'd absolutely been quite sober in the courtroom.

When Martin Thorn reported back to the courthouse on Friday, December 3, several jurors joined the crowd of reporters and spectators to hear his sentencing. It took all of eight minutes, for the county still pointedly regarded the entire matter as settled.

"Prisoner, arise," commanded the court clerk.

Judge Maddox gazed solemnly on his audience, then read slowly from his finding.

"Thorn," he began, "you are indicted for having deliberately designed and caused the death of William Guldensuppe. You have had a fair trial—defended most ably by an astute lawyer; by counsel, indeed, who could not have done more than they did for you." Howe's expression remained stoic; his fight was not over yet. "A jury found you guilty of murder in the first degree," the judge continued. "The punishment for that crime is death."

Thorn's face paled slightly, but he remained motionless.

"*Reflect upon it,*" Judge Maddox instructed, his voice lowered. "Reflect upon your past. Reflect upon the death of him who you have slain."

From the press tables, the reporters maintained a steady whisper of pencil points against paper and telegraph forms, and the crowd held its breath as Maddox straightened himself for the final pronouncement.

"The judgment of the court," he announced, "is that you shall be taken to the place from whence you came, and thence to the state prison in Sing Sing. There judgment shall be executed, and you shall be put to death according to law, in the manner provided by law, in the week beginning January tenth."

Martin Thorn had just five weeks left to live.

WHEN THE CONDEMNED MAN opened his eyes the next morning, it was still dark outside.

Six o'clock.

Thorn sat up on his jail cot, padded the short distance across the cold floor of his cell, and began smoothing out the creases in his trousers and brushing clean the only outfit he had left—a black coat, a shirt with a standing collar, and his blue polka-dotted cravat.

Breakfast, his jailer announced, and slid in his tray.

Thorn didn't much feel like eating; he dangled the morsels above his dog, and watched as Bill Baker snapped and pranced at them. When Captain Methven and Sheriff Doht arrived at the cell at seven-fifteen, Thorn was ready. He pulled on his thin summer coat, asked for his fedora—they couldn't find it, and gave him an old battered alpine hat instead—and then he turned to his dog. Bill Baker paused from pouncing repeatedly at a steam grate and tilted his head quizzically as his master was led away from the cell. "Good-bye, Bake," the man called back.

It was the only farewell Thorn made that morning.

There were two inches of slush and snow on the ground outside, and as the trio walked out to the Jackson Avenue streetcar in the darkness, Thorn slid on the ice; only Methven's beefy hand, manacled to his, kept him from hitting the sidewalk. He hadn't been outside much in the previous five months, and he had no winter clothes. When they reached the Thirty-Fourth Street ferry, he was shivering. The cabin of the boat was warmer but no more welcoming: The morning commuters immediately recognized the chained passenger, and once they reached the other side of the river a growing crowd was following him.

It's him, word shot across Grand Central Depot. The vast space—the marble colonnades, the luggage wagons being loaded for the Waldorf Astoria, the morning shoppers clutching Charles & Company praline bags—it all seemed to contract around the three men. The crowd was pressing on Thorn and his two jailers and into the scrum of *World, Journal,* and *Telegram* reporters that already surrounded them. *You must intervene*, they beseeched the station police, who then pushed the mob back into the onrush of commuters. But as Methven and Doht picked up smoking-car tickets for the next train—*three for the 8:05 smoker*—the masses cascaded wildly into adjacent lines, buying ticket after ticket to Sing Sing.

"They all want to see you," a *World* reporter marveled aloud. Thorn allowed himself a small smile as he was yanked by a manacled hand toward the train platform.

Inside the smoking carriage, the seats were crammed with onlookers, and there was nothing the conductor could do about it; they had bought tickets, after all. Even more were pressing their faces up against the glass where Thorn took a window seat on the left side of the carriage; it took another sweep of patrolmen to clear the unticketed gawkers off the platform. Thorn stared down, his hat pulled nearly over his eyes.

Cigar? Captain Methven offered.

Thorn shook his head; he wasn't interested. The train pulled forward with a jerk as the couplings tightened, and the last of the pursuing crowd pulled away; here, among the smaller crowd of gawkers who had bought their smoker tickets, Thorn at last looked up and watched as the landscape of the Hudson Valley slid by.

The reporters and sketch artists, sitting across from Thorn and his jailers, tried drawing him out: What were his thoughts on Mrs. Nack? But the prisoner wouldn't respond. Another tried a more clever opening: What did he think of the city elections a few weeks earlier?

"I wish that Tammany won," Thorn admitted. "I'd have voted for that ticket."

The thought seemed to depress his spirits further as he stared back out the train window. Captain Methven made a gruff attempt to cheer him up.

"Say, Martin." Methven nudged his prisoner. "Wouldn't you like to have your dog up here? He'll be lonely in jail."

"Yes." Thorn brightened a little. "If you will send him."

A *World* reporter quietly shook his head; maybe Methven and his prisoner didn't know Sing Sing well, but he'd accompanied condemned men there before, and he knew they'd never let Bill Baker into that place.

The train pulled up to Ossining station, where a second crowd had gathered. Thorn was hustled into a waiting hackney cab and past the onlookers, through the outskirts of the small town, and to the great stone gate that marked the entrance of Sing Sing. On the road in, crews of convicts in striped outfits worked in the freezing cold, breaking rocks and raking gravel under the gaze of men holding Winchester rifles.

His journey was almost over.

THERE WERE HUNDREDS of them out in the cold the next morning in Manhattan—and then thousands. They'd all read the newspaper accounts of Thorn's trip to Sing Sing, and then caught the notice beneath: *William Guldensuppe's viewing to-day, 115 East Third Street.*

The block of Third Street between First Avenue and Avenue A had never lacked for strange stories: At one end, a piano maker's wife had thrown herself from the top of a building; at the other was the home of a man recently arrested for assisting a high diver's illegal leap from the Brooklyn Bridge. The diver, as it happened, had not fared any better than the piano maker's wife. Conveniently, in the middle of this block sat the obliging funeral home of Herr Franz Odendhal. True, even this establishment had a bit of local infamy—an employee had once run off with the florist's wife, which made for some rather awkward moments in ordering memorial bouquets. But this Saturday morning they had a fine display ready for their latest casket.

At 10 a.m., Franz threw the doors open and the mourners poured inside. Facing them was a burnished oak coffin, and leaning against it, a photograph from life of the handsome, mustachioed masseur whom everyone in the city now recognized. At the back of the coffin rose a four-foot-high floral arrangement, ordered by his eight coworkers from the night shift at Murray Hill Baths, its blossoms spelling out a single word: COMRADE.

By now there were so many waiting outside that each was given about one second to view the body—they had to walk through the parlor briskly. It was just enough time to glance at the flowers, the photograph, and the brass plate at one end of the coffin. It bore the full name that the man himself had never used:

Christian W. Guldensuppe.
Died June 25, 1897.
Age, Forty-two Years.

As each New Yorker walked up, the glass top that Franz had placed over the coffin revealed the contents: a cleansed and carefully dressed man, wearing a suit and with his right hand laid upon his breast—protecting, it seemed, his stilled heart.

The body had no head.

Some ten thousand New Yorkers had filed past by two o'clock, and hundreds more lingered to follow a carriage procession to a ferry at the foot of Houston Street. The waiting boat soon slipped away from its mooring, its cargo bound for the Lutheran Cemetery across the river. And there, so long after that phone call to the bathhouse one warm June evening, Willie Guldensuppe finally got the Long Island home that Mrs. Nack had promised him.

THE ALLEGATIONS were terribly unfair, Mrs. Nack insisted to the *Journal* women's page reporter who visited her on Christmas Day. Having turned State's evidence in the first trial, she was still waiting for what she hoped would be a reduced sentence. In the meantime, she wanted the world to know that the crime wasn't her fault at all—it was the fault of her husband.

"Then Herman Nack was cruel?" the reporter pressed.

Mrs. Nack looked up and burst into tears.

"If he had not been, I would not be here now," she sobbed. "I would still be with him, for I loved him. If I did not, I would not have married, for my people didn't like him. But he said we need not mind that—we could be in this new country, and he would earn good wages, and I could learn a new business, and we would get rich.

"We both worked, but we didn't get rich." She dabbed her eyes. "We only got poorer."

And now, she sighed, she was here. Weeks had passed since Thorn was sent to Sing Sing, and on this day—Christmas Day—she was still in Queens County Jail, still assailed in the newspapers. Though the common wisdom among legal experts was that Mrs. Nack's confession meant that she'd escape the chair, the *Eagle* still pronounced her the "head devil" of the case, and Howe's office had been even blunter to the *Journal*.

"They should place her in the electric chair with Thorn," one of Howe's team snapped, before quickly adding, "*if* Thorn is to be placed there."

But for Mrs. Nack, passing her hours in jail making handcrafts, every page of the newspaper was trying reading. It wasn't just the cartoon in the *Evening Telegram* that showed the Woodside ducks proclaiming: "*Once again the town is ours!*" It was that the world outside was passing her by, what with the holiday and the coming of the New Year. One Christmas ad in the *World* rode the craze for Professor Röntgen's new discovery—"*Imagine Santa Throwing an X-Ray,*" it announced—with an illustration of the jolly old man irradiating the Third Avenue façade of Bloomingdale's to reveal the bounty of toys within. Beyond the *Herald*'s usual headlines of FIRE IN A MATCH FACTORY, the future beckoned with a proposal to put bike racks on trolley cars, and a promise that an eccentric British scientist had developed a photographic brain scanner: THOUGHTS PICTURED, it announced. The *Journal* had kept its headline circus running, too: Microscopic shrimp in the water supply inspired the headline FISH CHOWDER POURS FROM THE FAUCETS OF BROOKLYN HOUSES. But for the holiday season Hearst's men topped themselves with a new contest—the Prophecy Prize, which had readers stopping by the office to drop their predictions for 1898 into giant ironbound boxes in the lobby.

"Perhaps at the end of 1898 Queen Victoria will have passed away," editors helpfully suggested on the front page. "The problem of aerial navigation may have been solved, America may have annexed Cuba, a great war may have begun between European nations."

When the boxes were opened in a year's time, the best prediction would win $1,000. Yet there would surely be no prize for guessing the likely fate of Martin Thorn.

"Poor Martin," Gussie sighed. She could not help him now; and the paper flowers and lace heaped upon her cell's table would be of no comfort to the man.

Suddenly, her face brightened with an idea: "I cannot wish him a merry Christmas, but I can wish him a happy Christmas." She quickly jotted down a note on a sheet of paper, then puzzled over a second notion. "*And* I would like to send him a basket of fruit. Do you think they'll let me send it? . . . How will he get it?"

"I will see that he gets it," the *Journal* reporter assured her. "Then, if there is any answer I'll bring it back to you—"

"There won't be," Mrs. Nack cut her off.

"There *may* be."

Mrs. Nack shook her head slowly.

"I know him better than you," she said.

The *Journal* reporter picked up a basket of apples, bananas, and grapes from a fruiterer's near Grand Central, then promptly boarded the next train to Sing Sing. When she arrived, the warden reluctantly allowed her onto the cell block—but insisted on handing over the note and the basket himself.

"Martin," he called into the cell. "Here is a message from Mrs. Nack. A Christmas greeting."

He held out the envelope, and the prisoner emerged into the doorway to take it. He was not wearing the striped uniform of ordinary convicts; instead he wore the solid black outfit of a condemned man. The reporter watched as he ran his eyes over the words:

Dear Martin:

It is Christmas time. I send you greeting to your lonely cell at Sing Sing. I have found great peace with my own heart since I put my whole case in the Lord's hands. Let me say this to you, Martin, that I can send you no better gift than that you seek the Lord while he has given you time. Martin, it is determined by law that you must die . . .

His hands began to tear the sheet apart.

. . . Find peace before you go—then, you are not afraid what man can do.

AUGUSTA NACK

Thorn tossed the shredded pieces onto the floor.

The warden, unfazed, extended his other arm.

"And some fruit from her, too," he added.

The prisoner hesitated for a moment, and then, with a philosophical shrug, he took the basket.

"Any answer?" the reporter called from the hallway.

For a moment Thorn opened his mouth, as if to respond. But then, without a word, he shook his head and withdrew into his cell.

23.

A JOB FOR SMITH AND JONES

THE FRUIT FROM MRS. NACK was the only splash of color in Martin's cell. He had windowless walls on three sides, a fourth of iron bars, and the constant glare of electric bulbs. To be here, one inmate mused, was "like living, eating, sleeping, and bathing in a search-light." It illuminated the barest of existences: a steel cot, a lumpy straw mattress with a single pillow and a blanket, a tin cup, a basin, and a bucket.

Guards, soundless on their crêpe-soled shoes, constantly patrolled the Death Row hallway, so that the only escape was to be found in books from the prison library. Thorn had already devoured *The Old Curiosity Shop* and then more Dickens volumes, day after day. He had to—because he didn't have a table or pinochle cards, didn't even have a cell mate. But he was not alone. Though they couldn't see one another, by talking between the cells, Martin knew he was sharing Murderers Row with just two other men.

Hadley, said one.

Fritz, halloed the other.

Hadley Sutherland was a West Indian in for shooting his wife in their Brooklyn home; Fritz Meyer had gunned down a patrolman while robbing a church poor box on East Third Street. Hadley and Thorn were both scheduled to die in the electric chair on January 10. There were no clocks here, but the bananas in the fruit basket had scarcely ripened when the warden stopped by with a message from

Howe. It was New Year's Eve, he told Thorn, and he had a holiday present of sorts.

Your execution is delayed on appeal.

Hadley was not as fortunate. On what had been their appointed day, Thorn awoke to a thick curtain being pulled over his cell door, and then the sound of a manacled man shuffling past. The execution chamber was so close that it shared a wall with Martin's cell. A few minutes later, there was the distant hum of three electrical dynamos suddenly building up speed, then slowing back down into ominous silence.

Fritz? he called out.

Martin? the other answered.

But now there was no third.

Soon Mrs. Nack's basket would be gone, along with the torn note: *"I have found great peace with my own heart since I put my whole case in the Lord's hands."* But he didn't want to talk about the case, didn't want to think about her, didn't want to consider what her betrayal had probably bought—not even when the warden stopped by later that day with more news for him.

Manslaughter, he told the condemned man.

Thorn could see into the hallway behind the warden, where the keepers were clearing out Hadley's cell.

Fifteen years, the warden reported. *With good behavior, she'll be out in nine.*

Gussie had made her deal.

"I NEVER COULD EAT off *that* table," one woman in the crowd declared.

"I never could look at *that* clock," another added.

"Look at them!" cried the auctioneer, sweeping his arm over a table heaped with laces. "All elegantly knit by Mrs. Nack!"

The house was packed that Saturday morning. Scarcely three blocks from the Harlem drugstore where Thorn had been arrested, hundreds of women pressed into the ground-floor premises of the Standard Auction House. It had been given over that day to the property of one Augusta P. Nack, with the ground-floor sales-rooms on 125th Street magically transformed, fitted up to precisely resemble her newly vacated apartment on 439 Ninth Avenue. Here in the reconstituted parlor was a suite of red velvet furniture and a zither and a music box; there in the kitchen, cabinets clattered with the glassware from which Mrs. Nack and her lovers had once drunk. In her bedroom stood her white-and-gold-painted bedstead, and beside that a dressmaker's dummy attired in a rather garish gown with a crêpe waist of "crushed strawberry."

The sign in front of it read:

COSTUME

WORN BY

MRS. NACK

ON THE DAY OF THE

MURDER

Her outfit for dismembering her lover possessed, reporters dryly noted, "a low cut."

The second bedroom was occupied by the plain and melancholy wooden bed of Guldensuppe; and although his estate was supposed to have been sent on to his relatives in Philadelphia, the masseur's suspenders had gotten mixed up in the lot. So had one of his green neckties.

"The famous necktie!" an auctioneer bellowed. Nobody was sure why that item was famous, until one woman ventured that surely Mrs. Nack had thought of strangling him with it.

Circulating among the crowd were dime-museum managers, the sort of fellows immediately identifiable by loud suits and cigars. It was dime-museum men in Chicago who, a few weeks earlier, had very nearly gotten hold of Luetgert's sausage vat for display. New York promoters would not be so easily shaken off, and they were taking auction-house officials aside.

Five hundred dollars for everything, one offered.

The auctioneer shook his head. *Go higher.* Why, the *Journal* itself had already said it all in a headline: MURDER DEN A KLONDIKE. It was gold! The kitchen alone contained the stove—THE FAMOUS STOVE, they'd placarded it—where Mrs. Nack had burned her lover's bloody clothes.

"A message from Mrs. Nack, ladies and gentlemen!" yelled a staffer, waving a scrap of paper to the crowd as it surged forward. "A *real message* from Mrs. Nack, currently in Queens County Jail!"

This proved to be an old draft of a mail order for more corsets. But the crowd was happy and garrulous, clutching the favors that everyone had been handed at the entrance—business cards addressed from the apartment over Werner's Drug Store and inscribed with words that everybody now knew by heart: AUGUSTA NACK, LICENSED MIDWIFE.

THAT SAME WEEKEND, the owner of those cards was preparing for her departure from Queens County Jail. The cards, she insisted, had been for a respectable business.

"Those are terrible things my husband told about me. I want to ask you—" she demanded of a reporter, "how is it possible I had only three hundred dollars to draw from the bank at the time of the murder? Do you think if I had burned one baby's body, not to speak of more, I should not have been well paid? Go to the neighborhood and ask whether I could have done such things! The children all knew me—I was 'Nanty Nack'—the fairy who brought the last baby to their house. Go, ask their parents."

She shook her head at the injustice of it, and passed out the last of her paper flowers and lacework to her fellow prisoners. The humble earnings of her honest labor, she explained, was also what Thorn was after on the day of the murder. In fact, her entire conduct in the case had been an elaborate way to save herself from certain death at Thorn's hands.

"Explain to me why"—she jabbed a finger into the air—"when Thorn distinctly told me to go over to New York to buy the oilcloth,

I went to the nearest store and talked with the people, so that there was no doubt of identifying me?"

The reporter hid his amazement: Did she mean to say that this fiendishly complicated trail of circumstantial evidence was actually a distress call to detectives? That she *meant* to get arrested?

"I would have surely died but for *one thing*," she continued. "I had not brought money with me. You see, he had told me to draw the money from the bank and always carry it in my bosom. He thought I had done this, but I had not. He led me up stairs and when we reached there he told me to sit on the edge of the tub." She allowed the image of the headless Guldensuppe already draped into the tub to sink in with her listener. "I could only sit and sob until he suddenly said, *Did you bring money with you?* When I told him it was not drawn from the bank he was furious. That saved my life."

And that, she said, was when she managed to get the crime traced back to her.

"He said, *Very well, take the ferry over to New York and get some oilcloth, but don't go to any store on this side.* You know the remainder of the story."

The reporters did indeed know it. And they also knew that Mrs. Riger's sales register in Astoria showed that Augusta Nack bought the oilcloth on June 23—two days before the murder.

EIGHT MONTHS PASSED at Sing Sing. Winter turned to spring, with appeals piled up like dirty snow. They'd melted away in the summer until there was nothing left behind but a condemned man in a sweltering cell. Governor Black had refused to stay the execution.

"This is good news," Thorn said through the bars of his cell. "It's the best news I've had for months."

The warden was taken aback: This wasn't how most prisoners reacted to the governor turning them down.

"I *want* to die," Thorn explained with a shrug.

They'd tried every ploy already. Howe was known, after all, for disrupting courtrooms and wearing opponents out, and even the fetid air had seemed to conspire with him during the trial. So perhaps it was not entirely a surprise in May that a renovation crew opening the courtroom's ventilation ducts found one hundred dead rats crammed inside.

Howe didn't have much to say about that.

The rats hadn't worked. Neither had the intoxication claim. And the jury's visit to the Woodside cottage that Thorn had so nonchalantly neglected to join? Howe had claimed a mistrial, because *the defendant was not present during a presentation of evidence.* That argument had tied up the execution for months, though at length the superior-court judges didn't buy it; in fact, they didn't buy Howe, either. His $427 legal bill was cruelly knocked down to $127 by the state. Howe talked grandly to the press of taking the case to the U.S. Supreme Court, but with final appeals exhausted in the broiling heat—one year since the first mysterious parcels were found in the East River—a date of August 1 was now set for Thorn's execution.

And now Martin Thorn had one day left to live.

The day began with some measure of inconvenience. As soon as he finished his breakfast, his keepers called him out of his cell.

"Take all your clothes off, Martin," one of them directed.

It was a standard precaution, the same they'd used on Hadley on his last day. After Thorn stripped, they led him down to his final home, cell #1. It was slightly larger than the other cells, and arranged on the bed were black execution trousers and a new shirt. For once, the shirt wasn't also black. Thorn had always dressed well, and his pleas to the warden had been heard: Folded neatly atop the trousers was a crisp dress oxford—white, with light pink stripes. Thorn was delighted with it.

"My last clean shirt!" he yelled in mock triumph to the other inmates.

There were five condemned prisoners on the cell block now. Among them was Adrian Braun, a paranoid cigar maker whose domestic-assault charge turned capital after he stabbed his wife to death in the Sing Sing visitors' room. In Braun's lucid moments, Thorn found him fine company.

Thorn's neighbors weren't quite sure how to answer, though.

"Good luck!" Braun finally blurted.

Turning his attention to the rest of his new cell, Thorn also noticed what was missing.

"I want my books," he pleaded to a guard through the bars. It was the first time that morning that he'd actually sounded upset, and his relief was palpable when the guards moved the pile to his new cell.

"They are my friends," Thorn said as he hefted his books. He'd developed a fierce love of reading while on Death Row and even had managed to snare a coveted title from the prison library: *There's a cold-blooded scoundrel!" said Holmes, laughing as he threw himself down into his chair once more. "That fellow will rise from crime to crime until he does something very bad, and ends on a gallows."*

Well, if Sherlock Holmes wasn't quite a comfort on this day, at least he was entertaining. Thorn paused occasionally to chat across the cell walls with the other prisoners. One was reciting Heine poems, another chimed in with a dirty story, and a third started talking politics—namely, anarchy and socialism.

"I don't believe in it," Thorn shook his head. "Let a man keep what he earns."

"And what a man doesn't earn, let him steal," cracked Braun from his cell, before turning more serious. "Have you seen your mouse yet, Thorn?"

"No," Thorn called back. He'd caught one earlier in the summer and tamed it with portions of his prison ration. When the pet went missing earlier that week, it had nearly brought him to tears. "Smart little fellow, too—he'd eat out of my hand and all that."

But now Thorn was alone again in his cell.

"Rats desert a sinking ship," he added dryly to Braun and said a salutary set of prayers—for while religion had come slowly to him, he was covering his bets now. At six there arrived a final meal of roast beef, turnips, rye bread, and pudding—the foods of Thorn's youth in Prussia—and as the night finally fell outside, Thorn turned talkative with the priest dispatched to his cell as spiritual counsel. One of the keepers brewed a pot of coffee at the guard station, and cups were passed between the keepers, the priest, and Thorn. The prisoner didn't want to talk about his case; instead, he mused upon his childhood in his hometown of Posen. Those were happy days. Why dwell on the present?

I still remember, he said as midnight closed in. *I remember the sound of my father's hammer as he worked on shoes.*

"You must get some sleep, Martin," the priest said gently.

Thorn clasped his hand, then hung his clothes for the morning and settled into his cot. Soon he was so soundly asleep that the guards were startled when he suddenly sat up bolt upright at 4:30 a.m.

Fritz? he called out. *Adrian?*

The other inmates were still asleep.

"What are you doing, Thorn?" a keeper asked.

"Thinking about Posen," the prisoner mumbled—and then collapsed back into his slumbers.

THE NEXT MORNING, the curtains were drawn across the other inmates' cells. Warden Sage was bustling around his office, making preparations and welcoming his guests: the visiting physicians, electricians, and newspaper artists clutching thick pads of paper. All wore black for the occasion, and they mingled with nervous solemnity. More than two thousand applications had poured into the warden's office in the last week, but state law dictated that only twenty-eight observers were allowed at the death chamber. These men were the elite of the New York press and medical establishment. The old-timers could spot the yellow-press men by the sheer flash of their presence: *They've sent Smith and Jones.*

Hearst had deployed Langdon Smith, one of the *Evening Journal*'s top correspondents, and a man once famed as the country's fastest telegrapher. Standing by him was rival Haydon Jones, the *World*'s own speed artist. Barely out of art school, he'd been scooped up by Pulitzer's crew from the *Mail and Express* when it became clear that he was the best quick draw in town.

Follow me, the warden motioned the crowd. Smith and Jones tagged behind them, observing the location. The artist readied his favorite Blaisdell pencil and rakishly square Steinbach pad for the *World* litho crew, while Smith took notes for the *Journal* even as they crossed Sing Sing's grounds: *"The procession, black-clad and quiet, followed the Warden across the prison yard, where the dumb convicts were working: through the engine-room, where three noiseless dynamos were running, and on to the death chamber. An empty, high-ceilinged room, with broad glazed glass windows, a room without the softening effect of curtains or pictures, a room bare and spartan-like and well-fitted for the rigors of death."*

To the *World*'s man, the room was reminiscent of a small chapel—its only ornamentation a subtle Grecian meander painted around the walls, like a funeral urn, its totality bathed in the glare of sunlight. A few colored panes had been placed in the high skylights, giving the walls a ghostly green tint. As they sat down on the room's perimeter of hard pine benches, the crowd was already beginning to perspire under the rays of an August morning.

"Gentlemen"—the warden stood before them as the revving dynamos became faintly audible—"you will oblige me if you will not leave your places until after the physicians have declared the execution complete."

Before them, at the center of the far end of the room, stood the instrument of that execution: a heavy, plain-hewn oak chair with leather straps dangling idly from its sides. Above it spread black cables—"the tentacles of an electrical octopus," one awed reporter wrote—that snaked down and around the front legs, before creeping up to the screw cap at the back of the empty chair. Nearby, the state's electrician pointed to a board with a stark arrangement of three rows of six naked lightbulbs.

"By these lamps," the electrician explained, "we will test the current and see that we have the necessary power."

He tapped five bells to the dynamo room, then threw the switch. The lights rose in a row, each in succession, their filaments turning from a cherry-red glow to a blinding white radiance; the empty chair was coursing with electricity, the room ablaze with incandescent light. *1,750 volts at ten amperes,* he read from his gauge. When the power was cut, it took nearly thirty seconds for the angry glow of the test lights to finally die away.

The electric chair was ready.

Warden Sage opened the iron cell-block door and stepped out of the room with a guard. Reporters could hear the squeal of an iron door in the adjoining hallway and the low mutter of voices.

"The hour has come," the warden said.

"All right," they heard Thorn answer. "I want to thank you for your kindness."

The men appeared in the doorway: the warden, the guards, Father Hanselman, and the prisoner, who greeted his old newspaper acquaintances with a quick half smile. Thorn's gratitude to the warden showed on his sleeve, for Warden Sage had allowed a concession to the man's vanity: Thorn was wearing his best frock jacket and a white cambric tie. He sat down in the chair without any prompting, as if he were taking breakfast on an ordinary Monday morning.

"Dear God, this will be the birthday of a new life," intoned Father Hanselman. "Christ have mercy."

"Christ have mercy," Thorn dutifully repeated as his feet were lashed to the chair legs.

His eyes followed the guards as they placed sponges soaked in salt water against his calves and then against the base of his neck, the better to increase conductivity; over these they firmly buckled the cable fittings and the headpiece. A long black rubber sash was stretched across his face and around the back of the chair to hold his head in place; only his mouth was visible through a slit. Scarcely two minutes since he'd been led out of his cell, Thorn was now immobile and blindfolded.

"Christ, Mary, Mother of God," the priest chanted as he slid a small wooden crucifix into Thorn's right hand. "Christ have mercy."

The warden silently nodded to the electrician.

"Chri—" The prisoner's lips moved.

He never finished the word. Thorn's body was thrown into the straps by a massive shock. For ten seconds, then another twenty, then thirty more, his limbs convulsed and his neck swelled as the powerful current coursed into him, the amperage needle nearly twisting out of its gauge. A thin curl of smoke rose from his right calf, and when the electrician pushed the lever back up, Thorn's body slumped. White foam dripped from the slit of the faceless rubber mask.

The prison's physician stepped forward, stripped open Thorn's shirt, and lay the cold medallion of his stethoscope against the condemned man's chest. The only sound in the room was a pencil making quick slashing and cross-hatching across a sketch pad—for of all the newspaper artists there, only Haydon Jones had the presence of mind to catch Thorn in the moment before the lever was pulled. The others sat stunned and breathing in air that, a *Herald* writer noted, smelled "like an overheated flatiron on a handkerchief."

The doctor turned to the witnesses.

"The man is dead," he said.

24.

A STORY OF LIFE
IN NEW YORK

SMITH AND JONES hustled to get their stories and pictures out, and the other reporters followed hard on their heels. While the *Evening Telegram* announced MARTIN THORN GOES CALMLY TO HIS DEATH, and the *New York Sun* chimed in with THORN MET DEATH CALMLY, *Herald* readers were treated to a different execution altogether: MARTIN THORN DIES IN ABJECT TERROR. The *World*, always solicitous of its female readership, declared WOMAN MEDIUM COMMUNES WITH THORN JUST AS HIS SPIRIT WINGS ITS FLIGHT.

"It was all for thy sake, Augusta," they reported him calling out from the astral plane, "but I have forgiven and I died happy."

One man, though, was not so sure of that. As the reporters quickly exited the stifling death chamber, a different sort of witness pressed past them to the front of the room. Dr. Joseph Alan O'Neill was a surgeon with the New York School of Clinical Medicine, and he looked keenly at the lifeless body still slumped in the chair. It smelled of singed flesh, for one of the saltwater sponges had dried out, causing a burn hole nearly an inch deep under the electrode on Thorn's right calf. The body was still warm from the departed electrical current.

O'Neill opened his medical bag, revealing syringes and a ready supply of restoratives: nitroglycerin, strychnine, and brandy.

Shall I administer them? Dr. O'Neill asked the warden.

No, the prison official shot back. *You may not.* The law, the warden insisted, did not allow for resuscitation measures, but if Dr. O'Neill insisted on ascertaining that the patient was indeed dead, there was no language in the statute against that.

Then I will, Dr. O'Neill replied, and produced a stethoscope from his bag.

It was a tense moment. O'Neill was raising a delicate matter that few of the doctors still lingering in the room wished to acknowledge: that nobody was quite sure whether the electric chair actually worked. It had been introduced with great fanfare by the State of New York just eight years earlier, promising a new era of humane and instantaneous execution. But on the chair's first use, condemned prisoner William Kemmler had been left still breathing, with brown froth pouring from his mouth; some said he'd also caught fire. The nine-minute ordeal left witnesses so shaken that one deputy sheriff emerged in tears. Thorn, only the twenty-seventh man to go to Sing Sing's chair, faced a procedure that had hardly been perfected yet.

O'Neill bent over and rested the stethoscope on Thorn's skin. There was a motion underneath—a faint thrill in the carotid artery. That, he suspected, might just be blood draining from the head down to the trunk. But there were other disturbing signs. With swift and practiced movements, the doctor examined the cremasteric reflex, which retracted or loosened the testes; it was still working. O'Neill then lit his ophthalmoscope and pulled back Thorn's left eyelid; the pupil contracted beneath the blaze of light.

"If required, I should be very reluctant to sign his death certificate," the surgeon announced.

It was an admission many physicians made in utmost privacy after these executions—but not in front of the public. The prison doctor pointedly ignored O'Neill and directed two attendants to carry the body to an autopsy room. Thorn's skull and chest were quickly opened to reveal little of note.

Aghast, Dr. O'Neill fired off a dispatch titled "Who's the Executioner?" to the *Atlantic Medical Weekly.* "The law requires post-mortem mutilation," he noted. "It is, in fact, part of the penalty; for, as it reveals no cause of death and teaches nothing of interest to science, it is evident that *its purpose is to complete the killing.*"

Thorn suffered nothing less than a modern drawing and quartering, the surgeon charged, and another medical journal scorned the autopsy as "the prostitution of science." But the debate remained a quiet disagreement among colleagues. Reading the afternoon papers, one might never have guessed this most appalling irony of the case: that carried into an autopsy room and cut apart while faintly alive, Martin Thorn had met the same fate at Sing Sing that William Guldensuppe once suffered in a Woodside bathtub.

THE *EVENING JOURNAL* lavished attention that night on the execution, right down to helpful anatomical close-ups of Thorn's "Degenerate Ear" and "Pugnacious Nose." It was the end of an affair that had been very good to them: The Guldensuppe case had pushed Hearst's circulation past the *World*'s. He'd capitalized on this success with front-page attacks on crooked dealings in local trolley and gas franchises, stoked his paper's capacity even further with a baroquely engineered Hoe dectuple multi-color half-tone electrotype web perfecting press, and then trumpeted the serial debut of "the most startling and interesting novel of modern times"—something called *The War of the Worlds*. But it was freeing the comely Evangelina Cisneros that had shown William Randolph Hearst that *Journal* readers needed more than just Martian invaders to root against. They needed a real war.

THE WORST INSULT TO THE UNITED STATES IN ITS HISTORY, his paper had declared after obtaining a leaked letter from a Spanish diplomat that described President McKinley as weak and easily led. "A good war," the newspaper thundered, "might free Cuba, wipe out Spain, frighten to death the meanest tribe of money-worshipping parasites that has ever disgraced a decent nation." But a good war needed a good excuse, and early in 1898 Hearst had gotten it: a mysterious explosion that ripped open the USS *Maine* while docked in Cuba, sending the battleship and most of its men to the bottom of Havana Harbor.

"Have you put anything else on the front page?" Hearst demanded in a dawn phone call to his newsroom.

"Only the other big news—" his editor began.

"There is no other big news," Hearst replied. "This means war."

WAR! SURE! MAINE DESTROYED BY SPANISH, the *Journal* announced. Neither war nor the culprit was a sure thing—many suspected a coal fire belowdecks had doomed the ship—but Hearst was not to be deterred. THE WHOLE COUNTRY THRILLS WITH WAR FEVER, his paper insisted, and he proudly coined a national rallying cry: *"Remember the* Maine! *To hell with Spain!"* When McKinley finally declared war that spring, Hearst and his headlines left no doubts about their proud role in the matter:

HOW DO YOU LIKE THE JOURNAL'S WAR?

William Randolph Hearst liked it very much indeed. Having already issued his Murder Squad badges to pursue Thorn, he thought nothing of the next logical step: He offered the U.S. military $500,000 to raise a *Journal*-sponsored army regiment. His offer spurned, Hearst spent the money anyway: the Wrecking Crew poured out of his Park Row offices, this time headed for the next boats to Cuba. The paper's circulation, already the highest in the country when it had hit 300,000, now rocketed up to a dizzying half million, then a million, and then a million and a half.

It was now the greatest newspaper juggernaut the world had ever known.

Pulitzer was obliged to keep up, of course; he duly matched Hearst star Frederic Remington with his own Stephen Crane. The *World* charged that the *Journal*'s "war news was written by fools for fools." The *Journal* jeered that the *World* was so jealous that it stole the *Journal*'s wire reports. To prove it, the *Evening Journal* ran news of the death of one Colonel Reflipe W. Thenuz; the next morning's *World* ran a similar story on the ill-fated officer. Hearst's editors gleefully revealed that there *was* no Colonel Thenuz; reversing the colonel's first name and middle initial, though, revealed this message inadvertently run by the *World* "in cold type—in its own columns":

We Pilfer the News

Hearst had yet another humiliating trump card, which he knew the frail and nervous Pulitzer could not match: He sent *himself*. Soon the U.S. Navy was treated to the sight of the newspaper publisher tearing around Havana Harbor in a convoy of chartered yachts.

MUST FIND THAT FLEET! he roared in giant front-page headlines draped in patriotic red, white, and blue bunting, while inside, his paper offered up summer dessert tips for homemakers that included such "warlike dainties" as Ice Cream Soldiers and Lemon Ice Cannons. ("You will swallow bullets—of chocolate," it promised.) Hearst himself took to dodging actual bullets; after blithely ignoring press restrictions and taking some Spanish prisoners of war, the young publisher was spotted at the Battle of El Caney. A *Journal* correspondent, struck to the ground by a bullet to the shoulder, opened his eyes to see his own boss leaning over him, a ribboned straw hat on his head and a revolver strapped to his belt.

"I'm sorry you're hurt," Hearst beamed as the enemy rounds whistled past them. "But wasn't it a splendid fight? We must beat every paper in the world."

BACK IN NEW YORK, the Eden Musée was busy adding a score of patriotic new waxworks of Rough Rider charges and Manila Bay victories, and setting up pride of place for the latest in entertainment: the cinematograph. It had been scarcely a year since the first public cinema screenings in Paris and New York; not only did the Musée now have one of its own, its sign also announced the most eagerly awaited films of all: CINEMATOGRAPH WAR SCENES. While the war scenes were moved and spooled into place, other Musée staffers prepared a more familiar mannequin for a new scene down in its Chamber of Horrors. The Musée's old star wax attraction would now be seated in an oak chair festooned with ominous wiring and leather restraints convincingly riveted to its frame. The exhibit bore a stark caption: "The Electrocution of Martin Thorn."

Not many blocks away, the Empire Limited pulled in to Grand Central Depot bearing the genuine article; its baggage car disgorged a plain pine box, and handlers quickly moved it to a side entrance of the station, all under the watchful eye of a detective. There were worries that freak-show promoters might try stealing the remains, but so far the arrival of Martin Thorn had passed unnoticed and unannounced.

As a carriage bore the coffin toward Christian Herrlich's funeral parlor off Eighty-Third and First Avenue, though, word raced ahead: *He's here.* A thousand disappointed spectators had appeared at Herrlich Brothers' doors the night before, only to find that Thorn hadn't arrived yet. Even as the hearse drew quickly up the street, hundreds of onlookers were already gathering again. A dozen policemen from the Twenty-Seventh Precinct station house labored mightily to clear a path into the funeral home.

Out of the way! they yelled as the coffin passed through. *Move along.*

The undertaker barred the door to the surging crowd. Inside, sitting in the cool and darkened funeral parlor, was Martin Thorn's sister with her daughter and husband; alongside them stood three barbers from Thorn's old shop. They'd raised the money for their coworker's burial, and Thorn was quickly moved from his prison-issued pine box into a more respectable casket with silver handles. Beneath his dark curls, his head still bore red electrode marks; his young niece wept at the sight, and bent over to kiss his face.

After a few minutes, the brother-in-law leaned over for a word in the undertaker's ear. Herrlich open the door, and a boisterous line of New Yorkers poured in to view the executed man. As much as his exposed face, though, they gawked at the massive and luxuriant display of lilies of the valley decorating one end of the bier. It was a $45 delivery order—hardly the sort of expense the family or the barbers could have paid for. Who, then, had arranged for it to be delivered?

"Probably a woman," theorized a *Journal* reporter.

The undertaker just smiled, and an explanation became clear.

"Mrs. Nack?" a *Herald* reporter ventured.

"I will neither affirm," the undertaker replied, "*nor* deny your question."

And then he smiled again.

MRS. NACK had been busy indeed. As inmate #269 at Auburn Prison, she woke up each morning at seven sharp to find herself alone in a cell that was secured not with the usual iron bars but instead with a three-inch-thick oak door with a peephole—for the building still bore some touches of its origins as a hospital for the insane. After dressing in a blue-and-white-striped uniform of coarse awning cloth, the former midwife then spent her day in the prison's sewing room, where she labored quietly with other prisoners on a huge government order for 6,000 haversacks. She'd been a model prisoner, and for good reason: Soon she'd be able to earn the privilege of a bedside rug on her cell floor.

Word was leaking out, though, that while Thorn in his final days hadn't wanted to talk about his crime, he did admit one thing: Mr. Nack's wild charges about Gussie were *true*. She really had been disposing of fetuses in a kitchen stove and then dumping remains down a chute into the sewer system.

"He added," a reporter noted, "that it was very profitable. It was practically all profit."

A week after Thorn's burial, the *Journal* pounced on a damning discovery: Augusta Nack was quietly trying to arrange from behind bars the sale of two parcels of land in Cliffside, New Jersey. It was hardly the work of a poor midwife who had claimed to have only $300 to her name.

"Detectives have always believed that Mrs. Nack burned the bodies of babies," Hearst's paper charged. "Now, after Thorn's execution, like a confirmation of his charges, comes proof that Mrs. Nack is a woman of means." The imprisoned midwife maintained a stony silence, though not before another newspaper wittily nominated her for a Hall of Fame statue under the sardonic inscription of AUGUSTA NACK, SURGEON.

Some, though, were studying Nack and Thorn's methods more seriously. Mutilation murders now occurred with such alarming frequency that one medical journal declared that the Guldensuppe case had induced "Epidemic Hypnotic Criminal Suggestion." When a sawn-off trunk bobbed up in the East River the summer after Thorn's execution, the *Times* headline SECOND GULDENSUPPE CASE hardly covered it; there were also third, fourth, and fifth Guldensuppe cases. Still another trunk appeared on October 8, 1899: That morning, a woman's leg was found carefully wrapped in recent issues of the *World* and the *Journal* and tossed into the gutter in front of 160 West Seventeenth Street. Soon her midriff bumped up against the Thirtieth Street pier, and her chest washed ashore on Staten Island, where it was discovered by a boy out gathering driftwood.

Station houses around the city emptied out as the NYPD threw 200 detectives on the case. The discovery of coal dust on the wrappings quickly led to a house-to-house rifling of coal cellars.

"Everybody that shows the slightest hesitancy will regret it," one officer barked to a *Sun* reporter. "I will kick the door in and search every house on the block."

Newspapers roared to life again with offers of reward money, and Bellevue's morgue filled with would-be relatives; newspapers ran lists of missing women, and papers leapt at the clue that one of the newspaper wrappers had borne the small pencil notation of *16c.* That traced the paper to a dealer named Moses Cohen, the "C" newspaper concession on Sixteenth Street. Another witness, the captain of the barge *Knickerbocker,* reported a chillingly familiar sort of suspect fleeing the scene near the Thirtieth Street pier: a German male, aged about thirty-five. It was looking like the efforts of the police and the newspapers would bust open an insoluble case once again.

"The methods are largely those which would have appealed to Sherlock Holmes," the *Brooklyn Eagle* exulted. "The killers of Guldensuppe have paid the penalty for their crime and it is probable that within a few days we shall know who killed this woman."

The comparison was turning startlingly apt, for it looked like another German midwife might be the accomplice. The Prospect Place coal cellar of Alma Lundberg was found filled with bloody rags and quicklime, and she'd abandoned the house hurriedly after the first clues were found—perhaps running from a botched abortion. But the lead went nowhere, and other clues proved to be the usual nonsense—an overexcited servant girl, a missing beauty who turned up alive in Scranton, and an encore appearance by "the Great American Identifier," who this time gravely informed the police that the crime had been committed by two women.

There was also a more troubling development in the case. Examining the body, Deputy Coroner O'Hanlon determined that the cuts precisely matched those on Guldensuppe. Whoever had done this, he theorized, had been one of the many who had gawked at Guldensuppe's body in the Bellevue morgue.

"I believe that the persons who committed this murder saw the body of Guldensuppe more than once," the doctor warned. "The cutting up of this body is identical. These murderers copied Mrs. Nack and Thorn in everything."

OTHER CURIOUS REMEMBRANCES of the crime surfaced in the years after Thorn's execution. One of the first was a novel, *Three Men and a Woman: A Story of Life in New York*, by none other than the Reverend Robert Parker Miles, the minister whose young child had inspired the jail-cell confession of Augusta Nack. Along with the rushed-out *Guldensuppe Mystery* and the dime novel *The Headless Body Murder Mystery*, this became the third book on the case. Now living in Iowa, Miles restyled the crime a bit for his version; in his novel, the hard-drinking delivery driver Herman Nack became an earnest Viennese physician. But the story of a faithless wife who "plunges into a sea of gaiety" and then murder remained perfectly recognizable.

The real Herman Nack, though, was suffering even more than his fictional counterpart. "The death of Guldensuppe preyed upon his mind," one reporter noted; he found it hard to hold down delivery jobs whenever his name was recognized. In 1903, almost six years to the day after Guldensuppe's murder, Nack calmly abandoned his delivery wagon at the foot of Canal Street and drowned himself in the Hudson River.

The Woodside cottage proved nearly as ill starred. The modest home at 346 Second Street sat vacant for years after the last visit of the jury during Thorn's trial, for the building's reputation was so fearsome that the hapless Bualas were unable to rent it to anyone. The old bedroom upstairs where Guldensuppe was shot never quite recovered from the crime, either, for the district attorney had carelessly thrown the Bualas' baseboards into a bonfire during a fit of evidence-room housecleaning—though not before saving the two extracted bullets for himself and turning them into a jaunty pair of scarf pins.

At least one other man was determined to remain unfazed by the house.

"We have already put one haunted house out of business," Bill Offerman boasted to a *Tribune* reporter. As the president of the Brooklyn Society for the Extermination of Ghosts and Dispelling of Haunted House Illusions, Offerman and his fellow members—"thirty young men between the ages of seventeen and twenty-three"—had already rented and then camped out in a vacant Brooklyn home where a butcher had committed suicide. Armed with revolvers and lanterns, the Society held a weeklong stakeout to prove to fearful locals that the butcher did not, in fact, return each night to slit his own throat. Toward the end of the vigil, the bored debunkers amused themselves by testing out some new recruits.

"A skeleton in the dark hall, rigged up on wires, with electric lights for eyes, was enough to demonstrate that one young man was unfit for membership," Offerman noted drolly.

Now, he declared, his tried and tested group was ready to take on the infamous Woodside cottage. Their efforts did not rid the house of its reputation for bad luck: A few years later, a new tenant set up a pet shop in the house, only to die of rabies from a dog bite. A wine seller named Peter Piernot had fared little better after preserving the bathroom upstairs "as it was on the day of the murder" for curious customers. In the dead of a November night, Piernot ran half-naked and screaming from the premises and leaped aboard the next train out of Woodside. Before being placed in an insane asylum, Piernot babbled in horror to the police.

He was running, he told them, from the ghost of William Guldensuppe.

25.

CARRY OUT YOUR
OWN DEAD

"WHAT DO YOU WANT?" the frightened train passenger demanded. "I am not this woman you are looking for."

She was in the last seat of the third carriage on the Metropolitan Express—an unassuming country matron in a simple dress with white lace and a sensible black hat trimmed with fresh violets. But the crowd of reporters who boarded at Poughkeepsie wouldn't leave her alone. A tall, long-haired artist ostentatiously pulled out his sketch pad and drew on it rapidly.

"Why does he draw my picture?" she snapped. "I am the wife of a farmer named Ross, of Buffalo. Is my face of interest to any one? I hate newspapers, and I shall not say anything to them."

A glance at the latest *New York Journal* for July 19, 1907, explained everything. The papers had their usual horrors that day—CUT HIS THROAT BY ACCIDENT and SHE HEARD VOICES; LEAPED TO DEATH—and reporters were scrambling on the story of a Civil War vet in Central Park who threw hundreds of coins into the air; as they rained down on delighted children, the man pulled out a revolver and blew his head off. There was even another heat wave to report on. But there was no question at the *Journal* about the day's biggest story. A single gigantic headline roared out over the top half of their front page:

MRS. NACK

SET FREE

"Oh, Mrs. Nack," the farmer's wife said distantly. "What did she do? I never heard of Mrs. Nack."

"There are some here," a reporter in the train carriage answered tartly, "who remember you very well."

"Oh, you do? Well, I am not the same woman. I tell you I am not Mrs. Nack at all."

She arranged herself primly in her seat, hands folded across her purse, looking away from her tormentors. But it was no use; a train crewman stopped in the middle of his rounds, startled, and spoke volubly to her in German. His passenger was thinner now, with a few streaks of gray in her hair, but he'd recognized her immediately— because he'd been a spectator at Thorn's trial ten years earlier.

Mrs. Nack slumped back into her seat, defeated.

"I am glad to be out," she finally said. "I spent a long time in that awful prison. I have served my time, and I guess that pays my debt to the state."

So where was she going now?

"New York," she shrugged. "Because it is the only place I know. I do not quite know what I shall do. Maybe get a place as a seamstress or a housekeeper."

She considered what awaited her. The three men she had loved were all gone: one murdered, another executed, and the third a suicide.

"I have no family now," she said plainly. "My children are dead too."

When reporters asked about the murder, though, she pursed her lips into a tight frown and stared back out the train window. As the Metropolitan Express slid into Grand Central Terminal some ten minutes late, the platform boiled over with hundreds of people jostling in the July heat for a better look.

"Mrs. Nack!" reporters outside yelled. *"Mrs. Nack!"*

It was chaos. Mrs. Nack clutched her bags as she pressed forward into the crowd, swarmed by reporters and gawking New Yorkers. *Mrs.*

Nack! they yelled, jockeying for position. As the crowd pressed her up against an iron railing, she grew terrified.

"Go away!" she yelled. "I am not this Nack woman that you say I am! Go away!"

A lithe women's-page reporter scrambled to the front of the crowd and tried to whisper in her ear.

"Get away from me!" Mrs. Nack recoiled. "I know you all. You are bad, bad, bad. . . . Shall I scream? *Police!*"

A station policeman shoved through the crowd, clearing a path for her across the terminal. Near the entrance, a trio of women accosted her.

"We are friends of yours," they began. "You must remember—"

"I have no friends," she cut them off, then rushed away.

Outside was even worse: Ranks of tripod cameras lying in wait on Lexington Avenue went off all at once like lightning in her face. She began to run. "Reporters by the score," marveled a *Sun* reporter, "pestiferous kodakers, idlers, curiosity seekers, and fifty varieties of rubbernecks chased a pale faced, frightened woman in black in and among the trolleys, trucks and hansom cabs."

In front of the Grand Union Hotel, the frantic woman spotted an empty horse-drawn carriage.

"*Keb?*" the driver asked in a clipped accent.

"Yes!" cried Mrs. Nack as she clambered aboard. "Drive away from here quick!"

The cab jerked away with a snap of the driver's whip, followed by ten more reporter-filled carriages in hot pursuit.

"Go away!" she could be heard yelling from her carriage. "Get away!"

THE WORLD her cab galloped into was not the one she'd left ten years earlier. The Victorian era had ended, and a new century had begun. Humans had learned to fly. The police station where she'd been interrogated was gone; the courthouse and the jury's hotel were both burnt out. Along the stretches where she and Thorn had hurried in a horse-drawn funeral carriage, the streets of New York were now giving way to gleaming automobiles, and they rushed to a new entertainment called *cinema*.

The reporters didn't have autos, but it wasn't easy to get rid of them; she'd had to pay the driver six dollars to urge him on. Their cab rattled down to Thirty-Second Street, threw a hard right to Fifth Avenue, cut back up to Thirty-Eighth, then to Broadway, and then toward Hell's Kitchen. As her pursuers got lost in the traffic, Mrs. Nack relaxed a little and asked to see her old neighborhood.

"I suppose I shall find things a great deal different than they were when I was free in New York before," she had mused earlier to the *Herald*.

Many of the blocks by her old home were already gone, demolished to make way for Penn Station. There was little familiar left for her, just mocking echoes. Even the lawyer who had defended her, Manny Friend, had been gone for three years now. He died on the very afternoon he'd sent his premium check over to his life insurance company, after jovially instructing his clerk, "You'd better take it over now, as I might drop dead this afternoon."

Her legal tormentor was gone, too, for William Howe had passed away in 1902. In fact, he and Mrs. Nack had rather more in common than anyone realized. Before his career as America's top attorney, Howe had spent a stretch in the penitentiary himself. Recalled in obituaries as the son of an American minister, he was in fact the English child of a brothel keeper. Howe's first appearance before a judge had been not as a lawyer but as a defendant. In 1848 he was hauled before the bar as a young law-office clerk in London, accused of forging admission tickets to the Lyceum Theater. He narrowly escaped the charge by claiming it had been a practical joke, but he was less lucky the next time around. While employed as a clerk in Blackfriars, he was convicted in 1854 of impersonating a lawyer. Tossed into prison for eighteen months with hard labor, Howe emerged to reinvent himself across the ocean as the person he'd once only pretended to be: not just a real attorney, but one of the greatest in the country.

But for Mrs. Nack, starting over would not be so easy.

Her cab pulled up to the Forty-Second Street entrance to the

Hotel Markwell, where the manager recognized her. She wasn't welcome there. A few blocks and one alias later, the Hotel Rand was hardly an improvement: Its proprietor was Wilson Mizner, a colorful character whose lobby sign read CARRY OUT YOUR OWN DEAD. Mizner had a fighter's battered knuckles—"I got those knocking down dames in the Klondike," he claimed—but the quiet woman who signed in as "Mrs. A. Ross, Buffalo" was too much even for him. As reporters descended on his hotel late that night, Mizner ordered "Mrs. Ross" to leave first thing next morning. *I don't want your money,* he told her. *Just get out.*

"I have had enough misery for one woman," she sobbed, and collapsed in the hallway with her bags. "What interest can anyone have in the past? Are they not satisfied?"

But by the next day, Augusta Nack was beginning to see the value of the past.

"I am selling this story," she informed the *New York Times* as she marched into its offices. "What arrangements is your paper making to pay me?"

To her chagrin, she was told that this was not how the *Times* operated. It was, however, how the *Journal* did. Some things hadn't changed. Even so, Hearst's paper had become almost unrecognizable to Mrs. Nack in her decade away. Along with the downright futuristic sight of newspaper photographs, the *Journal* now carried such inconceivable captions as "Remarkable Photograph Showing Fatal Crash Between Autos Going 50 Miles Per Hour." Life outside prison, it seemed, had gotten faster while she was gone—and louder. Hearst's paper was now more squat and squarish in shape, and some already believed an outright tabloid format would be "the 20th Century newspaper." Pulitzer's *World* had already tested out an issue in this potent new form; tabloids were cheap to print, after all, and easier to read on the crowded new subways. Hearst hadn't quite made the shift yet, but he was halfway there: His paper already looked coarser, its front-page headlines a Klaxon call of massive type, sometimes in crude wooden-type letters that were seven inches tall. In the *Journal*'s early days, only the beginning of a war could summon up crude and gargantuan typesetting; but in this new century every day was a conflict, every day a panic. BUILDING FALLS; 40 KILLED, blared one copy from that week. WOMAN KILLS MAN IN UNION SQUARE, roared another.

There were far more subtly disturbing stories out that day, too—such as word that Kaiser Wilhelm was becoming fascinated by the notion of sending armed zeppelins across the English Channel. ("The young German Emperor gets peevish sometimes," the paper mused.) But after Mrs. Nack's visit, she had booming type of her own on the *Evening Journal*'s front page:

MRS. NACK CONFESSES!

Readers looking inside the paper discovered that indeed she had confessed . . . to her love for William Guldensuppe.

"Guldensuppe and I were happy until Martin Thorn came," she insisted. "He was younger and extremely good looking, but I had no love for him. I told him I could never love him. God knows I did not dream of what was going to happen. I should have given him over to the police as a dangerous man. But I did not think of it."

The entire crime from start to finish, she continued, had been his doing. In fact, she hadn't even known Thorn was upstairs in the Woodside cottage.

"I heard a shot, an exclamation of pain, and a fall. Then it flashed over me in an instant that Thorn had killed the man I loved. He slowly came down the stairs and towards me. I shut my eyes because I thought he was going to kill me. He thought I had fainted and went to get me a glass of water. When he came with the water he said: *Gussie, darling, I did it for you.*"

Her tale sounded curiously theatrical—which indeed it was.

"A theatrical company has made me an offer to go on stage," she admitted, "but I don't think I shall accept. I am going to write a book of my life, and when people read that they will see."

But first she'd have to find a place to live, a place where she could be left alone—"anywhere—everywhere—just so I can lose my identity," she explained. Maybe, she wondered aloud, she'd have to pull together enough money to move back to Germany. The $300 the police seized when arresting her was presumably still in a bank some-where, but with her lawyer long dead, she wasn't sure where to start looking.

Instead, she was busy seeking lodging; the very next place she'd gone to after the Hotel Rand also rejected her. Visiting the towering World Building to hawk her story again that day, she looked out over the sprawling city that spurned her. Augusta Nack no longer knew New York, but New Yorkers still knew her.

"This," she muttered, "is worse than prison."

ONE YEAR LATER, a call came upstairs to the head matron of the Tombs; there was, one of the jail staff informed her, "a lady wear-ing diamonds" waiting for her on a bench in the lobby. The matron puzzled over who it might be as she walked down to the entrance of the jail.

"How do you do, my dear?" her visitor called out as she rose. "Oh, it is so good to see you again!"

The head matron stood back, mystified. Her visitor was a respectable-looking middle-aged woman, finely adorned with a gold watch and a diamond brooch, and utterly unfamiliar to her.

"Who are you?" she finally asked.

Her visitor looked about a little conspiratorially, then leaned in. "I am Mrs. Nack."

The matron was startled, and quickly led her former star prisoner into her office. It had been some eleven years since she'd last seen her—so long, in fact, that the entire jail had been rebuilt since she left.

"I have just returned from Germany, where I went to see my old mother," Mrs. Nack explained as they sat down. "I had a good time in the old home, but I wanted to come back to America. I wouldn't live in Europe if you paid me. This is the place to make money."

Mrs. Nack had seen the takings at the Tombs and at Auburn Prison; the first was almost mythically corrupt, and a state audit later found Auburn a "brutal" place of "wanton waste and extravagance." Mrs. Nack had already been on the receiving end of that cruelty and graft. "You do not have enough to eat," she recalled of Auburn.

"When I was in solitary confinement I received one slice of bread and two ounces of water a day. I thought I would commit suicide, and I tried to open a vein in my arm with a pin. I sucked out the blood and it moistened my lips, and I did not die."

But as long as you were the one standing outside the cell, it was clearly a good business to get into.

"I would like to get a place as a matron or a head keeper in a prison," Mrs. Nack earnestly explained to the flabbergasted jailer. "I know something about the business. Such a place would just suit me."

The matron, a reporter dryly noted, "made no offer to help."

For others, though, the Guldensuppe case launched new careers. Both Judge Smith and Judge Maddox went on to state supreme court appointments soon afterward. For District Attorney William Youngs, the case was followed by a plum promotion: He became Teddy Roosevelt's private secretary, and later the U.S. attorney in New York. After retiring, he even tried the other side of the reporter's notebook and ran a newspaper himself. He drew upon his experience in the first Thorn mistrial to urge the adoption of an alternate-juror rule. The state government in Albany being what it was, it only took another thirty-three years for his sensible proposal to become law.

The chemist whose forensic evidence was spurned for Thorn's trial, Professor Rudolph Witthaus, also went on to great success. Witthaus was brilliant, disturbing, and arrogant to the end, testifying in major murder cases over the next two decades, including such star-studded scandals as the shooting of Stanford White. It was his expertise in poisons, though, that made his fame. He could view stomach membrane under a microscope and pick out the dazzling crystals of arsenic poisoning—or "inheritance powder," as it was dubbed. That same flesh could be minced and boiled and mixed with lye and benzene; if the slurry fluoresced under an ultraviolet light, that was chloroform poisoning. Blasted with the rotten-egg stink of hydrogen sulfide, it would also turn yellow for mercury poisoning. Witthaus's skills were in such demand that in one 1900 case he charged the city a dizzying $18,550 for his services. He could have used some of that consulting himself, as his heirs would later claim that a paramour had kept the dying professor in a chemical haze while filing three conflicting wills. Witthaus, it turned out, died leaving a poisoning case probably only he could have solved: his own.

At least one vital advance was already being made for his successors, though. For all of Witthaus's tools, he had often been frustrated by the evidence ruined by drunk and incompetent coroners, who were still appointed out of political patronage. Emil Hoeber had been one such appointee—and a man not opposed to being bribed with, say, a nice gold watch. The office proved so hopelessly corrupt that in 1915, the year of Witthaus's death, the coroner's job was abolished altogether and replaced by a trained medical examiner. With that, New York City forensics had finally stepped—a little belatedly—into the modern era. Were a Guldensuppe case to come to trial again, no DA would need to feel embarrassed to call forth a coroner or a chemistry professor to testify.

Among police officers, the old "river mystery" remained legendary: Whenever a head was found buried in a basement or a vacant lot, it was promptly dubbed "Guldensuppe's head." Those who really had searched for his head, though, went on to upstanding careers. The first officer to interrogate Mrs. Nack, Captain Samuel Price, rose to become one of the most recognizable detectives in the city and eventually the head of the Detective Bureau in the Bronx. Another key officer at the Harlem find, George Aloncle, became one of the city's top safecracking experts. And even Captain Stephen O'Brien— who lost his Detective Bureau post after triumphantly wrapping up the case—went on to address the bewildering rise of automobiles by founding the city's Traffic Squad. Fittingly enough for the man famed as "the honest cop," after first observing traffic squads in London, Paris, and Berlin, O'Brien submitted a travel-expense report so scrupulously penny-pinching that he was ribbed about it on the force for years afterward.

But the man most marked by the Guldensuppe case was Arthur Carey, the demoted police officer who'd opened the package found in the bushes near the Harlem River. His pursuit of the oilcloth provided a key break in solving the case; his star rose again, and he was made the first head of the NYPD's newly formed Homicide Bureau.

For three decades he was New York City's "Murder Man," famed for being so relentless that he once questioned a suspect in the middle of the funeral of the man's murdered wife. In one Chinatown murder case, he interrogated a suspect for thirty hours, until they both nearly broke down. Carey became a city institution, teaching the homicide course in the NYPD's detective academy. Along with training in weapons and crowd control, the police academy also imparted to recruits a new lesson: Never run roughshod over a crime scene. Spurred by the meticulous new methodologies developed in Austria, police were now exhorted to leave them untouched, and to neatly number and photograph each piece of physical evidence wherever it had fallen. They weren't to touch anything if they could help it; though fingerprints were still ignored in New York City back in 1897, by the time of Mrs. Nack's release, dusting for them had become a standard procedure. The identification of Guldensuppe's body and the murder scene—once so precarious that Howe had nearly used them to overturn the whole case—would in this new era have been clinched by Carey through fingerprints from the body and at Woodside.

By the time Carey retired, he'd personally overseen more murder investigations than possibly any police officer before or since—more than ten thousand, by a *Times* estimate. But it was the Guldensuppe case that stayed with him. Carey always recalled what his first big case and its "hundred different sources" taught him.

"In a murder case there is no one obvious clue," Carey mused, "but all clues are good."

And it was just one such murder case, as it turned out, that would bring Augusta Nack into the news again.

IT WAS A WARM JUNE EVENING in 1909 when a man—a European immigrant, perhaps thirty-five years old—approached a young boy not far from the newsrooms of the *Journal* and the *World*.

"Do you want to make five cents?" the man asked.

The boy was to guard two large parcels wrapped in black oilcloth, then wait for the man to come back to pick them up. Minutes ticked by, then an hour; there was no sign of the man or the nickel. Just as the boy was losing hope, a passing dog caught a scent and began frantically trying to tear at the packages.

Inside them, sliced cleanly in two, was a freshly murdered man with no head.

As Officer Carey hurried over from his newly formed Homicide Bureau, newspaper reporters dashed out of their offices and onto the scene unfolding just down the street. Written in blood on the inside of the oilcloth were the words *Black Hand*; but this, it was surmised, was a murderer's ruse to fool the police into blaming an Italian gang. Before a day had passed, the head was discovered under the Brooklyn Bridge, and newspapers had their real victim: a Russian housepainter named Samuel Bersin.

VICTIM CARVED UP LIKE GULDENSUPPE, one paper announced, while the *Evening Journal* declared CASE MOST PUZZLING SINCE GULDENSUPPE. This time the police were ready. Scores of detectives tracked the distinctive oilcloth pattern and piled into pawnshops, where they soon found Bersin's missing jewelry. Reporters followed in hot pursuit, pouncing on the latest theories: Sammy was murdered by a jealous husband; Sammy was robbed for his diamond rings; Sammy was a Russian Jewish anarchist caught in a political squabble. But the most palpable clue was also the most alluring one: Everyone who knew Sammy knew that he had romantic rivals for the hand of a comely Russian émigré named Jennie Siegel.

Among those swept up in the dragnet around the case was one unexpected bystander: Augusta Nack. With memories of the Guldensuppe case revived, reporters discovered the infamous Mrs. Nack hiding in plain sight just blocks from her old apartment.

"Mrs. Nack has taken the name of Augusta Huber," a wire-service article revealed, "and now manages and owns a small fancy goods store at No. 357 Ninth Avenue." Within hours, Mrs. Nack's new identity had been exposed to both her neighbors and to newspaper readers across the country; within a month of the Bersin murder, she was in bankruptcy court, her business in ruins. And with that, Augusta Nack vanished from public view again—this time, it seemed, for good.

But for old-timers on the force, the memory of Gussie Nack was not so easily lost. Still working the streets of New York decades later, they'd recognize her face with a start, then pass quietly onward. Even so, Chief Inspector Ernest Van Wagner admitted that there'd never been any question among these detectives that it was Nack herself "who actually designed and planned" the murder of William Guldensuppe.

But had she also carried it out?

It is worth considering why the detectives in the case remained insistent on Mrs. Nack's equal guilt, even decades later. *Neither Thorn's explanation nor hers fit the evidence.* The medical examiner, in examining Guldensuppe's body, found signs of a desperate fight: a deep stab wound from a knife plunged straight down, wounds to the hand from where he'd grabbed at a blade, and additional glancing or angled stab wounds. These wounds were clean of any fibers, indicating that he'd been attacked while naked. And upon Mrs. Nack's arrest, the jail matron had discovered bruises on her arm that corresponded in age to the day of the crime. Finally, there was one last humble piece of physical evidence left unaccounted for in the Woodside bedroom. It was the only thing there, in fact, other than the two bullets and a discarded cartridge box: an empty cabernet bottle.

None of these clues were explained in the trial, in Thorn's story to Gotha, or in either murderer's testimony on the stand. But it *is* possible to conceive of one explanation of what happened that afternoon—one that accounts for all of the evidence. Guldensuppe was stabbed while naked, and stabbed from above when he least expected it. Only one person could have led Guldensuppe to the bedroom of a vacant house, offered him wine, stripped him naked, straddled atop him—and then plunged a knife straight down into his chest.

That person was not Martin Thorn.

Guldensuppe would have reached out and grabbed at his assailant's arm and hand, leaving bruises—and was stabbed across the palm and clumsily in the chest. That is when Martin Thorn would have stepped out from a closet to finish his rival off with a gunshot to the head.

Neither Mrs. Nack nor Thorn could admit to this. Thorn's story to John Gotha—the hapless friend who admired his way with cards and women—would quietly omit that he'd triumphed over Guldensuppe by watching him tryst with Gussie. And once Thorn and Mrs. Nack went to trial, each was determined to establish that *only the other had been upstairs to commit the murder.* If they'd acted in concert, neither could breathe a word of the actual plot. And if DA Youngs suspected the truth, there was nothing to be gained by airing it; he lacked hard evidence against Mrs. Nack. As it was, the prosecution managed to keep the salacious details of Guldensuppe's anatomy away from the public. The appalling way he was killed would also remain safely distant from Victorian eyes and ears.

Those who knew better couldn't quite shake off the chill of seeing Mrs. Nack walk free. She had never really left her old streets—the place where she'd considered herself to be the beloved "Nanty Nack" of young mothers and their families alike. There, Chief Inspector Van Wagner wrote in 1938, she could still be found, covered under the cloak of passing decades.

"I last saw her a few years ago," the old detective wrote, "smilingly selling cheap candy in her little store to the unsuspecting and innocent children of her neighborhood."

EPILOGUE: THE LAST MAN STANDING

REPORTERS RECALLED the Nack and Thorn case for years to come, but by the time Walter Winchell hailed it in 1948 as "the first of the great newspaper trials," he was already speaking of events from his own infancy. The star reporters were long gone: George Arnold, who traced the famed red-and-gold oilcloth for the *Journal*, had one of the more peaceful retirements by capping off his long newspaper career with a venture into writing novelty songs. The *World*'s crack reporter, Ike White, went on to expose dozens of Wall Street fraud operations, and courthouse correspondent Julian Hawthorne landed in prison himself for promoting a nonexistent silver mine.

The yellow-journalism era had taken a toll, though, on Joseph Pulitzer. At the end of the mighty battles over Guldensuppe and Cuba, his advisors estimated that the *Journal* had burned through about $4 million in Hearst's family coffers—but that another $5 million was left. That was more than enough to throw knockout blows at the *World*. The blind and ailing Pulitzer wavered, and finally emerged from the soundproofed mansion where he had ruled by the dictates of a telegraph. He and Hearst met quietly—their one face-to-face meeting—and negotiated a deal. What if they split up the market? The *Journal* could become the carnivalesque one-cent paper of the masses, and the *World* would return to being a more respectable two-cent paper, bent once again on bloodying the *Sun* and the *Herald*.

Just as important, the two papers would band together to fight labor unrest in their ranks.

The *World* and the *Journal*, famed for their crusades against cartels, were now secretly plotting one of their own.

After a year of delicate maneuvering, their resulting agreement went unsigned. Ultimately, though, the *World* inched away from sensationalism of its own accord. Joseph Pulitzer never was very happy playing against Hearst's one-upmanship; in his final years, he quietly came to admire the sober reliability of the *New York Times*. After Pulitzer's death in 1911, the *World*'s proprietor was rehabilitated in historical memory; the yellow-journalism wars faded away, replaced by the rosy glow of bequests to Columbia University and to the writing awards that still bear his name.

Hearst, though, remained unrepentant. He had always delighted in the blockbuster Sunday editions that the yellow revolution fostered—"a Coney Island of ink and wood pulp," as one contemporary put it—and he relished the sensational headlines that made them sell. But just as he challenged his spiritual godfather in Pulitzer, and Pulitzer had turned on James Bennett, so too was Hearst attacked. Now it was by Joseph Patterson, a young Chicagoan that Hearst had once hired as a China correspondent. Patterson's founding in 1919 of the New York *Daily News* upped the stakes in newspaper journalism once again; printed in a bold tabloid format, the paper made its fame by sneaking a shoe-mounted camera into the electrocution of murderess Ruth Snyder and snapping a picture at the moment the switch was thrown. And like Pulitzer and Bennett before him, Hearst seemed rather appalled by his own journalistic progeny. He tried buying out Patterson, and when that didn't work, he launched his own version—the *New York Daily Mirror*. The tabloid war long fomented by Hearst had now truly begun, with square front pages and fist-high headlines socking New Yorkers as they stepped out of the subway.

William Randolph Hearst had always cut a bigger figure than just his newspapers, though. Yet even after parlaying his populism and grandstanding into runs for mayor, then governor, and inevitably for president—he finally settled for a couple of terms in Congress—he never quite recaptured the youthful excitement of his Murder Squad. As the media baron's holdings expanded into dozens of newspapers, and his persona grew to the mythical proportions immortalized in *Citizen Kane*, one contemporary mused that the Guldensuppe case remained "a lark and a triumph which he enjoyed more keenly" than any party nomination.

"Ah well, we were young," he later reminisced. "It was an adventure."

IT SEEMED AS IF that final word on the Guldensuppe case might remain with Hearst himself. But when the media baron died in 1951, there was still another man who hadn't forgotten about the case— one man still standing. That man was Ned Brown.

The cub reporter who first found Mrs. Nack's apartment rose in time to write the *World*'s "Pardon My Glove" boxing column. He outlasted the newspaper itself; Ned worked in its newsroom until its final hours in 1931, then graduated to a long career handling publicity for Jack Dempsey and editing *Boxing* magazine. But he never stopped filing ringside newspaper reports, and when his fellow boxing writer A. J. Liebling profiled him in 1955, it was as much in admiration of an era as of a man: Ned was the last Victorian holdout in the New York sports pens.

"Being a newspaperman gave you stature then," the old man fondly recalled. "Everywhere except in society. It didn't cut any ice there."

Ned then went on to outlive Liebling, too. In fact, he also outlived nearly every New York newspaper. After the *World* went under, it combined with the *Evening Telegram* to become the *New York World-Telegram*. Then it swallowed the *Sun* to become the *New York World-Telegram and Sun*. Then it was mashed together with the remnants of the *Journal*, the *Herald*, and the *Tribune* to become the *New York World Journal Tribune*. And then it died.

But Ned Brown lived on.

Nothing could knock Ned to the mat; the same inquisitive blue eyes that searched Mrs. Nack's mantelpiece for a picture of

Guldensuppe would go on to witness the Manson trial and Watergate. In an age of *Kojak* and *Dirty Harry,* he still recalled the days when *journalists* carried badges. Yet although news evolved from carrier-pigeon dispatches to satellite broadcasts, the business remained curiously familiar; when Rupert Murdoch started his chains, and Ted Turner bought his first TV stations, it was already old news to Ned Brown. He'd seen it all before. Hearst's saturation coverage of sensational local crime—creating a suspenseful narrative out of endless news updates from every angle, whether there was anything substantive to cover or not—had already anticipated the round-the-clock cycle of broadcast news.

When Ned Brown died in 1976, he was well into his nineties—nobody was quite sure how old he was anymore. It wasn't long since he'd made a final bow to the public; evicted from his apartment by the Hudson River, the one possession the old man had bothered to retrieve was his tuxedo.

"I need that suit for my social life," he explained to a reporter.

With him ended the living memory of Augusta Nack and Martin Thorn. Even the case files had been destroyed years earlier by the Queens County Courthouse in a fit of housekeeping. As they were on their way to the incinerator, though, one curious reporter picked out a yellowed evidence envelope and opened it up.

It held little inside—just six duck feathers and a mystery.

SOURCES

PRIMARY SOURCES

Newspapers may be the first draft of history, but most of what they cover never gets a second draft. This book is the first on the entire Guldensuppe affair, and it's indebted to the several thousand newspaper articles about this case that I gathered by examining each day's reporting from more than a dozen daily newspapers:

Brooklyn Daily Eagle (BE)

New York Commercial Advertiser (NYCA)

New York Evening Post (NYEP)

New York Evening Telegram (NYET)

New York Herald (NYH)

New York Journal (NYJ)

New York Evening Journal (NYEJ)

New York Journal and Advertiser (NYJA)

New York Mail and Express (NYME)

New York Press (NYP)

New York Sun (NYS)

New York Evening Sun (NYES)

New York Times (NYT)

New York Tribune (NYTR)

New York World (NYW)

New Yorker Staats Zeitung (NYSZ)

I'm also fortunate to have both court records and memoirs written by the journalists and detectives from the case:

Carey, Arthur. *Memoirs of a Murder Man.* New York: Doubleday, Doran, 1930.

Collins, Frederick L. *Homicide Squad: Adventures of a Headquarters Old Timer.* New York: Putnam, 1944.

Court of Appeals of the State of New York: People of the State of New York Respondent, Against Martin Thorn, Appellant. Jamaica, NY: Long Island Farmer Print, 1898.

Edwarde, Charles. *The Guldensuppe Mystery: The True Story of a Real Crime.* New York: True Story, 1897.

O'Neill, Joseph Alan. "Who's the Executioner?" *The Atlantic Medical Weekly,* vols. 9–10 (September 17, 1898): 184–85.

Pulitzer, Joseph. *Joseph Pulitzer Papers, 1880–1924*. Washington, D.C.: Library of Congress.

Van Wagner, Ernest. *New York Detective*. New York: Dodd, Mead, 1938.

ADDITIONAL SOURCES

Annual Report of the Committee on the Fire Patrol to the New York Board of Fire Underwriters. New York: Economical Printing, 1894.

Ashley, Perry J. *American Newspaper Journalists, 1873–1900*. Detroit: Gale Research, 1983.

Baldasty, Gerald. *The Commercialization of News in the Nineteenth Century*. Madison: University of Wisconsin Press, 1992.

Bell, Suzanne. *Crime and Circumstance: Investigating the History of Forensic Science*. New York: Praeger, 2008.

Bleyer, Willard. *Main Currents in the History of American Journalism*. Boston: Houghton Mifflin, 1927.

Blum, Deborah. *The Poisoner's Handbook: Murder and the Birth of Forensic Medicine in Jazz Age New York*. New York: Penguin Press, 2010.

Brandon, Craig. *The Electric Chair: An Unnatural American History*. Jefferson, NC: McFarland, 1999.

Branigan, Elba. *The History of Johnson County, Indiana*. Indianapolis: B. F. Bowen, 1913.

Brian, Denis. *Pulitzer: A Life*. Hoboken, NJ: Wiley, 2001.

Brodie, Janet Farrell. *Contraception and Abortion in Nineteenth Century America*. Ithaca, NY: Cornell University Press, 1997.

Bromley, G. W. *Atlas of the City of New York, Borough of Queens*. New York: G. W. Bromley, 1909.

Brown, Henry Collins. *In the Golden Nineties*. Hastings on Hudson, NY: Valentine's Manual, 1928.

Byrnes, Thomas. *Professional Criminals of America*. New York: Cassell, 1886.

Cahn, Julius. *Julius Cahn's Official Theatrical Guide*, vol. 9. New York: Julius Cahn, 1904.

Campbell, W. Joseph. *Yellow Journalism: Puncturing the Myths, Defining the Legacies*. New York: Praeger, 2003.

———. *The Year That Defined American Journalism: 1897 and the Clash of Paradigms*. New York: Routledge, 2006.

Churchill, Allen. *Park Row: A Vivid Re-Creation of Turn of the Century Newspaper Days*. New York: Rinehart, 1958.

Cole, Simon. *Suspect Identities: A History of Fingerprinting and Criminal Identification*. Cambridge: Harvard University Press, 2001.

"Conspiracy Charge Against William Howe, William Thompson, Gavin Rickards." *Proceedings of the Old Bailey*, September 18, 1854. Old Bailey Online, oldbaileyonline.org, Ref #t18540918–997.

Copquin, Claudia Gryvatz. *The Neighborhoods of Queens*. New Haven, CT: Yale University Press, 2007.

Creelman, James. *On the Great Highway: The Wanderings and Adventures of a Special Correspondent*. Boston: Lothrop, 1901.

Crouthamel, James. *Bennett's New York Herald and the Rise of the Popular Press*. Syracuse: Syracuse University Press, 1989.

Dennett, Andrea. *Weird and Wonderful: The Dime Museum in America*. New York: New York University Press, 1997.

Dicken-Garcia, Hazel. *Journalistic Standards in Nineteenth-Century America*. Madison: University of Wisconsin Press, 1989.

Douglas, George H. *The Golden Age of the Newspaper.* Westport, CT: Greenwood Press, 1999.

Dreiser, Theodore. *Newspaper Days.* Edited by T. D. Nostwich. Philadelphia: University of Pennsylvania Press, 1991.

Eden Museé: Monthly Catalogue. N.d.

Flint, Austin. *Collected Essays and Articles on Physiology and Medicine.* New York: Appleton, 1903.

Ford, James L. *Forty-Odd Years in the Literary Shop.* New York: Dutton, 1921.

Forrest, Jay W. *Tammany's Treason.* Albany, NY: Fort Orange Press, 1913.

Gilfoyle, Timothy J. "America's Greatest Criminal Barrister." *Journal of Urban History* 29, no. 5 (July 2003): 525–54.

Gregory, Catherine. *Woodside, Queens County: A Historical Perspective, 1652–1994.* Woodside, NY: Woodside on the Move, 1994.

Harlow, Alvin Fay. *Old Bowery Days: The Chronicles of a Famous Street.* New York: Appleton, 1931.

Houck, Max. *Forensic Science: Modern Methods of Solving Crime.* New York: Praeger, 2007.

Hughes, Rupert. *The Real New York.* New York: Smart Set, 1904.

Important Events of the Century. New York: United States Central Publishing, 1876.

Ingersoll, Ernest. *Handy Guide to New York City.* New York: Rand McNally, 1897.

Ireland, Alleyne. *An Adventure with a Genius: Recollections of Joseph Pulitzer.* New York: E. P. Dutton, 1931.

James, W. I. *The Headless Body Murder Mystery, or Old Cap. Collier Searching for Clews; Old Cap. Collier Library #711.* New York: Munro's, 1897.

Jeffers, H. Paul. *Commissioner Roosevelt: The Story of Theodore Roosevelt and the New York City Police, 1895–1897.* New York: John Wiley, 1996.

Johnston, Alva, and Reginald Marsh. *The Legendary Mizners.* New York: Farrar, Straus and Young, 1953.

Juergens, George. *Joseph Pulitzer and the New York World.* Princeton, NJ: Princeton University Press, 1966.

King, Moses. *King's Handbook of New York City.* Buffalo, NY: Moses King, 1893.

Kobbé, Gustav. *New York and Its Environs.* New York: Harper & Brothers, 1891.

Korom, Joseph. *The American Skyscraper, 1850–1940.* Branden Books, 2008.

Lardner, James, and Thomas Reppetto. *NYPD: A City and Its Police.* New York, Henry Holt, 2000.

Lee, Alfred McClurg. *American Journalism, 1690–1940.* New York: Routledge, 2000.

Lee, James Melvin. *A History of American Journalism.* Boston: Houghton Mifflin, 1917.

Liebling, A. J. *Liebling at* The New Yorker: *Uncollected Essays.* Albuquerque: University of New Mexico Press, 1994.

Loerzel, Robert. *Alchemy of Bones: Chicago's Luetgert Murder Case of 1897.* Champaign: University of Illinois Press, 2007.

Lofton, John. *Justice and the Press.* Boston: Beacon Press, 1966.

Longworth, Thomas. *Longworth's American Almanac, New York City Register, and City Directory.* New York: Thomas Longworth, 1834.

Marcuse, Maxwell. *This Was New York.* New York: LIM Press, 1969.

McAdoo, William. *Guarding a Great City.* New York: Harper & Brothers, 1906.

McKerns, Joseph P. *Biographical Dictionary of American Journalism.* Westport, CT: Greenwood Press, 1989.

Miles, Robert Harrison Parker. *Three Men and a Woman: A Story of Life in New York.* New York: G. W. Dillingham, 1901.

Molineaux, Roland. *The Room with the Little Door.* New York: G. W. Dillingham, 1903.

Moran, Richard. *The Executioner's Current.* New York: Random House, 2002.

Morgan, Wayne, and Charles Lincoln Van Doren. *A Documentary History of the Italian Americans.* New York: Praeger, 1974.

Morris, James McGrath. *Pulitzer: A Life in Politics, Print, and Power.* New York: HarperCollins, 2010.

Moss, Frank. *The American Metropolis: From Knickerbocker Days to the Present Time.* New York: Collier, 1897.

Mott, Frank Luther. *American Journalism: A History, 1690–1960.* New York: Macmillan, 1962.

Nasaw, David. *The Chief: The Life of William Randolph Hearst.* New York: Houghton Mifflin, 2000.

"Note: Proof of the Corpus Delicti Aliunde the Defendant's Confession," *University of Pennsylvania Law Review,* 1955: 638–49.

O'Brien, Frank Michael. *The Story of the Sun: New York, 1833–1918.* New York: George H. Doran, 1918.

Palmer, Frederick. "Hearst and Hearstism." *Collier's,* September 22, 1906. In *A Calvacade of Collier's.* New York: A. S. Barnes, 1959.

Prison Association of New York. *Annual Report of the Prison Association of New York for the Year 1895.* State of New York, 1896.

Procter, Ben. *William Randolph Hearst: The Early Years, 1863–1910.* Oxford: Oxford University Press, 1998.

Reel, Guy. *The National Police Gazette and the Making of the Modern American Man, 1879–1906.* New York: Palgrave Macmillan, 2006.

Researches of the Loomis Laboratory of the Medical Department of the University of the City of New York. No. 1. New York: Douglas Taylor, 1890.

Rovere, Richard R. *Howe & Hummel: Their True and Scandalous History.* New York: Farrar, Straus & Giroux, 1947.

Seitz, Don. *Joseph Pulitzer: His Life and Letters.* New York: Simon & Schuster, 1924.

Spitzka, E. C. "Cases of Masturbation (Masturbatic Insanity)," *Journal of Mental Science* 33 (1887): 238–54.

Srebnick, Amy Gilman. *The Mysterious Death of Mary Rogers: Sex and Culture in Nineteenth-Century New York.* Oxford: Oxford University Press, 1997.

Stashower, Daniel. *The Beautiful Cigar Girl: Mary Rogers, Edgar Allan Poe, and the Invention of Murder.* New York: E. P. Dutton, 2006.

Stevens, John D. *Sensationalism and the New York Press.* New York: Columbia University Press, 1991.

Swanberg, W. A. *Citizen Hearst: The Monumental and Controversial Biography of One of the Most Fabulous Characters in American History.* New York: Scribner's, 1961.

Sweetser, M. F. *How to Know New York City.* New York: J. J. Little, 1898.

Tifft, Susan, and Alex S. Jones. *The Trust: The Private and Powerful Family Behind the New York Times.* New York: Back Bay Books, 1999.

Trow's New York City Directory. 1860, 1879, 1890 eds. New York: Trow City Directory.

Turner, Hy. *When Giants Ruled: The Story of Park Row, New York's Great Newspaper Street.* Bronx, NY: Fordham University Press, 1999.

Villard, Oswald. *Some Newspapers and Newspaper-Men.* New York: Alfred A. Knopf, 1926.

Waldman, Bette S., and Linda B. Martin. *Nassau, Long Island, in Early Photographs, 1869–1940.* New York: Dover, 1981.

Warren, Samuel. *Famous Cases of Circumstantial Evidence.* Jersey City, NJ: Frederick D. Linn, 1879.

Whyte, Kenneth. *The Uncrowned King: The Sensational Rise of William Randolph Hearst.* Berkeley, CA: Counterpoint, 2009.

Wilson, James Harrison. *The Life of Charles A. Dana.* New York: Harper & Brothers, 1907.

Winkler, John K. *W. R. Hearst: An American Phenomenon.* New York: Simon & Schuster, 1928.

———. *W. R. Hearst: A New Appraisal.* New York: Hastings House, 1955.

Witthaus, Rudolph, and Tracy Becker. *Medical Jurisprudence, Forensic Medicine and Toxicology.* New York: William Wood, 1894.

Wood, Francis Carter. *Chemical and Microscopical Diagnosis.* New York: Appleton, 1905.

Wyeth, John Allan. *With Sabre and Scalpel: The Autobiography of a Soldier and Surgeon.* New York: Harper & Brothers, 1914.

NOTES

1. THE MYSTERY OF THE RIVER

3 *"OH! YES, IT IS HOT ENOUGH!"*   NYET, June 25, 1897.
3 *riverside refreshment stalls . . . the new 700-foot-long promenade pier*   "Large Public Pier Opened," *NYET*, June 26, 1897.
3 *a confection of whitewashed wrought iron*   "New Public Pier," *NYW*, June 27, 1897.
3 *tenements on Avenue C*   Edwarde, *Guldensuppe Mystery*, 9.
4 *flat caps and straw boaters*   "River Gives Up a Murder Mystery," *NYH*, June 27, 1897.
4 *a mysterious ironclad in the shape of a giant sturgeon*   "Flyer for the Sea Afloat," *NYH*, June 26, 1897.
4 *Jack McGuire spotted it first*   Edwarde, *Guldensuppe Mystery*, 10.
5 *The police knew just whom to blame*   "River Gives Up A Murder Mystery," *NYH*, June 27, 1897.
5 *five schools that were allowed to use cadavers*   "Boy's Ghastly Find," *NYW*, June 27, 1897.
5 *The city had yet to buy its first horseless carriages*   Lardner and Reppetto, *NYPD*, 152.
6 *morgue keeper had been arrested*   See *New York Times* coverage of March 23, 1896, January 10, 1897, and April 2, 1897.
6 *tobacco would get a reporter the run*   Dreiser, *Newspaper Days*, 492.
6 *resident tomcat*   "Bellevue Cat a Prisoner," *NYT*, January 15, 1900.
6 *"That horrible place"*   Dreiser, *Newspaper Days*, 492.
7 *obligatory seventy-two hours . . . . Each day a dead-boat pulled up*   King, *King's Handbook*, 461.
7 *the coffin room, where another attendant hammered*   Wyeth, *With Sabre and Scalpel*, 362.
7 *Brady forcibly checked his mother*   "Wealthy Woman Committed," *NYT*, June 27, 1897; and "Rich Woman Insane," *NYEJ*, June 26, 1897.
7 *"There is a mystery here"*   *NYW*, June 27, 1897.

2. A DETECTIVE READS THE PAPER

9 *his Harlem tenement on 127th Street*   "Fragments of a Body Make a Mystery," *NYW*, June 28, 1897.
9 *"let's go cherrying!"*   Ibid.
9 *Just one house was visible . . . twelve-foot drop*   "Strange Murder Mystery Deepens"   *NYH*, June 28, 1897.
10 *Sedgwick and 170th*   *NYH*, June 28, 1897.
10 *he called out*   *NYW*, June 28, 1897.
10 *"I was walking a post"*   Carey, *Memoirs*, 49.
10 *everyone in the department called it: Goatsville*   Lardner and Reppetto, *NYPD*, 63.
10 *Carey had been in Goatsville ever since*   "Detectives in New Jobs," *NYT*, July 20, 1895.

11 *easily a hundred pounds. . . . They'd needed a stretcher and towing ropes*   "River Mystery Grows in Horror," *NYP,* June 28, 1897.

11 *captain was another Byrnes appointee . . . . renting out on-duty police*   "The Killilea Fiasco," *NYT,* May 17, 1896.

11 *the annual police parade was canceled*   Lardner and Reppetto, *NYPD,* 112.

11 *in that morning's New York* Herald   *NYH,* June 28, 1897.

12 *It was a sort druggists used*   *NYW,* June 28, 1897. NB: This *World* report was the only one to specifically note the use of druggist's seine twine, a telling minor detail that others—including their own reporters—then overlooked or forgot.

12 *adhered another piece of brown paper*   Carey, *Memoirs,* 49. NB: The piece of paper bearing the stamp of Kugler & Wollens is noted in Carey's account, and *it is only in his account.* The stamped paper is not cited in any newspaper, or indeed in the trial. Given the insatiable hunger newspapers had for reproducing illustrations of any clue in the case, the reasonable supposition is that they never saw this one. The exiled Carey was clearly hungry for a real case, and he was by far the earliest to make a good guess—startlingly so—at where the crime had been committed and how the body had been disposed of. I can't help but wonder whether, rather like the newspaper reporters, Carey wasn't above pocketing a hot lead for himself.

12 *ramshackle and roiling retail polyglot*   Marcuse, *This Was New York,* 54.

12 *pouncing on on-duty officers*   Lardner and Reppetto, *NYPD,* 112.

13 *you could tell the old and new officers apart*   "Conlin Leads a Long Line," *NYTR,* June 2,1897.

13 *one of the world's largest*   "The Bowery Savings Bank," *World's Work* 4 (1902): 2229.

13 *retired with a fortune of $350,000*   Lardner and Reppetto, *NYPD,* 83.

13 *John Jacob Astor IV owned*   "The Building Department," *NYT,* December 30, 1899.

13 *For decades . . . the Marsh family*   Longworth, *Longworth's American Almanac* (1834), 471; and *Trow's New York City Directory* (1860), 571.

13 *it became a German beer saloon*   Important Events, *132.* NB: John Volz's shortlived saloon is featured in an ad on this page.

13 *Ernst Kugler*   *Trow's New York City Directory* (1890), 163.

13 *outlasting a previous partner*   Ibid. (1879), 115.

14 *used to wrap a saw*   Carey, *Memoirs,* 49.

14 *it smelled of the store*   *NYP,* June 28, 1897.

14 *four feet wide and fourteen and a half feet long*   "East River Mystery," *NYT,* June 28, 1897.

14 *nearest distributor: Henry Feuerstein*   *NYH,* June 28, 1897.

14 *other distributor that Buchanan & Sons used*   "A Queer Murder Mystery," *NYTR,* June 28, 1897.

14 *Claflin, had been arrested*   "Will Arrest Mr. Claflin," *NYT,* May 27, 1897.

15 *something like fifty more shops to visit*   *NYW,* June 28, 1897.

3. THE JIGSAW MAN

16 *Ned Brown just about had the place to himself*   Liebling, *Liebling at* The New Yorker, 169.

16 *walls placarded with exhortations*   Dreiser, *Newspaper Days,* 625.

16 *clear out to the East River*   Ibid., 632.

17 *ridden cavalry in Sheridan's Shenandoah Valley campaign* Morris, *Pulitzer*, 24.
17 *Pulitzer, then a penniless veteran, was thrown out of it* Bleyer, *Main Currents*, 334.
17 *two miles of wrought-iron columns to support the world's largest pressroom* Morris, *Pulitzer*, 286.
17 *425-ton golden dome* Ibid., 287.
17 *its gilded surface could be seen for miles out to sea* Ibid., 272.
17 *"Is God in?"* Brian, *Pulitzer*, 153.
17 *a circulation of twenty thousand* Churchill, *Park Row*, 27.
17 *attention-grabbing promotions* Ibid., 39. NB: The idea of the Mars billboard was slightly less loony than it may sound; astronomers like Thomas Dick proposed decades earlier that a giant geometric ditch could be dug out in Siberia, and perhaps be set aflame, the better to send a signal of intelligent life to our fellow astronomers on Mars. The *World* scheme of sending an actual message to Mars was shelved, alas, when someone at a promotion meeting asked: "What language shall we print it in?"
18 *Circulation had risen fifteenfold* Liebling, *Liebling at* The New Yorker, 165.
18 yellow journalism, *they called it* Campbell, *Yellow Journalism*, 25.
18 *the day's front-page grabber* *NYW,* June 27, 1897.
18 *today it was just the substitute editor. . . . Ned was to run over* Liebling, *Liebling at* The New Yorker, 169. NB: The description of Ned Brown, as well as his conversations with editors and other reporters, is drawn entirely from Liebling's September 24, 1955, *New Yorker* article "The Scattered Dutchman," reprinted in *Liebling at* The New Yorker. Although the article contains a few errors and chronological inconsistencies, it was by far the most ambitious account ever attempted regarding the Guldensuppe case. That it's a Liebling piece makes it a joy to read—he writes tartly of the victim's "brisket" arriving "in installments"—and he conveys what it was like to be a denizen of Newspaper Row in the old days. The article focuses largely on the opening stages of the case, and in particular on revealing Ned Brown as the *World*'s near-miss reporter.
19 *"At first," O'Hanlon admitted* *NYW,* June 28, 1897.
19 *lungs was still spongy and the heart was filled* *NYT,* June 28, 1897.
19 *between the victim's fifth and sixth ribs* *NYW,* June 28, 1897.
20 *blood had entered into the surrounding tissue* Ibid.
20 *alive and naked when stabbed* *NYT,* June 28, 1897.
20 *"Both wounds were made"* *NYH,* June 28, 1897.
20 *The victim had cut his hand* *NYP,* June 28, 1897.
20 *"That he was knocked down"* *NYW,* June 28, 1897.
21 *the two segments were pushed together* Edwarde, *Guldunsuppe Mystery*, 17.
21 *Magnusson's friends and neighbors had been urging her to visit* *NYTR*, June 28, 1897.
22 *"If they had only been able to account"* *NYW,* June 28, 1897.
22 *A few among the reporters took notice* *NYT,* June 28, 1897.
22 I knew it was a murder all along "River Gives Up a Murder Mystery," *NYH,* June 27, 1897.
22 *the patrolman's report claimed . . . a patent falsehood* *NYW,* June 27, 1897.
22 Herald *reporter who had fetched the coroner* *NYH,* June 27, 1897.
22 World *reporter who started knocking* *NYW,* June 27, 1897.
22 *hadn't secured the crime scene* Ibid.
22 *Hogan ventured. . . . out of their jurisdiction* NYH, June 27, 1897.
23 *sweeps of women . . . walking along Broadway* "Moss Gets on Chapman's Trail," *NYET,* June 28, 1897.

23 *his own pet theory*   *NYT,* June 28, 1897.
23 *an unnerving sense of recognition*   Liebling, *Liebling at* The New Yorker, 186.

4. THE WRECKING CREW

24 *"may have been a Hebrew"*   "River Mystery Grows in Horror," *NYP,* June 28, 1897.
24 no alcohol in his stomach. . . . Nor was there food   "Louis A. Lutz the Victim?" *NYEJ,* June 28, 1897.
24 *"It appears to me"*   "Dr. Weston Says Body Was Boiled," *NYET,* June 28, 1897.
25 *CANNIBALISM SUGGESTED*   *NYH,* June 30, 1897.
25 *"A butcher may have done it"*   "Strange Murder Mystery Deepens," *NYH,* June 28, 1897.
25 *a recent Chicago murder*   Loerzel, *Alchemy of Bones.*
25 *"as white as marble. . . . body had been washed"*   *NYH,* June 28, 1897.
25 *a* Press *reporter suggested*   *NYP,* June 28, 1897.
25 *The* World *knew just the man to ask*   *NYW,* June 28, 1897.
26 *scores of reporters were fanning out*   "World Men Find a Clue," *NYW,* June 29, 1897.
26 *"God damn it,* get excited!"   Churchill, *Park Row,* 86.
27 *You could tell when New York was having a peaceful day*   Ford, *Forty-Odd Years,* 260.
27 *sent reporters off to tail detectives and swipe evidence*   Liebling, *Liebling at* The New Yorker, 166.
27 *"Events seem to indicate"*   signed W. R. Hearst editorial, *NYEJ,* June 29, 1897.
27 *race riots in Key West*   "Inviting a Race War," *Boston Daily Globe,* June 28, 1897.
27 *stealing electricity off high-voltage streetcar lines*   "Up-to-Date Burglars in Ohio Tap Trolley Wires for Electricity"   *NYH,* June 29, 1897.
27 *a $15 dog*   "Millionaires War Over a $15 Dog," *NYEJ,* June 27, 1897.
27 *Hire four launches*   "Picture of the Murder," *NYJ,* June 29, 1897.
27 *crowded with bereaved families*   "Undurchdringlithes Dunkel," *NYSZ,* June 29, 1897.
28 *could barely make their way inside*   *NYW,* June 29, 1897.
28 *John Johnson and Adolph Carlson*   "The Body Not Identified," *NYCA,* June 29, 1897.
28 *"Japanese." . . . Another mysterious visitor*   "Dark Crime of River and Wood," *NYH,* June 29, 1897.
28 *presumptive widow of Mr. Robert Wood*   *NYH,* June 29, 1897.
29 *Brooklyn gas engineer Charles Russell*   "No Clew Yet Found," *NYTR,* June 29, 1897.
29 *bartender John Otten*   "No Light on Murder Mystery," *NYP,* June 29, 1897.
29 *printer John Livingston, or . . . Edward Leunhelt*   *NYH,* June 29, 1897.
29 *Manhattan bricklayer:*   *NYCA,* June 28, 1897.
29 *he refused to talk*   *NYW,* June 29, 1897.
29 *"bicycle attorney"*   "Drivers in Trouble," *NYJ,* June 29, 1897.
29 *"I feel sure it is my uncle's body"*   *NYEJ,* June 28, 1897.
30 *"Oh, Dick!"*   *NYW,* June 29, 1897.
30 *dancing a little jig . . . as page proofs were laid out*   Winkler, *W. R. Hearst,* 71.
30 *"The public . . . likes entertainment better"*   Stevens, *Sensationalism,* 87.
31 *$20 gold piece he used*   Churchill, *Park Row,* 46.

31 *piss pots emblazoned with their portraits*   Winkler, *W. R. Hearst*, 58.
31 *"I am possessed of the weakness"*   Procter, *William Randolph Hearst*, 41.
31 *"chambermaid's delight"*   Ibid., 78.
31 *"in the Silurian era"*   Campbell, *Yellow Journalism*, 3.
31 *"Smash as many as you have to"*   Winkler, *W. R. Hearst*, 110.
31 *"polychromous effervescence"*   Whyte, *Uncrowned King*, 187.
31 MAN WITH THE MUSICAL STOMACH   Stevens, *Sensationalism*, 84.
32 *word arrived of the upcoming four o'clock* World   Liebling, *Liebling at* The New Yorker, 178.
32 *$500 REWARD*   *NYW,* June 28, 1897.
33 *Run an Extra Final Edition*   Liebling, *Liebling at* The New Yorker, 179.
33 *$1,000 Reward:*   *NYEJ,* June 28, 1897.

5. JILL THE RIPPER

34 *reader guesses included*   "Theories of the Multitude," *NYEJ,* June 29, 1897.
35 *Hearst loved promotion*   Turner, *When Giants Ruled*, 124.
35 *"a wooden-legged burglar"*   Lee, History of American Journalism, *373.*
35 *"Take all or any part of that"*   Turner, *When Giants Ruled*, 123.
35 *Park Row sidewalk . . . was wearing thin*   Swanberg, *Citizen Hearst*, 83.
35 *"We must beat every paper"*   Churchill, *Park Row*, 87.
35 *Wreckers dedicated to homicide coverage*   Procter, *William Randolph Hearst*, 99.
36 *"One might as well have tried"*   Edwarde, *Guldensuppe Mystery*, 30.
36 *"Did love or jealousy have aught"*   *NYW,* June 29, 1897.
36 *five men gathered around the dissecting table*   "Light on the Murder Mystery," *NYW,* June 30, 1897.
36 *Ferguson sensed a chilling familiarity*   "May Be Cyklam's Headless Body," *NYP,* June 30, 1897. NB: The quotes from Ferguson that follow are from this account.
37 *detectives coursed uptown*   Ibid.
37 *a lone cub reporter could be seen*   Liebling, *Liebling at* The New Yorker, 186.
38 *bites by mad dogs*   "Hints for Dog Bites," *NYCA,* June 29, 1897.
38 *A Romanesque space with white marble floors*   Advertisement in Cahn, *Theatrical Guide.*
38 *"The House of a Thousand Hangovers"*   "Miscellany," *Time,* December 7, 1925. NB: The baths' demolition occasioned the magazine's recollection of its old days. These same baths, incidentally, also figured in the infamous Becker-Rosenthal murder case of 1912.
38 *Ned idly let a question drop*   Liebling, *Liebling at* The New Yorker, 187. NB: Liebling's article is the sole source for the account in this section of Brown's exploits.
40 *It was the new issue of the* Evening Journal   "The Real Clew to the Murder Mystery," *NYEJ,* June 29, 1897.
41 *For the first time ever, color was being used*   Stevens, *Sensationalism*, 92.
41 *"I learned from some neighbors"*   "Saw Two Men with Package in a Saloon," *NYET,* June 29, 1897.
41 *a slender* Times *reporter attempted to try on one of Max's suits*   *NYT,* June 29, 1897.
41 *the* Times *theorized . . . that two escapees*   *NYT,* June 29, 1897.
41 THE DEAD MAN'S VALISE   "Police Work on a New Clue," *NYEJ,* June 29, 1897.
41 *"The German seems to regard"*   "Theories of Prominent Persons as to How the Murder Was Committed," *NYJ,* June 29, 1897.

41 *"The solution of the whole matter hangs upon the oilcloth"* "The Rest of the Roll," Ibid.
42 *Carey . . . hadn't made it to Queens or Long Island* *NYT,* June 29, 1897.
42 *throwing* thirty men *into tracking the oilcloth* Bleyer, *Main Currents,* 368.
42 *a* Journal *team at the dry-goods store of one Max Riger* "Murder Mystery Is Solved by the Journal," *NYEJ,* June 30, 1897.

6. THE BAKER IN HELL'S KITCHEN

45 *another heat wave* "Scorching Heat for the Freshmen," *NYET,* June 30, 1897.
45 *unshaven and tough-looking fellow* "Mr. and Mrs. Nack Under Arrest; Guldensuppe's Legs Found in Brooklyn" *NYET,* June 30, 1897.
45 *gangster Mallet Murphy* Marcuse, *This Was New York,* 63.
45 *two men clambered aboard* *NYEJ,* June 30, 1897.
45 *"Mr. Nack?"* "Murder Charged to a Midwife," *NYP,* July 1, 1897.
46 *Garfield Drug Company on Thirty-Fourth* *American Druggist and Pharmaceutical Record* 30 (1897): 22.
46 *carriage-jackers Oscar Piper and Walter McDevitt* *NYEJ,* June 30, 1897.
46 *tried escaping twice . . . .* *"I have absolutely no idea . . . "* Ibid.
46 *nine coworkers from the Murray Hill Baths* "May Be Guldensuppe," *NYT,* July 1, 1897.
46 *VICTIM THOUGHT TO BE THEODORE CYKLAM* *NYW,* June 30, 1897.
46 *elbowed aside by Pulitzer's ace reporter Ike White* Liebling, *Liebling at* The New Yorker, 191.
46 *Ike's pet theory* *NYW,* June 30, 1897.
47 *not unknown for reporters to tail detectives* Liebling, *Leibling at* The New Yorker, 166.
47 *The* Herald, *it seemed, had boozily stumbled* "Police Say Murder Mystery Is Solved," *NYH,* July 1, 1897.
47 *overheard by reporter Joe Gavan* Collins, *Homicide Squad,* 55.
47 *Hearst alone made a personal visit* Ford, *Forty-Odd Years,* 260.
48 *"that antique and shabby"* McAdoo, *Guarding a Great City,* 3.
48 *under constant watch by the competition* Jeffers, *Commisioner Roosevelt,* 87.
48 *more than 100,000 arrests a year* "New York at Its Best and Worst," *NYW,* July 1, 1898.
49 *chief had more than 250 detectives* "Police Chief's Suggestion," *NYT,* December 1, 1897.
49 *new rank hadn't even gone through . . . . on the force for more than twenty years* Lardner and Reppetto, *NYPD,* 114.
49 *walls and floors of the office had been carefully muffled* Ibid., 88.
49 *"I went to work at two o'clock"* *NYEJ,* June 30, 1897.
50 *"I get up at about 1 or 2 and go over the ferry"* *NYP,* July 1, 1897.
50 *I was so drunk that I had to stay in bed"* *NYEJ,* June 30, 1897.
50 *"What the deuce"* *NYP,* July 1, 1897.
50 *Bakery's owner vouch . . . Nack had actually led Strack's saloon* *NYP,* July 1, 1897.
51 *$20 monthly lease; she'd given notice* *NYP,* July 1, 1897.
51 *detective now sitting on her sofa . . . . another detective stood* Edwarde, *Guldensuppe Mystery,* 62.
51 *"pleasing, yet repellant, appearance"* *NYT,* July 1, 1897.
51 *"I gave her a bit of my mind"* *NYET,* June 30, 1897.

51 *Krauch had been watching her apartment*   *NYH*, July 1, 1897.
52 *fashionable tulle-trimmed hat that she'd quickly donned*   *NYET*, June 30, 1897.
52 *"My name is Augusta Nack"*   Edwarde, *Guldensuppe Mystery*, 69.
52 Speak louder   Ibid.
53 *Pauline Riger . . . had been listening all along*   "Mrs. Nack Will Be Formally Charged with Murdering Guldensuppe"   *NYEJ*, July 1, 1897.
54 *bumping up against the USS* Vermont   *NYT*, July 1, 1897.
54 *in the middle of his hallway, were two severed human legs*   Edwarde, *Guldensupe Mystery*, 77.

7. THE UNDERTAKER'S NEIGHBOR

55 *Werner's indispensable assistant was vacationing*   *NYH*, July 1, 1897.
55 *The young millionaire made the landlord an offer*   Churchill, *Park Row*, 90.
56 *Pulitzer had increasingly taken*   Ibid., 57.
56 *"We must smash the interloper"*   Procter, *William Randolph Hearst*, 85.
56 *The* Times *had briefly gone bust*   Tifft and Jones, *The Trust*, 36.
56 *Dana . . . stopped coming to his office*   Wilson, *Charles A. Dana*, 513.
56 *"When I came to New York"*   Juergens, *Joseph Pulitzer*, 350.
56 *The* World's *unmatched circulation*   Stevens, *Sensationalism*, 86.
57 *"undesirable class of readers"*   "Views of New Journalism," *NYT*, March 4, 1897.
57 World *had dubbed the Missing Head Mystery*   *NYW*, July 2, 1897.
57 *"The sensational journals of the city"*   "The Sensational Journals of the City," *NYCA*, June 29, 1897
57 *"The freak journals"*   "Vociferous Journals," *NYT*, June 30, 1897.
57 *Hearst's men had cut the cords*   Churchill, *Park Row*, 90.
57 *Price, Krauch, and O'Donohue . . . spent the next few hours unpacking*   *NYEJ*, July 1, 1897.
58 *small trapdoor in the ground floor . . . motley assortment*   Ibid.
58 *Neighbors watched from the adjacent buildings*   Ibid.
58 *avenue that was turning increasingly chaotic . . . police were holding back*   *NYH*, July 1, 1897.
58 *Vockroth, had rented a horse and surrey to Nack*   "More Murder Clues," *NYME*, July 1, 1897.
59 *another boarder had lived in the apartment*   *NYEJ*, July 1, 1897.
59 *in February when Guldensuppe had beaten his rival*   *NYT*, July 1, 1897.
59 *knife, a broken saw, and then a revolver . . . a dried spray of blood*   *NYEJ*, July 1, 1897.
59 *that evening's* Journal *headline*   *NYEJ*, June 30, 1897.
59 *sent out beefy guards*   Stevens, *Sensationalism*, 93.
59 *"When patting oneself on the back"*   Editorial, *NYEJ*, July 1, 1897.
60 *signed Guldensuppe . . . not Gieldsensuppe*   "Fear and Strain Weaken Mrs. Nack," *NYP*, July 2, 1897.
60 *couldn't find missing money she claimed*   "Now Formally Accused," *NYTR*, July 3, 1897.
60 *a jail matron found it hidden in her corset*   "The Murder Mystery," *NYTR*, July 2, 1897.
60 *The matron also noticed bruises*   "Murder Will Out," *NYEP*, July 1, 1897.
60 *having her fingernails pared and scraped*   "Police Couldn't Weaken Her," *NYET*, July 2, 1897.
60 *"If that body belonged to William Guldensuppe"*   "The Identification Upset," *NYW*, July 2, 1897.

60 One was a Bowery waiter . . . other was a babbling metal-polish peddler   NYT,
    July 1, 1897.

60 home address that proved to be a lumberyard   NYP, June 30, 1897.

61 "He is a freak"   NYW, June 30, 1897.

61 "She has a temper"   NYP, July 1, 1897.

61 Herald writer heard Herman Nack claim   NYH, July 1, 1897.

61 "She is strong enough?"   NYP, July 1, 1897.

61 Friend, had marched into the Mulberry Street   "To Protest Her Innocence,"
    BE, July 2, 1897.

61 World editors were doubling down   "Murder Mystery Is a Mystery Still," NYW,
    July 1, 1897.

62 willing to testify that the body was not his   "The Identification Upset," NYW,
    July 2, 1897.

62 Mrs. Clark, it turned out, had been caught up in a divorce   "Police Seeking
    Thorn," NYT, July 2, 1897.

62 "always mixed up in several affairs"   "Mrs. Nack Spends Hours on Detective
    Chief O'Brien's Rack," NYEJ, July 2, 1897.

62 Journal reporters sat down with Frank   Ibid. NB: The remainder of this chap-
    ter's dialogue is drawn from this account.

63 the illicit service that some midwives quietly provided   Brodie, Contraception and
    Abortion, 54.

8. THE WIDOW'S FRIEND

64 finally been promoted to acting inspector   "More Murder Clues," NYME, July 1,
    1897.

64 a composer of novelty tunes   "Ex-Inspector O'Brien Dead," NYT, July 3, 1913.

64 on the table and chairs . . . O'Brien had arranged the tools   NYET, July 2, 1897.

64 "the most cold blooded woman"   "Trying to Trace Thorn," BE, July 3, 1897.

64 alienists wandered in and out   "An Expert Alienist Studies Mrs. Nack," NYH,
    July 4, 1897.

65 readers were treated to close-ups   NYEJ, July 1, 1897.

65 "I made an especial study"   NYH, July 4, 1897.

65 "masturbatic insanity"   Spitzka, Cases of Masturbation, 238.

65 presiding over the electric chair's rather messy debut   Moran, Executioner's Current,
    19.

65 "Did you know . . . she has never reported a live birth"   NYH, July 4, 1897.

65 "I cannot understand how detectives could expect such a clumsy trick"   "World-Wide
    Hunt for Martin Thorn," NYEJ, July 3, 1897.

66 "She is a decided liar. . . . Streuning buried a child of hers"   "Looks Black for the
    Midwife," NYH, July 2, 1897.

66 lost their own five-year-old daughter to diphtheria   NYP, July 1, 1897.

66 a servant girl who let burglars   "A Servant's Intelligence Suspected," NYEP,
    July 1, 1897.

66 a would-be parachute inventor   "Hung by One Foot in Midair," NYH, July 1,
    1897.

66 a severed black-stockinged leg   "Found a Woman's Leg," NYEJ, July 1, 1897.

66 the druggist who hanged himself   "Rope His Last Resort," Ibid.

66 "My name . . . is Sophie Miller"   "Mrs. Nack at the Bar of Justice," NYH,
    July 2, 1897.

67 Hearst's print room hastily jammed the two crucial words   "Mrs. Nack Will Be
    Charged with Murdering Guldensuppe," NYEJ, July 1, 1897.

67   *spent the afternoon working barbershops . . . over a shave*   Collins, *Homicide Squad*, 61.

68   *he'd quit on the spot last week*   NYH, July 2, 1897.

68   *"As soon as I saw . . . I thought right away of Thorn"*   NYW, July 2, 1897.

69   *a particular fondness, Keehn said, for widows*   NYH, July 2, 1897.

69   *"He used to laugh at Guldensuppe"*   NYW, July 2, 1897. NB: The dialogue in the remainder of this section is all drawn from this *World* account.

70   *his face prickling painfully*   Collins, *Homicide Squad*, 61.

9. THE DISAPPEARING SHOEMAKER

71   THE IDENTIFICATION UPSET   NYW, July 2, 1897.

71   World *reporters in turn humiliated Mrs. Riger*   NYW, July 2, 1897.

71   THE WORLD DESPERATE   NYEJ, July 2, 1897.

71   *One of Nack's neighbors signed . . . that Pulitzer had a $10,000 slush fund*   Ibid.

72   STILL TWENTY FOUR HOURS BEHIND THE NEWS   Ibid.

72   *reporters hired Mrs. Nack's surrey and horse*   "Murder Will Out," NYW, July 3, 1897.

72   *His name was Henry Wahle, and he lived in Woodside*   "Mrs. Nack's Confession," NYW, July 4, 1897.

72   *Mrs. DeBeuchelare's dairy*   Gregory, *Woodside*, 77.

72   *Mr. Jacobs kept that greenhouse*   Ibid., 75.

73   *Four Manhattan detectives marched*   NYW, July 4, 1897.

73   *A general store by the trolley stop*   Gregory, *Woodside*, 84.

73   *Greenpoint Avenue Hall . . . rube entertainments*   Gregory, *Woodside*, 89.

73   *fire chief and a coroner were convenient neighbors*   "Murder Traced in Duck Tracks," NYH, July 4, 1897.

73   *"Mrs. Hafftner," she introduced herself*   NYW, July 4, 1897.

74   *near one end of the block was the stop for the NY & Queens County trolley*   Copquin, *Neighborhoods of Queens*, 207.

74   *a dreary little house, coated in cheap brown paint*   NYH, July 4, 1897. NB: Second Street has since been renamed Fifty-Fifth Street; its northern intersection of "Anderson Avenue" is now Thirty-Seventh Avenue. The location of the cottage, based on a graphic from the September 20, 1897, NYEJ (which pinpoints the cottage), as well as a 1909 Bromley map of Queens (plate 13), would place the crime scene on the west side of Fifty-Fifth Street, roughly a quarter of a block south of the intersection with Thirty-Seventh Avenue. This side of Fifty-Fifth is now completely covered by warehouses; a single old house wedged in across the street is the sole indication that it was once a residential block.

74   *the remains of a man's shoe*   "Murder Still a Mystery," NYT, July 5, 1897.

75   *The bathroom . . . shaved samples off the floor*   NYW, July 4, 1897.

75   *scooped up a bucket of the mud*   NYT, July 4, 1897.

75   *Reporters were pouring over on the East River ferries*   Edwarde, *Guldensuppe Mystery*, 87.

75   *Something like—"Help! Help! Murder!"*   "Is Thorn in New York?" BE, July 4, 1897.

75   *"I clean my windows every Friday afternoon"*   Edwarde, *Guldensuppe Mystery*, 89.

76   *She'd only seen one come out*   "Dying Screams Heard by Three," NYH, July 5, 1897.

76   WORLD WIDE HUNT   NYEJ, July 3, 1897.

76 WANTED—*For the murder*   "Heard Murder Cried," *NYT,* July 4, 1897.
76 *NYU maintained its newly built Loomis Laboratory*   *Researches of the Loomis Laboratory,* 7.
77 *first guide to preserving crime-scene evidence*   Bell, *Crime and Circumstance,* 192.
77 *the first book on cadaver fauna*   Ibid., 216. NB: Specifically, the two books are Hans Gross's *Handbuch für Untersuchungsrichter als System der Kriminalistik* (1893) and Jean Pierre Mégnin's *La faune des cadavres* (1894).
77 *match the microscopic shells on a dead man's muddy boot*   Witthaus and Becker, *Medical Jurisprudence,* 353.
77 *A careful practitioner might even extract*   Ibid., 354.
77 *featured asphalt floors for easy hosing down*   *Researchers of the Loomis Laboratory,* 70.
77 *"Witthaus looks like a sea-lion"*   "Dr. Witthaus Found Deadly Poison," *NYW,* January 11, 1900.
77 *Carey had collared a physician . . . . Witthaus who'd gotten the goods*   Carey, *Memoirs,* 42.
78 *original handwritten manuscript*   "Witthaus Bought Copies as Real Art," *NYT,* July 16, 1916.
78 *Witthaus was battling an allegation of attempted murder*   *NYT,* January 24, 1898.
78 *There wasn't a speck of blood*   "Mrs. Nack's Oilcloth," *NYME,* July 2, 1897.
78 *saw and knife weren't even the right fit*   *NYME,* July 2, 1897.
78 *strategy had secured a conviction*   *NYET,* July 2, 1897.
78 *Byrnes had publicly dared Jack the Ripper*   Lardner and Reppetto, *NYPD,* 88.
79 *telltale viscera of dismemberment*   Flint, *Collected Essays,* vol. 2, 516.
79 *Buala was bustling around his wine shop*   *NYW,* July 4, 1897.
79 *"I do not remember these people"*   *NYW,* July 4, 1897. NB: The remainder of the dialogue in this section is drawn from this *World* account.
80 *same as in the "Fred" letters*   Ibid.
80 *It had been postmarked only yesterday*   "Den of Murderers Located," *NYP,* July 4, 1897.

10. THE SILENT CUSTOMER

81 *Detective J. J. O'Connell . . . . and his partner, Detective Boyle, were arriving in Queens*   "Dying Screams Heard by Three," *NYH,* July 5, 1897.
81 MURDER TRACED IN DUCK TRACKS   *NYH,* July 4, 1897.
81 THE HOUSE OF DEATH   *NYW,* July 4, 1897.
81 HAIR PULLING MATCH   *NYP,* July 4, 1897.
81 *Den of Murder*   Ibid.
82 *rumor had spread of a $1,000 bounty*   "Blood in the House of Mystery," *NYW,* July 5, 1897.
82 *constable struggled to keep the masses at bay*   Ibid.
82 *Nobody knew where to find the caretaker*   *NYH,* July 5, 1897.
82 *O'Connell and Boyle wrenched open a window*   Ibid.
82 *"Yes, that's the same rig"*   *NYW,* July 5, 1897.
82 *"That's the same carriage"*   Ibid.
82 *wine bottle*   "Mrs. Nack May Be Indicted," *NYT,* July 6, 1897.
82 *small cardboard bullet box*   "Queens County Wants Mrs. Nack," *NYEJ,* July 6, 1897.
83 *he'd worked as a plumber. . . . exposed and disassembled the plumbing*   "Murder Still a Mystery," *NYT,* July 5, 1897.

83 *a sea of children. More than a thousand of them*   *NYH*, July 5, 1897. NB: This remarkable figure is also given in the same day's *Evening Telegram*.

83 *cyclists were getting drunk and crashing wildly* . . . . *"Between drinks"*   *NYW*, July 5, 1897.

83 *water out from a spring in Trains Meadow*   Gregory, *Woodside*, 78.

83 *meter showed a whopping 40,000-gallon spike* . . . "The amount of water"   Edwarde, *Guldensuppe Mystery*, 92.

84 *"The legs . . . are not in the morgue"*   "Guldensuppe's Legs Gone," *NYTR*, July 6, 1897.

84 *"Guldensuppe has gained more fame"*   *NYH*, July 6, 1897.

84 *"One of the theories"*   *NYT*, July 6, 1897.

84 *"I desire"*   *NYP*, July 4, 1897.

84 *announced the recipients of his $1,000 reward*   "These Men Got the $1000," *NYEJ*, July 5, 1897.

85 *gouged a stain out of the floor*   *NYW*, July 5, 1897.

85 BLOOD IN THE HOUSE OF MYSTERY   Ibid.

85 *Teichmann test*   Wood, *Chemical and Microscopical Diagnosis*, 17.

85 *Mrs. Nack was beginning to waver*   *NYW*, July 4, 1897.

86 *Thorn, he assured the* Journal   "Heard Victim's Appeal," *NYEJ*, July 5, 1897.

86 *and the* Tribune   *NYTR*, July 6, 1897.

86 *he added to the* Press   "Thorn May Be Caught in Canada," *NYP*, July 5, 1897.

86 *and the Brooklyn Eagle*   "Is Thorn in New York?" *BE*, July 4, 1897.

86 *To the* Mail and Express, *he was "positive"*   "No News of Thorn," *NYME*, July 5, 1897.

86 *turned up later that evening in the morgue's pickling vat*   "Guldensuppe's Legs Vanish," *NYH*, July 6, 1897.

86 *logging one sunstroke case after another*   "Heat in the City," *NYW*, July 7, 1897.

86 *Louisville embezzler and a Brooklyn con man*   "Nack Hearing Postponed," *NYT*, July 7, 1897.

86 *A suicide found in a Jersey City*   *NYT*, July 5, 1897.

86 *body that veteran stage actor George Beane found*   Ibid.

87 IS THIS MARTIN THORN?   *NYT*, July 5, 1897.

87 *Pauline told a* Journal *reporter*   "Queens County Wants Mrs. Nack," *NYEJ*, July 6, 1897.

87 World *reporters located Thorn's older brother*   "Saw Thorn on Wednesday," *NYW*, July 6, 1897.

88 *last confirmed sighting of Thorn was by a moving company*   *NYW*, July 6, 1897.

88 *woman in the Detective Bureau's office*   "Thorn Has Confessed to the Murder," *NYEJ*, July 7, 1897.

88 *detectives waited impatiently at the 125th Street El station*   *NYEJ*, July 7, 1897.

88 *"I can't go back on a friend"*   *NYEJ*, July 7, 1897.

88 *uttered a single word: "Haircut"*   "Martin Thorn Is a Prisoner," *NYH*, July 7, 1897.

88 *shed his usual brown derby for a white fedora and shaved*   Edwarde, *Guldensuppe Mystery*, 96.

89 *quarter past nine that night*   *NYH*, July 7, 1897.

89 *Spear's Drug Store ruled the busy Harlem corner*   *NYW*, July 7, 1897.

89 *Spear himself was manning the till, and his clerk Maurice*   "Martin Thorn Is Captured," *NYW*, July 7, 1897.

89 *the real profits, which lay in the slot telephone*   *American Druggist and Pharmaceutical Record* 31 (1897): 113.

89 *city after city on the East Coast was reporting relentless heat*   "The Whole Country Overheated," *NYW*, July 7, 1897.

89 *Laborers in soiled overalls*   *NYH*, July 7, 1897.
90 *"Let's go take a drink"*   *NYEJ*, July 7, 1897.
90 It's a holdup, *Maurice frantically signaled*   *NYW*, July 7, 1897.
90 *"I am Martin Thorn."* . . . *"And I am Inspector O'Brien"*   Edwarde, *Guldensuppe Mystery*, 109.

11. A CASE OF LIFE AND DEATH

93 *"I've thought so for five minutes"*   "Thorn Indicted with Mrs. Nack," *NYP*, July 9, 1897.
93 *Along with the .32 revolver, a closer search*   "Indicted for the Murder," *NYT*, July 9, 1897.
93 *O'Brien, McCauley, and Price, along with*   *NYH*, July 7, 1897.
93 *They reached Houston and Bowery just after ten p.m.*   *NYH*, July 7, 1897.
94 *AN ELECTRICAL EXECUTION*   *NYEP*, July 6, 1897.
94 *A plainclothes scrum double-marched Thorn*   *NYH*, July 7, 1897.
94 *they'd been scraped by forensics*   "Thorn Murdered Guldensuppe," *BE*, July 7, 1897.
94 *Witthaus himself had come*   "Thorn's Friend Betrays Him," *NYW*, July 8, 1897.
94 *Thorn's body had been scrupulously measured*   "Thorn Says He Alone Is Guilty," *NYH*, July 9, 1897.
95 *Bertillon's wondrous anthropometric system*   Houck, *Forensic Science*, 26.
95 *India had adopted a new system*   Cole, *Suspect Identities*, 87.
95 *inspector worked quietly at his desk, saying nothing for hours*   *NYH*, July 7, 1897.
95 *Thorn's gaze fell upon the piles of letters*   *NYW*, July 8, 1897.
95 *"I at present live in a furnished room"*   *NYH*, July 9, 1897. NB: The remainder of this scene's conversation is from this *Herald* account.
97 *four in the morning, when O'Brien finally let his prisoner collapse*   *NYW*, July 8, 1897.
97 That's him   Ibid.
97 *"Looks pretty bad."* . . . *"I don't fear death"*   Ibid.
97 *"Hit him!"*   "Gartha [*sic*] Tells of the Murder," *NYH*, July 8, 1897. The remainder of the description of Gotha's ruse is drawn from the *Herald* account.
98 *"I first met Thorn nine years ago"*   "Thorn Warns Mrs. Nack in Court," *NYEJ*, July 9, 1897.
99 *"old—prematurely old"*   Rheta Childe Dorr, "The Prodigal Daughter," *Hampton's Magazine* 24 (1910): 526.
99 *"He had the look of a man going to the electric chair"*   *NYH*, July 9, 1897.
99 *"I met him at a saloon"*   Edwarde, *Guldensuppe Mystery*, 100.
100 *"He nearly severed the head"*   Ibid., 103.
100 *"It's done"*   *NYH*, July 8, 1897.
101 *"He told her"*   Edwarde, *Guldensuppe Mystery*, 103.
101 *With hot water running at full blast*   *NYW*, July 8, 1897.
101 *"As the boat neared the slip"*   Edwarde, *Guldensuppe Mystery*, 105.
101 *He fretted that he hadn't shaved*   "Lured to His Death," *NYME*, July 7, 1897.
101 *"I saw by newspaper reports"*   "Gartha Tells of the Murder," *NYH*, July 8, 1897.
102 *"Mr. Gotha, I do not want to detain you"*   "Thorn Says He Alone Is Guilty," *NYH*, July 9, 1897.
102 *"'I wish to God I had not told you'"*   Edwarde, *Guldensuppe Mystery*, 106.
102 *he'd instantly understood what it meant*   *NYEJ*, July 9, 1897.

12. HEADS OR TAILS

103 *"Going fishing?"*   "Mrs. Nack Sees Martin Thorn," *NYET,* July 9, 1897.

103 *These were naphtha boats*   *NYEJ,* July 8, 1897.

103 *grapplers, salvagers who worked the docks*   "How the Grappler Earns His Bread," *NYT,* May 5, 1901.

103 *A couple of dozen grapplers . . . on six launches*   *NYEJ,* July 8, 1897.

103 *"Three cheers for Guldensuppe!"*   "Still Seeking the Head," *NYT,* July 12, 1897.

103 *Captain Schultz . . . was in a droll mood*   *NYET,* July 9, 1897.

103 *"Heads you win, tails you lose!"*   Ibid.

104 *"These men know how to find"*   *NYEJ,* July 8, 1897.

104 *Street urchins were stripping off . . . diving among the rakes*   Ibid.

104 *The riverbed was a good twenty-five feet*   "Diver Hunts Head," *NYW,* July 9, 1897.

104 *"Something's caught!"*   Ibid.

104 William E. Chapman . . . *came chugging up*   Ibid.

104 *already run an operation with hooks*   "Valise and Clothes of the Murdered Man Found," *NYJ,* June 29, 1897.

104 *veteran deep-sea diver Charles Olsen*   *NYW,* July 9, 1897.

105 *all they were pulling up were stones and tin cans*   "Mrs. Nack Faces Martin Thorn," *NYP,* July 10, 1897.

105 *130 feet of rubber hose to Olsen's diving suit*   *NYW,* July 9, 1897.

105 *The door of the narrow three-story brick boardinghouse*   *NYEJ,* July 7, 1897. NB: The remainder of this scene is drawn from this *Evening Journal* account, except for the quote that follows.

106 *"Do you recognize me?"*   *NYH,* July 8, 1897.

107 *copy after copy of murder coverage*   "Lured to His Death," *NYME,* July 7, 1897.

107 *from the* World   *NYW,* July 7, 1897.

107 *the* Journal   NYEJ, July 7, 1897.

107 *the* Herald   *NYH,* July 8, 1897.

107 *"My God!" was gleefully illustrated*   *NYEJ,* July 7, 1897.

107 *witnessed them discovering a bullet hole*   *NYEJ,* July 8, 1897.

107 *"Blood Spots on Martin Thorn's Undershirt"*   *NYEJ,* July 8, 1897.

107 *"the* Evening Journal*'s pen and pencil"*   Editorial, Ibid.

107 *"a nail made the bullet hole"*   *NYW,* July 9, 1897.

108 *Thorn did indeed resemble a man who'd walked up to Dr. O'Hanlon*   Ibid.

108 Herald *had been the city's colossus, with a circulation of more than 190,000*   Reel, *The National Police Gazette and the Making of the Modern American Man,* 48.

108 *1874 hoax claiming escaped circus tigers*   Ibid.

108 *Thorn pondering aloud how one might lure*   *NYH,* July 9, 1897.

109 *reduced to profiling the Woodside duck*   "Thorn Said to Have Confessed," *NYP,* July 8, 1897.

109 *detectives marched into the* World *offices*   *NYW,* July 9, 1897.

109 *Mr. Valentine's turnip giveaway*   "Turnips Free for All," Ibid.

110 *Old-timers . . . recalled "the Kelsey Outrage"*   *NYEJ,* July 9, 1897.

110 *no jury had been able to convict*   *NYT,* "The Kelsey Murder Mystery," November 6, 1876.

110 *"as dead as Kelsey's nuts"*   Carol Richards, "The Kelsey Outrage Gets More Outrageous," *Newsday,* February 3, 2001.

110 *assistant DA had been busy insisting . . . didn't particularly need Guldensuppe's head*   "Mrs. Nack Warns Thorn in Court," *NYH,* July 10, 1897.

111   *he couldn't recognize Nack and Thorn . . . detectives grumbled, he feared a conviction*
"Mrs. Nack May Be Indicted," *NYT,* July 6, 1897.

111   *attempted to keep the coroner from touching his precious baseboards*   *NYW,* July 8,
1897.

13. QUEEN OF THE TOMBS

112   *Intended for a city of 300,000 . . . now served 1.8 million*   "Tombs an Unfit
Prison," *NYT,* June 29, 1895.

112   *throwing the stairways akimbo, and letting sewage ooze*   Gilfoyle, "America's
Greatest Criminal Barrister," 528.

112   *tin plates perched on the rim of a malodorous toilet*   "A Disgrace to the City of
New York," *Annual Report of the Prison Association,* 79.

113   *murmur passed among the inmates . . .* "It's Mrs. Nack!"   "Thorn Warns Mrs.
Nack in Court," *NYEJ,* July 9, 1897.

113   *Dressed in a black coat and a straw boater*   "Mrs. Nack Sees Martin Thorn,"
NYET, July 9, 1897.

113   *"Come on up the bridge, Thorn"*   *NYEJ,* July 9, 1897.

113   *stubble, the result of a suicide watch*   *NYET,* July 9, 1897.

113   *"Have you any counsel?"*   *NYEJ,* July 9, 1897.

114   *"We appear for Mrs. Thorn"*   "Mrs. Nack Meets Thorn in Court," *NYW,*
July 10, 1897.

114   "Schweige still"   *NYEJ,* July 9, 1897.

114   "Halt den Mund und Spricht nicht!"   "Im Anklagezustand," *NYSZ,* July
10, 1897.

114   *"Mrs. Nack and Martin Thorn Refuse to Talk"*   Signed editorial, *NYEJ,* July
13, 1897.

114   The Guldensuppe Mystery. . . . *hit the streets just days later*   Edwarde, *Guldensuppe Mystery.* NB: The Library of Congress's copy of *The Guldensuppe Mystery* bears a Received stamp of July 24, 1897. The last dated event noted in the
text is July 8, so the book was completed, printed, and shipped to Washington,
D.C., within this astonishingly short interval.

115   *Lower East Side summer-school teacher . . . turned into a mock trial*   "Murder
Trial in School," *NYT,* July 24, 1897.

115   *masseurs were now slyly referred to as "Gieldensuppers"*   "A Gieldensupper Arrested," *NYS,* September 14, 1897.

115   *"That's not Thorn the police got!"*   "The Question of Jurisdiction," *NYTR,*
July 18, 1897.

115   THE MURDER OF WILLIAM GULDENSUPPE   Advertisement, *NYT,* July 18, 1897.

115   *one of the city's most popular tourist destinations . . . a top-floor workshop that
could whip up a body within twenty-four hours*   Dennett, *Weird and Wonderful,* 115.

115   *the Chess Automaton . . . a Klondike gold-rush mining camp*   "Notes of the
Stage," *NYTR,* July 25, 1897.

116   *Woodside Horror*   *NYTR,* July 25, 1897.

116   *"Your face possesses a charm"*   *NYW,* July 7, 1897.

116   *"I'm no freak," Nrs, Nack snapped*   "Howe's Move for Thorn and Mrs. Nack's
Novel Charity," *NYW,* July 16, 1897.

116   *Thorn passed the days in cells #29 and #30*   "Dredging for the Head Hopeless," *NYEJ,* July 10, 1897.

116   *tutoring cell mates in pinochle*   "Martin Thorn's School for Card Players,"
NYEJ, July 14, 1897.

117   *Boylan . . . so weighted down with stolen silverware*   "John Boylan Laden Down with Silver," *NYEJ*, July 8, 1897.

117   THE HORRIBLE MURDER IN NEW YORK   *Aberdeen Weekly* (Scotland), July 9, 1897.

117   *Japan and Spain were considering an alliance*   "Japan and Spain May Be Allies," *NYP*, July 16, 1897.

117   *reports of massive strikes by coal miners*   "Strike Battle on Ohio River," *NYH*, July 9, 1897.

117   *his own starring role . . . he'd miss the city elections*   "Thorn's Vanity Betrayed Him," *NYW*, December 5, 1897.

117   *businessman named Horton. . . . "Where's the head?"*   "Thorn and Mrs. Nack in Court," *NYTR*, July 22, 1897.

117   *"The new industry of finding William Guldensuppe's head"*   "Guldensuppe's Head," *NYH*, July 14, 1897.

118   *mystically body-homing loaves of black bread*   "Says Tombs Fare Makes Her Ill," *NYP*, July 13, 1897.

118   *an intrepid* Herald *reporter to discover why*   *NYH*, July 14, 1897.

118   *Three more boys spotted a head floating*   "Italian Boys Find a Head," *NYT*, July 27, 1897.

118   *"decomposed mass" frightened passing ferry passengers*   "A Head, Not Guldensuppe's," *NYT*, September 2, 1897.

118   *A grisly find made in an Upper West Side boardinghouse*   "Not Guldensuppe's Skull," *NYTR*, July 20, 1897.

118   *girl from Woodside found an actual chunk*   "Guldensuppe Death Mask," *NYT*, September 20, 1897.

118   *Woodside child promptly discovered a brown derby*   *BE*, September 22, 1897.

118   *"Woodside is undergoing a boom in the agricultural line"*   "Yellow Sleuth's Work," *NYS*, September 23, 1897.

119   *Allegations emerged that* someone . . . *had paid a couple of local utility workers*   *BE*, September 22, 1897.

119   *more than half a million in circulation*   "It Breaks All Records," *NYEJ*, August 23, 1897.

119   *Perrin H. Sumner . . . "the Great American Identifier"*   "Habeas Corpus for Martin Thorn," *NYH*, July 16, 1897.

119   *nearly bankrupted an Indiana college*   Branigan, *History of Johnson County*, 293.

119   *run Florida real estate swindles*   "Perrin H. Sumner Sued," *NYT*, November 13, 1907.

119   *fleeced would-be fiancées*   "Perrin H. Sumner Dies in the Subway," *NYT*, March 20, 1914.

119   *passed off worthless mining stock*   "Telegraphic Brevities," *Harvard Crimson*, May 18, 1883.

119   *descended on the Bellevue morgue to identify an unclaimed suicide*   *NYW*, February 1, 1892.

120   *professor spent July embarrassingly tied up in divorce proceedings*   "Professor Witthaus Must Pay It," *NYTR*, August 3, 1897.

120   *human blood, he declared*   "Human Blood Stains," *BE*, August 23, 1897.

120   *a whopping dredging bill*   "Police Board Meeting," *NYT*, August 19, 1897.

120   *O'Brien lost his own: He was relieved of his post*   "Sleuth O'Brien Bounced," *NYS*, August 31, 1897.

120   *"I have been described in a paper as a 'murderess'"*   "Mrs. Nack Talks Freely to the World," *NYW*, August 6, 1897. NB: The remainder of this scene is drawn from this *World* account of the interview.

14. THE HIGH ROLLER

123   *Mitchell hastily sent for a stenographer*   "Nack's Awful Charge Against His Wife," *NYW*, September 3, 1897.

123   *"She said lots of bad things"*   Ibid.

123   *They were joined by Detective Samuel Price*   Ibid.

124   *"My wife left me in 1896"*   "Murders by Scores Laid to Mrs. Nack," *NYEJ*, September 2, 1897. NB: All but the last line of remaining dialogue in this section is from this *Evening Journal* account.

124   *Dr. Weiss of Tenth Avenue . . . F. W. Werner, quietly assisted*   "Says the Accused Out-Heroded Herod," *NYEJ*, September 3, 1897.

125   *"There is something at the back of that"*   *NYW*, September 3, 1897.

125   *"It's a lie!" . . . "Fool!"*   *NYEJ*, September 3, 1897.

126   SAYS THE ACCUSED MURDERESS OUT-HERODED HEROD   *NYW*, September 3, 1897.

126   *so was the death of John Gotha's ninety-five-year-old father-in-law*   "Mrs. Nack Gains Time," *NYW*, July 13, 1897.

126   *Dr. Weiss claimed to have no idea . . . nor did Mrs. Nack's landlord*   *NYW*, September 3, 1897.

126   *Alois Palm tried rather unsportingly*   *NYEJ*, September 3, 1897.

126   *Even Mrs. Nack's friends faulted her*   "Mrs. Nack's Neighbors," *NYW*, July 4, 1897.

126   *"she was a high roller"*   *NYEJ*, September 3, 1897.

127   *Guldensuppe had kept Gussie from leaving*   *NYW*, September 3, 1897.

127   *Mrs. Nack had gone to one Ernest Moring . . . hire him to kill her ex-husband*   "*Journal* Completes Case Against Martin Thorn," *NYEJ*, September 4, 1897.

128   World *reporter ascended the rickety stairs*   "Diploma Mills for Midwives," *NYW*, September 18, 1897.

128   A SCHOOL FOR BARBARITY   *NYW*, September 22, 1897.

128   DIPLOMA MILL FOR MIDWIVES   *NYW*, September 18, 1897.

128   *"Out of 55,000 live births"*   *NYW*, September 3, 1897.

128   *suspicions ran strong that "Madame Restell". . . . had dumped her body*   Reel, *The National Police Gazette and the Making of the Modern Man*, 38.

128   *designated villainess both for moralizing* Herald *journalists and for the American Medical Association*   Srebnick, *Mysterious Death of Mary Rogers*, 86.

128   *state criminalized abortion soon afterward*   Ibid., 85.

128   *laws made it illegal to even discuss*   Brodie, *Contraception and Abortion*, 257.

128   *The better practitioners were often immigrants*   Ibid., 228.

129   *"Their methods are so hidden"*   *NYW*, September 3, 1897.

129   WOMEN FARM, MEN COOK   *NYW*, August 2, 1897.

129   SHE'S PRETTY, EVEN IF SHE IS A LAWYER   *NYJ*, October 17, 1897.

129   *"Really . . . the newspapers are becoming"*   *NYH*, August 9, 1841, quoted in Stashower, *Beautiful Cigar Girl*, epigraph.

129   *another indictment had just been handed down*   "Indicted in Queens," *NYW*, September 16, 1897.

130   *handed over to Undersheriff Baker . . . and slipped out the Leonard Street exit*   "Taken to L.I. City Jail," *BE*, September 16, 1897.

130   *One thousand New Yorkers were waiting*   "Mrs. Nack and Thorn in New Cells," *NYS*, September 17, 1897.

130   *He'd become used to the sound of pile drivers and hammers*   "Nack . . . Cottage" (title partly destroyed), *NYEJ*, September 17, 1897.

130   *"I rented the Woodside cottage"*   Mrs. Nack's Window of Spectres, *NYEJ*, September 4, 1897.

130 *blurted out to* Journal *reporter Lowe Shearon* "Justice's Bar," *NYEJ*, September 15, 1897.

131 *"That is all rot"* *NYEJ*, September 4, 1897.

131 *Mrs. Nack had pulled an upper-floor unit* *NYEJ*, September 14, 1897.

131 World *sent . . . Harriet Hubbard Ayer* "Mrs. Nack's Own Story of the Killing of Guldensuppe," *NYW*, October 3, 1897.

131 *Ayer was a household name . . . whose cosmetics empire had fallen apart* "Mrs. Harriet Ayer Dead," *Chicago Daily Tribune*, November 26, 1903.

131 "Must I be locked in?" *NYW*, October 3, 1897. NB: The remainder of this section is drawn from this *World* account.

15. KLONDIKE WILLIE

134 *Rockaway Ed was a trusty. . . . second only to a "bum boss"* "Dist. Att'y Youngs Says Journal Gives the Last Link of Evidence," *NYJA*, October 7, 1897. NB: Rockaway Ed's dealings with Nack and the *Journal*, although repeated to some degree in other newspapers, is drawn from this *Journal* account.

135 *writers and artists at the ready to make a copy* "Mrs. Nack's Strange Letter to Thorn Captured by the Jailers," *NYJA*, October 6, 1897.

135 *the text that would appear in the next morning's paper . . .* "Dear Martin" *NYJA*, October 6, 1897.

137 *"Where is it?" Sheriff Doht demanded* *NYJA* October 6, 1897.

137 *The fragments bearing Thorn's writing were reassembled. . . .* "My dear" *NYJA*, October 7, 1897.

138 *The watch on Thorn's cell was instantly doubled* "Mrs. Nack Has Lost Hope," *NYT*, October 7, 1897.

138 *"I am sorry." DA Youngs sighed* *NYJA*, October 7, 1897.

138 *He had tried to induce vomiting . . . hung a picture of a man's disembodied head* "The Soup Was Too Rich," *NYTR*, October 8, 1897.

138 *Mrs. Nack also tried denying the note* "Nack and Thorn Plan Suicide," *NYH*, October 7, 1897.

139 *the block of brick tenements past the corner of Forty-Second and Tenth* *Annual Report of the Committee on the Fire Patrol*, 108. NB: All the details of this block except for the mattress shop are drawn from this source.

139 *Mssr. Mauborgne's Mattress Renovating* *NYT*, classifieds, June 13, 1897.

139 *Where's Guldensuppe's head?* "Thorn's Brother-in-Law Sunk the Missing Head," *NYJ*, October 12, 1897.

139 *tantalizing story: that one Frank Clark had heard a boozy confession* *NYW*, October 6, 1897.

140 *"He often boasted," Clark recalled* *NYJ*, October 12, 1897.

140 *visit to the ailing forger by the district attorney* *NYW*, October 6, 1897.

140 Journal *came piling into Menker's hallway* *YJ*, October 12, 1897.

141 *letter had arrived in Coroner Hoeber's office* "Did Thorn Admit Murder?" *BE*, August 6, 1897.

141 My dear sir: I cannot "Hoeber Jumped on Friend," *NYTR*, July 8, 1897.

142 *One claimed that it was* Guldensuppe *who'd been hiding* "Another Guldensuppe Letter," *NYT*, August 17, 1897.

142 *At least two more claimed that Guldensuppe was alive* "Letters to Hoeber," *BE*, August 9, 1897; and "Guldensuppe or Edwards?" *NYT*, August 10, 1897.

142 *"I have always believed that he had gone to Europe"* "Martin Thorn Has Hope," *NYW*, August 5, 1897.

142 Kindly do not believe any of the cards *NYT,* August 10, 1897.

142 *Yet another missive, sent by Mrs. Lenora Merrifield* "Guldensuppe Case Stirs Up Cranks," *NYEJ,* August 13, 1897.

142 Guldensuppe is alive, and taking revenge on Thorn *BE,* August 9, 1897.

143 *"The police do not expect to see Guldensuppe"* W. R. Hearst, editorial, *NYEJ,* July 3, 1897.

143 *Evangelina Cisneros, the pretty eighteen-year-old daughter. . . . Hearst preferred the latter explanation* Ibid., 317.

143 *another* Journal *operative—the hotshot reporter Karl Decker—to Cuba* Whyte, *Uncrowned King, 325.*

143 *Disguised with a sailor's outfit and a cigar* Ibid., 328.

143 *EVANGELINA CISNEROS RESCUED BY THE JOURNAL* *NYJ,* October 10, 1897.

143 *A NEW IDEA IN JOURNALISM* *NYEJ,* October 3, 1897.

143 *offensives against a gas trust and crooked paving contractors* Procter, *William Randolph Hearst,* 101.

144 *"Every one will sympathize with the* Journal's *enterprise"* Whyte, *Uncrowned King,* 330.

144 *"The newspapers of your country"* Creelman, *On the Great Highway,* 187.

144 *"It is epochal"* W. R. Hearst, editorial, *NYJA,* October 13, 1897.

144 *a fine profusion of ads . . . the Lady Push Ball Players* advertisement, *NYEJ,* September 4, 1897.

144 *"Organize a great open-air reception"* Creelman, *On the Great Highway,* 171.

144 *Rooms were hired at the Waldorf, reservations made at Delmonico's* Whyte, *Uncrowned King,* 332.

145 "scooped every day of its existence" Ibid.

145 *THE PAPER SUFFERS AN EXCESSIVE STATESMANSHIP* telegram, October 27, 1897. Pulitzer Papers, container 2.

145 *firing of a reporter for using the word "pregnant"* Morris, *Pulitzer,* 379.

145 *MAKE SALARIED ARTISTS* telegram, November 16, 1897. Pulitzer Papers, container 2.

145 *I REALLY DON'T EXPECT TO BE IN NEW YORK* telegram, October 29, 1897, ibid.

145 *Brisbane, who jumped ship for the* Journal Morris, *Pulitzer,* 334.

145 *Brooklyn Eagle . . . a curious development in Germany* *BE,* October 13, 1897.

145 *"reputable merchants of Hamburg," were departing for New York* *BE,* October 15, 1897.

145 *GULDENSUPPE ALIVE?* *BE,* October 14, 1897.

16. CORPUS DELICTI

149 *A thick fog blanketed the Hudson* *NYT,* November 6, 1897.

149 *"The* Fürst Bismarck *has been sighted"* "Looks in Vain for Mrs. Nack," *NYEJ,* November 5, 1897.

149 *Hamilton Fish was on board* "A Young Wheelman Hurt," *NYT,* November 6, 1897.

149 *one Josephine Vanderhoff had turned up* "No Bail for Martin Thorn," *BE,* July 19, 1897.

149 *Edwards's minister visited to view the pickled* "Didn't Know Guldensuppe," *NYT,* August 28, 1897.

150 *they immediately identified the abandoned valise* "Edward's Satchel Murray Says," *NYTR,* August 29, 1897.

150 *explain the enigmatically marked-up slates* "Murrays Identify Valise," *NYT,* August 29, 1897.

150 *daughter examined the corpse's hands*   Ibid.
150 *Chicago trial had concluded for the infamous sausage-maker Adolph Luetgert*   *NYT,* October 22, 1897.
150 *nothing but five bone fragments*   "On These Five Bones Hang Luetgert's Fate," *NYEJ,* October 10, 1897.
150 *Thorn eagerly read the wire reports*   *NYEJ,* November 5, 1897.
150 *No Carl and Julius Peterson were listed*   "Ready for the Thorn Trial," *NYTR,* November 7, 1897.
151 *Open twenty-four hours a day*   Rovere, *Howe & Hummel,* 126.
151 *When seventy-eight brothel madams were arrested*   Ibid., 6.
151 *loud green and violet waistcoats*   Ibid., 16.
151 *defended 650 murder and manslaughter cases*   Ibid., 5.
151 *"You cannot prove a* corpus delicti"   *NYW,* October 12, 1897.
151 *DA's office laughed Howe off*   *NYT,* July 13, 1897.
151 *The notion had originated with Lord Chief Justice Sir Matthew Hale*   "Proof of the Corpus Delicti Aliunde the Defendant's Confession," 639.
151 *revived in America in 1819 after the Boorn brothers case*   Ibid., 646.
151 *combination safe filled with coal*   Rovere, *Howe & Hummel,* 25.
151 *staff amused themselves by serving one another*   Ibid., 27.
151 *they'd found nothing in the desks*   Ibid.
152 *"I cannot see how the District Attorney can get around the identification"*   "Mrs. Nack Offers to Confess All," *NYW,* October 12, 1897.
152 *Danish preacher Soren Qvist*   Warren, *Famous Cases,* 14. NB: Warren's account of Soren Qvist, along with a number of nearly identical ones published in English in the late nineteenth century, is curiously lacking in specific dates—and may indeed be drawing its information from an earlier Danish fictionalization of the case, the 1829 novel *The Rector of Veilbye.* That tale, though, is drawn from an apparently factual account of a 1626 case.
152 *"Then there was the Ruloff case"*   "Dredging for the Head Hopeless," *NYEJ,* October 7, 1897.
152 *two hapless detectives on the next steamer to Hamburg*   Carey, *Memoirs,* 51.
152 *secretly paying a witness to move to Japan*   Rovere, *Howe & Hummel,* 51.
152 *blaming a stabbing on the man's four-year-old daughter*   Ibid., 69.
152 *"Well . . . when you see Guldensuppe walk"*   "Thorn's Victim Rebuilt," *NYEJ,* July 23, 1897.
152 *carpenters added extra benches*   "Heavy Demand for Seats," *BE,* November 7, 1897.
153 *They'd spent nearly two hours shifting tables*   *BE,* November 7, 1897.
153 *he had a table custom-built for the case*   *NYEJ,* November 5, 1897.
153 *galleries were saved for sketch artists*   "Ready for the Thorn Trial," *NYTR,* November 7, 1897.
153 *Sheriff Doht was flooded with ticket requests*   *NYEJ,* November 5, 1897.
153 *being converted into a newsroom*   *BE,* November 7, 1897.
153 *housewives . . . hung Room for Rent signs*   *NYEJ,* November 5, 1897.
154 COURT TO PRINTING PRESS   *NYEJ,* November 6, 1897.
154 *prosecution of a recent Columbia graduate*   "College Man Confesses Crime," *NYW,* November 9, 1897.
154 *murder trial of a man who gunned down a police officer*   "Traced by a Time-piece," Ibid.
154 *husband driven mad by his wife's incessant whistling*   "Whistling Drove Him Mad," Ibid.
155 *"Martin Thorn is the same as any other man"*   Editorial, *NYEJ,* November 9, 1897.

155 *"Every day there will be some fifty different pictures of scenes"*   "Murder Pictures," *NYT,* November 7, 1897.

155 *hundreds of potential jurors . . . waited*   "Five Jurors to Try Thorn for His Life," *NYEJ,* November 8, 1897.

155 *Harriet Ayers was easy to spot . . . as was novelist Julian Hawthorne*   "Thorn on Trial," *NYP,* November 9, 1897.

155 *gray-haired janitor shuffled up*   *NYEJ,* November 8, 1897.

155 *police captain read that morning's newspaper*   "Thorn's Counsel Happy," *BE,* November 9, 1897.

155 *district attorney was balding and bespectacled, wearing an off-the-rack suit*   "The Trial of Martin Thorn," *NYCA,* November 8, 1897.

156 *"He's dead"*   *NYEJ,* November 8, 1897. NB: With the following exception, the remainder of this scene is drawn from this account.

156 *lottery wheel with slips of paper bearing jury-pool names*   "Thorn's Trial Opens," *NYME,* November 8, 1897.

157 *"That is not Mr. Blomquist"*   "Thorn's Jury Selected," *NYT,* November 9, 1897.

157 *"How long have you lived in this country?"*   *NYEJ,* November 8, 1897.

157 *they had interviewed Blomquist*   "Thorn's Life Is in the Balance," *NYH,* November 9, 1897.

157 *"Have you an opinion"*   *NYEJ,* November 8, 1897.

158 *"I think he's guilty"*   *NYT,* November 9, 1897.

158 *Another two men confessed that they were over seventy*   *NYH,* November 9, 1897.

158 *the judge had to empty the room out twice*   *NYT,* November 9, 1897.

158 *a bell rang out lunchtime*   *NYEJ,* November 8, 1897.

158 *all the local establishments were out of food within minutes*   *NYH,* November 9, 1897.

158 *peremptory challenges, he admitted to reporters, were following a pattern*   "The Thorn Jury Completed," *NYTR,* November 9, 1897.

158 *"I'm going at every talesman with extreme care"*   *NYH,* November 8, 1897.

159 *first approved juror was a retired oysterman named Jacob Bumstead*   *NYT,* November 9, 1897.

159 *appeared to be counting the gaslights*   *NYEJ,* November 8, 1897.

159 *"Thorn is a very average specimen"*   "Martin Thorn's Trial Begun, with Singular Celerity," *NYW,* November 9, 1897.

159 *They had run through sixty-four candidates*   *NYH,* November 9, 1897.

159 Press *journalist had wickedly spread the rumor*   "Thorn on Trial," *NYP,* November 9, 1897.

159 *"This . . . is magnificent"*   "Testimony Begun in Trial of Thorn," *BE,* November 9, 1897.

17. COVERED IN BLOOD

160 *Long Island Rail Road's special jury car*   *NYH,* November 9, 1897.

160 *held ordinary jobs*   "Link by Link Thorn's Chain Is Forged," *NYEJ,* November 9, 1897.

160 *a warning sign from the sheriff*   "Thorn on Trial," *NYP,* November 9, 1897.

160 *The farmers had stayed up . . . playing cards*   *NYH,* November 9, 1897.

160 *puzzling over the newfangled electrical switches*   "Thorn in the State's Toils," *NYH,* November 10, 1897.

161 *janitor was still sweeping out clouds of dust*   *NYEJ,* November 9, 1897.

161 *precious white slips that read "PASS ONE"* "Life Against Life, Lie Against Lie," *NYW*, November 11, 1897.

161 *only just gotten over a neck rash* *NYEJ*, November 9, 1897.

161 *flower in Howe's lapel* *BE*, November 9, 1897.

161 *"About a half-pint of diamonds"* "Thorn Jury Discharged," *NYT*, November 13, 1897.

161 Herald *man was keeping track of the betting pools* *NYH*, November 10, 1897.

161 *anonymous note that warned* Ibid.

161 *sitting with a handkerchief atop his bald head* *NYH*, November 9, 1897.

161 "Hear ye! Hear ye!" "Rapidly Nearing the Supreme Test," *NYET*, November 9, 1897.

161 *"This is one of the most remarkable crimes"* *NYH*, November 10, 1897. NB: The remainder of this section is primarily drawn from the *Herald*'s transcription.

162 *air in the room had already grown foul again* *BE*, November 9, 1897.

163 *picked out some friends of his in the gallery* *NYT*, November 9, 1897.

163 *signing autographs at just fifty cents a pop* . . . The Headless Body Murder Mystery *NYET*, November 9, 1897. NB: This is title #771 (1897) from the very popular Old Cap. Collier dime-novel series. Dime novels were only haphazardly preserved, so that there is currently only one known surviving copy, at the University of Texas at Austin.

163 *"Where were you shortly after 1 o'clock"* *NYEJ*, November 9, 1897.

163 *"like a ghastly pack of cards"* "Mrs. Nack Has Confessed," *NYT*, November 10, 1897.

164 *"Is this the part of the body found by you?"* *NYEJ*, November 9, 1897.

164 One Telegram *writer dryly observed* *NYET*, November 9, 1897.

164 *"He is a good little boy"* "Mrs. Nack Has Confessed the Murder," *NYW*, November 10, 1897.

164 *"Was there any one else there"* *NYEJ*, November 9, 1897. NB: The remainder of this section is drawn from this *Evening Journal* account, except as noted.

165 *corner seat in the jury box was right next to the exhibit table* "Mrs. Nack Has Confessed the Murder," *NYH*, November 11, 1897.

165 *looked like he was about to turn green* "The Thorn Jury Completed," *NYTR*, November 9, 1897.

166 *Isaac Newton . . . failed to see anything funny* *NYT*, November 10, 1897.

166 *"Did you see these three portions together"* *NYW*, November 10, 1897. NB: The remainder of this section is drawn from this account, except for the Aimee Smith exchange noted below.

168 *"Do you remember the case of . . . Aimee Smith?"* *NYH*, November 10, 1897.

168 *first four pages of tonight's issue would be devoted to the case* *NYEJ*, November 9, 1897.

169 *Spanish overture to President McKinley* "Cabinet Like Spain's Reply," *NYT*, November 10, 1897.

169 *vote by the Georgia legislature* "Voted 91 to 3 Against Football," *NYP*, November 9, 1897.

169 *"Dynamite Dick" had been gunned down* "Dynamite Dick Shot Dead," *NYT*, November 10, 1897.

169 *"Interest in the case is not wholly"* *BE*, November 9, 1897.

169 *"We will disprove"* *NYEJ*, November 9, 1897.

169 *betting on Thorn now ran at roughly even odds* *NYH*, November 10, 1897.

169 *Barberi had been the first woman ever sentenced* *NYT*, July 16, 1895.

169 *already been turned into a Broadway play* Morgan and Van Doren, *Italian Americans*, 320.

169   *Barberi was a free woman, sitting in the gallery right beside the lawyer*   "Mrs. Nack Saw Thorn with a Dirk Knife," *NYEJ*, November 10, 1897.

170   *"What are you doing here, anyway?"*   *NYW*, November 10, 1897.

18. CAUGHT IN THE HEADLIGHT

171   *Mrs. Nack's lawyer was followed*   *NYH*, November 10, 1897.

171   *a melodrama set in Chinatown*   "The First Born a Hit," *NYT*, October 6, 1897.

171   *Friend walking purposefully away, leaving before*   *NYH*, November 10, 1897.

172   *wake up everyone from Captain O'Brien*   *NYT*, November 10, 1897.

172   *to Sheriff Doht*   *NYW*, November 10, 1897.

172   *Howe's house on Boston Avenue . . . darkened and quiet*   "Mrs. Nack Confesses," *NYTR*, November 10, 1897.

172   *a reporter secretly on his payroll*   Rovere, *Howe & Hummel*, 35.

172   *during big cases he worked out of the Park Avenue*   *NYH*, November 10, 1897.

172   *immense cast-iron castle painted a blinding white*   Korom, *American Skyscraper*, 77.

172   *"Yes, I've heard the news"*   *NYH*, November 10, 1897.

172   *Another knock came at the door . . . a* World *reporter*   *NYW*, November 10, 1897.

172   *"I had the* most perfect case"   *NYH*, November 10, 1897.

172   *counsel . . .* for Nelson Weeks   *BE*, April 20, 1897.

172   *body in the Aimee Smith case had* not *been quickly identified*   *BE*, March 9, 1897.

173   *Newton was in direct charge of the Thorn case's body parts*   *NYT*, November 10, 1897.

173   *"I cannot understand one thing"*   *NYH*, November 10, 1897.

173   *Californians and even Londoners woke that morning to the news*   "A Murderess Tells Her Dark Secret," *Oakland Tribune*, November 10, 1897; and "The New York Turkish-Bath Murder," *Pall Mall Gazette* (London), November 10, 1897.

174   *men in the crowd sprinted . . . women, slowed by their long skirts*   "Life Against Life, Lie Against Lie," *NYW*, November 11, 1897.

174   World *reporter dubbed it the Flower Garden*   Ibid.

174   MRS. NACK HAS CONFESSED THE MURDER   *NYW*, November 10, 1897.

174   *Thorn went pale and stiffly passed the newspaper*   "Mrs. Nack's Story Told," *NYT*, November 11, 1897.

174   *"Augusta Nack," announced the court clerk*   *NYEJ*, November 10, 1897.

174   *smoothing her skirt as she sat*   "Mrs. Nack's Awful Story Told," *NYP*, November 11, 1897.

174   *Her appearance, the* Times *sniffed*   *NYT*, November 11, 1897.

174   *"My name is Augusta Nack"*   *NYEJ*, November 10, 1897. NB: I have drawn from different news reports as indicated for the testimony that follows. Many of the physical gestures and tone of voice, however, are drawn from the particularly detailed rendition given in the November 11, 1897, report in the *New York Press*.

175   *transfixed spectator . . . nearly toppled over*   *NYW*, November 11, 1897.

175   *"Wanted his head?"*   "Story of Murder Told by Mrs. Nack," *BE*, November 10, 1897.

175   *"He came one evening in my house"*   *NYEJ*, November 10, 1897.

176   *"I told Guldensuppe that he should come with me"*   *NYW*, November 11, 1897.

176   *"I had the key, and I went inside"*   *NYEJ*, November 10, 1897.

176   *not another sound in the room save for the furious* scritch scritch   *NYP*, November 11, 1897.

177   *"He had a bottle of ammonia"*   "Thorn's Trial Is Postponed," *NYET*, November 11, 1897.

177 *"Here is a photograph"*   *NYEJ*, November 10, 1897.
177 *favorite diamond pendant*   "Passed Away Very Suddenly," *BE*, September 2, 1902.
178 *"Mrs. Nack. . . . You have told us"*   *NYEJ*, November 10, 1897.
179 *"How long did this frightful love continue?"*   *NYH*, November 11, 1897.
180 *"You prepared to go Europe, didn't you?"*   *NYEJ*, November 10, 1897.
182 *"Mrs. Nack, don't you remember"*   *NYH*, November 11, 1897.
183 *"a scene of disorder in the court room"*   "Mrs. Nack Tells Her Story," *NYCA*, November 10, 1897.
183 *collapsed in a far corner of the jury box*   *NYH*, November 11, 1897.

19. SCYTHE AND SAW

184 *gathered around the Garden City Hotel billiard table*   "New Jury to Try Thorn," *NYT*, November 12, 1897.
184 *crowds scoured the floors . . . and locals pointed out the chairs*   "Thorn Confesses His Part in the Murder," *NYEJ*, November 11, 1897.
184 *"Yes, yes, yes—no, no, no"*   "Thorn Trial Ends; Jury Discharged," *NYEJ*, November 12, 1897.
184 *his rose-and-scarlet scarf . . . diamond-encircled moonstone*   "Thorn Jury Discharged," *NYT*, November 13, 1897.
184 *the size of an egg*   *NYEJ*, November 12, 1897.
184 *"The gallery was nearly full of Long Island folks"*   *NYT*, November 13, 1897.
185 *Howe jokingly shook a fist*   "Thorn's Trial Is Postponed," *NYET*, November 12, 1897.
185 *"Larsen had a very narrow escape"*   "Thorn Juror Under the Knife," *NYH*, November 12, 1897.
185 *In the Cancini case of 1857, he noted*   *NYEJ*, November 11, 1897.
185 *"You! You insignificant little imp!"*   "Jury Discharged in the Thorn Trial," *BE*, November 12, 1897.
186 *"This . . . is the case of my life"*   *NYT*, November 13, 1897.
186 *cheers and congratulations from his staff*   "Thorn's Trial at a Standstill," *BE*, November 11, 1897.
186 *"a damnable spider"*   "Thorn Eager to Testify," *NYT*, November 14, 1897.
186 *"From my first interview I found him saturated with chivalry"*   "New Trial for Martin Thorn," *NYH*, November 12, 1897.
186 *million-dollar operation in breach-of-promise cases*   Rovere, *Howe & Hummel*, 77.
186 *John Barrymore, because he didn't give a damn*   Ibid., 95.
186 *"She is the biggest liar unhung"*   *NYEJ*, November 11, 1897.
187 *"Mrs. Nack admitted that she herself had cremated Guldensuppe's clothes"*   "Mrs. Nack Identifies the Saw," *NYEJ*, November 17, 1897.
187 *stern, bespectacled Bronx landlady named Ida Ziegler*   "Lawyer Howe's New Witness," *NYT*, November 21, 1897.
187 *"On one Sunday. . . . I believe it was prior"*   "Thorn's New Witness," *NYW*, November 21, 1897.
187 *the accused barber had been left unshaven. . . . barber showed up at Thorn's cell with manacles*   "Thorn Handcuffed Getting a Prison Shave," *NYW*, November 20, 1897.
188 *Howe associate led a short impresario and a willowy actress*   "Anna Held Meets Thorn—A New Trial and Jury," *NYW*, November 12, 1897.

189 *THORN CONFESSES HIS PART IN THE MURDER* *NYEJ*, November 11, 1897.

189 *women's fashion plates with actual photographed faces* "An Advance View of Striking Autumn Fashions," *NYW,* August 29, 1897.

190 *Pulitzer anxiously telegraphed from Maine* Telegram, December 15, 1897. Pulitzer Papers, container 2.

190 Evening Telegram *ceased publication altogether* "Evening Telegram Suspends and Resumes," *NYEJ*, November 22, 1897.

190 "All the News That's Fit to Print" Campbell, *The Year That Defined American Journalism*, 70.

190 COCAINE PHANTOMS HAUNT HIM *NYEJ*, November 22, 1897.

190 *one could also find all these headlines* *NYH*, November 22, 1897.

190 *far more column inches on crime and accidents than other cities* Baldasky, *Commercialization of News*, 155.

190 "*The two stories of Nack and Thorn have reached an equilibrium*" W. R. Hearst, editorial, *NYEJ*, November 12, 1897.

191 *They tallied some 1,147 letters* "Three New Jurors and a New Judge for Thorn," *NYEJ*, November 22, 1897.

191 *latest ad for the Eden Musée waxworks* advertisement, *NYT,* November 20, 1897.

191 *THE INVASION OF NEW YORK* *NYJ*, November 14, 1897.

191 *THE STORY OF MY LIFE* Ibid.

192 *Augusta Nack was quietly led out of her cell* "Mrs. Nack Has an Outing," *NYS*, November 15, 1897.

192 "*Can you point out the place?*" "Digging Ends," *NYEJ*, November 15, 1897.

193 "*Did you find the saw?*" *NYS*, November 15, 1897.

193 *lost his job at the Astoria Model Bakery* "Nack Lives in Dread," *NYW,* November 13, 1897.

194 "*What do you think of the strange course*" "Mrs. Nack Tells New Secrets," *NYEJ*, November 13, 1897.

194 *newspapers gloated after word of her failed carriage trip* "Thorn Denies That He Is a Jailbird," *NYH*, November 16, 1897.

194 *laborers worked with scythes to clear* "Find Saw as Mrs. Nack Said," *NYEJ*, November 16, 1897.

194 *rusting eighteen-inch surgeon's saw—a Richardson & Sons model* "Thorn's Saw Is Found," *BE*, November 16, 1897.

20. A WONDERFUL MURDER

195 *Malwine Brandel clutched a bouquet . . . begging Sheriff Doht to let her inside* "Women Who Watch the Trial with Morbid Interest Tell the Journal Why," *NYJ*, November 25, 1897.

196 *the de rigueur accessory of the trial—opera glasses* "Mrs. Nack Again on View," *NYS*, November 25, 1897.

196 *Tessie . . . from Greenpoint* *NYJ*, November 25, 1897.

196 *Maddox on the bench—the last judge having excused himself* "Five Jurors Chosen to Try Thorn," *BE*, November 22, 1897.

196 "*I go to the Tombs to sing*" *NYJ*, November 25, 1897.

196 *LOOK MORE INTELLIGENT THAN THE FORMER LOT* *NYP,* November 23, 1897.

196 *two farmers, a florist, a property agent, an oyster dealer, and fully seven builders* "Twelve Men Chosen to Try Martin Thorn," *BE*, November 23, 1897.

196 *Clara Nunnheimer. . . . A fresh-faced and beaming* "Thorn's Trial Continues," *NYT,* November 25, 1897.

196 *"Do you recall the 25th of June?"* New York v. Thorn, 142.
197 *Nor could he rattle a thirteen-year-old girl* Ibid., 174.
197 *"kind of diagonally across from Mr. Buala's property"* Ibid., 156–57.
197 *"Did you ever see William Guldensuppe naked?"* Ibid., 75. NB: The revelations regarding the identification of Guldensuppe by his "peculiar" penis occur solely in the trial transcript; no other source of the time even dared to hint at them, instead referring to his being identified by his "finger."
198 *"He had very peculiar privates"* Ibid., 82.
198 *"The most peculiar thing was his penis"* Ibid., 87.
199 *"A very peculiar penis"* Ibid., 101.
199 *fruit jar, sealed with red wax* "Saw Martin Thorn at Woodside House," *BE*, November 24, 1897.
199 *"something looking much like small sections of tripe"* *NYT*, November 25, 1897.
199 *"Has that changed its appearance?"* New York v. Thorn, 103.
200 *"Church—or golf?"* "Thorn Jurors at Golf Contest," *NYET*, November 25, 1897.
200 *the Garden City had been designed by Stanford White* Waldman and Martin, *Nassau, Long Island*, 62.
200 *One juror . . . stuffed buckwheat pancakes into his pockets* "Hot Cakes in His Pocket," *NYEJ*, November 23, 1897.
200 *Church, a stout minority of five argued* *NYET*, November 25, 1897.
200 *Hundreds milled about, hoping to gain an audience* "Four Thanksgivings Behind Bars," *NYW*, November 26, 1897.
201 *"I can say . . . that I really knew what Thanksgiving is today"* "What Thorn Told Captain O'Brien," *NYEJ*, November 25, 1897.
201 *"Show your passes!"* "Gotha Betrays Thorn to the Jury," *NYEJ*, November 26, 1897.
201 *"It's a disgrace to have women in attendance"* "Human Flies at Thorn's Trial," *NYW*, November 27, 1897.
201 *"To show crime in its vulgarest"* W. R. Hearst, editorial, *NYEJ*, November 11, 1897.
201 BRAZEN WOMEN AND BAD AIR *NYW*, November 27, 1897.
201 *"more offensive than ever"* "Mrs. Nack Held as Trump Card," *NYP*, November 27, 1897.
202 *and so, the press pool surmised, was Herman's new wardrobe* *BE*, November 27, 1897.
202 *"Just a crazy barber"* *NYP*, November 27, 1897.
202 *Sullivan identified the bullets* New York v. Thorn, 340.
202 *NYPD pistol instructor noted that their caliber matched* Ibid., 346.
202 *Detective O'Connell, the former plumber* Ibid., 351.
202 *Thorn smiled at the sight of his old friend* *NYEJ*, November 26, 1897.
202 *Thorn's informant looked puffy and tired* "Gotha Repeats Thorn's Story," *NYET*, November 26, 1897.
203 *"I asked him if he done the murder"* New York v. Thorn, 299. NB: The remainder of this section is drawn from the trial transcript.
205 *Howe was thunderstruck* *NYW*, November 27, 1897.
205 CROWD MAY BREAK RECORDS *BE*, November 28, 1897.
205 *attorneys were making a pilgrimage* "All Eager to Hear Thorn," *NYT*, November 29, 1897.
205 *"No women"* "Martin Thorn a Good Witness," *NYET*, November 29, 1897.
205 *Scores of women promptly laid siege* "Thorn's Bid for Life," *NYW*, November 30, 1897.

206 *"I have been watching them"*   "Thorn's Story Told, His Life at Stake," *NYH*, November 30, 1897.

206 *women who had gotten in under the pretense*   "Thorn Testifies in His Own Behalf," *BE*, November 29, 1897.

206 *"The killing of Guldensuppe germinated"*   "Thorn Talks for His Own Life," *NYTR*, November 30, 1897.

207 *"In a long career in the court"*   "Jurors Paled at Thorn's Grewsome Evidence," *NYJA*, November 30, 1897.

207 *"Will Your Honor pardon me if I sit down"*   *New York v. Thorn*, 369.

208 *Howe rose and walked to the jury box*   *BE*, November 29, 1897.

208 *Then the defendant leveled his gaze squarely at the twelve men*   "Thorn's Account of the Murder," *NYEP*, November 29, 1897.

21. MRS. NACK'S OFFICE

211 *Hearst even joked*   W. R. Hearst, editorial, *NYEJ*, November 26, 1897.

211 *$60,000 windfall*   "Patrick J. Gleason Dead," *NYT*, May 21, 1901.

211 *her lucky piece of coral*   "Luetgert Predicts Thorn's Conviction," *NYW*, November 24, 1897.

211 *carried a rabbit's foot—a present from his wife*   "Fears Thorn's Collapse," *NYW*, November 23, 1897.

211 *"The case for the people was complete without her"*   *NYH*, November 30, 1897.

211 *"Where do you live?"*   *New York v. Thorn*, 387.

212 *her voice small and precise, free of artifice*   *NYW*, November 30, 1897.

212 *"Do you remember"*   *New York v. Thorn*, 387.

212 *"Is that all your evidence?"*   *NYH*, November 30, 1897.

213 *"I ask . . . that the jury be permitted to view the bath tub"*   *New York v. Thorn*, 495.

213 *Thorn . . . wasn't interested in joining them*   Ibid., 501.

213 *While a private trolley was requisitioned for the jurors, reporters jockeyed*   "Martin Thorn's Case Is in the Hands of the Jury," *NYEJ*, November 30, 1897.

214 *He hadn't allowed his charges to read . . . "nothing but hotel menu cards"*   "Fight for Thorn's Life Is On Again," *NYH*, November 24, 1897.

214 *Good Thing Club*   "Thorn Jurors' Bright Idea," *NYH*, November 29, 1897.

214 *genially hazed their police escort by loading his rifle with blanks*   "Thorn Will Say the Woman Did It," *NYH*, November 28, 1897.

214 *referred to as Mrs. Nack's Office*   "Thorn Confesses It All," *NYT*, December 1, 1897.

214 *"All off here for Woodside cottage!"*   "Thorn's Fate in Jury's Hands," *BE*, November 30, 1897.

214 *The place had hardly changed*   *NYT*, December 1, 1897.

214 *shooing gawkers to a perimeter*   *NYH*, December 1, 1897.

215 *Sullivan busily threw open the shutters*   "Thorn's Life in Jury's Keeping," *NYET*, November 30, 1897.

216 *Judge Maddox hadn't yet finished his cigar*   *NYEJ*, November 30, 1897.

216 *tugged down on his pin-striped vest*   Ibid.

217 *so loud that the chandeliers jangled*   *NYJA*, November 30, 1897.

217 *"Now, as to your visit to the cottage"*   *NYEJ*, November 30, 1897.

218 *"Remember that the scenes of this day will never"*   *BE*, November 30, 1897.

218 *"Put these things together in a mosaic"*   *NYEJ*, November 30, 1897.

219 *it was 2:25*   *NYEJ*, November 30, 1897.

219 *a single black-veiled woman nearly hidden*   "Thorn Found Guilty," *NYTR*, December 1, 1897.

220   *"So long as Mr. Howe kept in a sphere above the actual evidence"*   "The Jury's Declaration at Thorn's . . . " (title damaged), *NYJA*, December 1, 1897.

220   *"It is not believed that he cut* himself *up"*   editorial, *BE*, November 27, 1897.

221   *reporters could make out raised voices*   "Jury in Three Hours Finds Thorn Guilty," *NYJA*, December 1, 1897.

221   *poring over the intercepted jailhouse correspondence*   "Martin Thorn Convicted," *NYS*, December 1, 1897.

221   *"Remove your hats!"*   *NYT*, December 1, 1897.

221   *"Gentlemen of the jury, have you agreed upon a verdict?"*   "Jury Finds Thorn Guilty of Murder," *NYH*, December 1, 1897.

22. THE SMOKER TO SING SING

222   *"I suppose Howe will get a new trial"*   *NYH*, December 1, 1897.

222   *wrestling with his adopted mutt*   "Thorn Sentenced to Die In January," *BE*, December 3, 1897.

222   *"I had no motive to kill Guldensuppe"*   *NYH*, December 1, 1897.

222   *"Martin!" his sister sobbed*   "Martin Thorn Is Breaking Down," *NYW*, December 3, 1897.

223   *"It doesn't make any difference to me"*   *NYH*, December 1, 1897. NB: The remainder of this scene is drawn from this account.

224   *"I am smoking a cigar"*   "Howe Calls Doht a Liar," *BE*, December 1, 1897.

224   *Garden City Hotel dutifully filed*   "Thorn Trial Expenses," *NYS*, December 3, 1897.

224   *Detective Sullivan's fruitless trip to Hamburg*   "Mrs. Nack May Escape Death," *NYW*, December 2, 1897.

224   *the entire cost of the case might balloon to $40,000 or $50,000*   "Luxurious Thorn Jurors," *NYT*, December 3, 1897.

224   *hotel bill consisted of the usual pettiness*   "Thorn Jury Bill Edited," *BE*, January 13, 1898.

224   *The jury was incompetent to render a verdict*   "The Thorn Jury Wine Bill," *NYT*, January 8, 1898.

225   *"I saw no wine drunk"*   "Thorn Jurors Swear They Had No Wine," *BE*, January 9, 1898.

225   *"Prisoner, arise"*   *BE*, December 3, 1897. NB: The remainder of the scene is drawn from this account.

226   *Thorn sat up on his jail cot*   "Thorn Taken to Sing Sing," *BE*, December 4, 1897.

226   *he turned to his dog*   "Martin Thorn in Sing Sing," *NYET*, December 4, 1897.

226   *two inches of slush and snow*   "Thorn Must Die Within Five Weeks," *NYW*, December 4, 1897.

226   *Thorn slid on the ice*   "Almost Fell Twice," *NYJ*, December 5, 1897.

227   *crowd was pressing on Thorn and his two jailers*   *NYET*, December 4, 1897.

227   *"They all want to see you"*   "Thorn's Vanity Betrayed Him," *NYW*, December 5, 1897. NB: The remainder of this scene is drawn from this account.

228   *a piano maker's wife had thrown herself*   "The Suicidal Mania," *NYT*, May 13, 1881.

228   *man recently arrested for assisting a high diver's illegal leap*   "Jumped from the Bridge," *NYT*, July 5, 1897.

228   *employee had once run off with the florist's wife*   "Mrs. Spengler Went Wrong," *NYT*, September 9, 1892.

228   *burnished oak coffin*   "Guldensuppe's Body Buried," *NYTR*, December 6, 1897.

229 *his right hand laid upon his breast* NYT, December 6, 1897.
229 Journal *women's page reporter who visited her on Christmas Day* "Mrs. Nack's Christmas Present to Thorn," *NYJA*, December 26, 1897.
230 *"head devil" of the case* "Maudlin Sympathy," *BE*, December 6, 1897.
230 *"They should place her in the electric chair with Thorn"* "Mrs. Nack May Escape Death," *NYW*, December 2, 1897.
230 "Imagine Santa Throwing an X-Ray" Bloomingdale's display ad, *NYW*, December 5, 1897.
230 *FIRE IN A MATCH FACTORY* NYH, December 4, 1897.
230 *proposal to put bike racks on trolley cars* "Brooklyn Trolleys May Carry Cycles Next Season," *NYJ*, December 10, 1897.
230 *THOUGHTS PICTURED* NYH, November 28, 1897.
230 *FISH CHOWDER POURS* NYJ, December 15, 1897.
231 *the Prophecy Prize* "What Do You Think Will Happen in the Year 1898?" *NYJA*, December 19, 1897.
231 *"Poor Martin." Gussie sighed* NYJA, December 26, 1897. NB: The remainder of this section is drawn from this account.

23. A JOB FOR SMITH AND JONES

233 *windowless walls on three sides* NYW, December 5, 1897.
233 *"bathing in a search-light"* Molineux, *Room with the Little Door*, 21. NB: Though an erstwhile work of fiction, Molineux's book is well worth finding for its account of life on Sing Sing's Death Row—namely, because he was a convicted poisoner sent there just a couple of years after Thorn. Molineux's conviction was one of the next great "newspaper trials" after Thorn's, although he was later released after a retrial.
233 *Thorn had already devoured* The Old Curiosity Shop NYT, December 6, 1897.
233 *Sutherland was a West Indian in for shooting his wife* "Died in the Electric Chair," *Sun* (Baltimore), January 11, 1898.
233 *warden stopped by with a message from Howe* "A Stay for Martin Thorn," *NYT*, January 1, 1898.
234 *Hadley was not as fortunate* "Went to His Death Cheerfully," *NYW*, January 11, 1898.
234 *"I could never eat off* that *table"* "Ghastly Vanity Fair," *NYW*, January 16, 1898.
235 *salesrooms on 125th Street magically transformed* "May Go To-Morrow," *BE*, January 13, 1898.
235 *in the reconstituted parlor was a suite* NYW, January 16, 1898.
235 *"a low cut"* "Mrs. Nack's Effects," *BE*, January 16, 1898.
235 *the plain and melancholy wooden bed of Guldensuppe* NYW, January 16, 1898.
235 *dime-museum men . . . Luetgert's sausage vat* "Would Exhibit Luetgert's Vat," *NYJ*, December 24, 1897.
236 *MURDER DEN A KLONDIKE* NYEJ, January 14, 1898.
236 *THE FAMOUS STOVE* NYW, January 16, 1898.
236 *handed at the entrance—business cards* BE, January 16, 1898.
236 *"Those are terrible things my husband told"* "Mrs. Nack's Story," *BE*, January 18, 1898. NB: The remainder of this scene is drawn from the *Eagle*'s interview.
237 *appeals piled up* "Calmly Martin Thorn Awaits His Fate of Death," *NYW*, July 28, 1898.

237 *"This is good news"*   "Martin Thorn to Die, and He Is Glad of It," *NYW,* July 31, 1898.

238 *found one hundred dead rats*   "Dead Rats in the Ventilators," *BE,* May 29, 1898.

238 *Howe had claimed a mistrial*   "Trying to Save Thorn's Life," *NYT,* July 29, 1898.

238 *bill was cruelly knocked down to $127*   "W. F. Howe's Cut Down," *NYT,* June 19, 1898.

238 *Howe talked grandly to the press of taking the case to the U.S. Supreme Court*   "Martin Thorn Must Die," *NYW,* June 8, 1898.

238 *"Take all your clothes off, Martin"*   "Murderer of Guldensuppe, Martin Thorn, Will Pay the Penalty and Be Killed Today," *NYW,* August 1, 1898.

238 *a crisp dress oxford*   *NYW,* July 31, 1898.

238 *There were five condemned prisoners*   *NYW,* August 1, 1898.

239 *"I want my books"*   Ibid.

239 *snare a coveted title from the prison library*   *NYP,* August 2, 1898.

239 *chat across the cell walls with the other prisoners*   *NYW,* August 1, 1898.

239 *"Have you seen your mouse yet, Thorn?"*   "Thorn Dies in the Chair for Guldensuppe's Murder," *NYEJ,* August 1, 1898.

240 *Sage was bustling around his office, making preparations*   *NYEJ,* August 1, 1898.

240 *only twenty-eight observers were allowed*   *NYW,* July 28, 1898.

240 *Hearst had deployed Langdon Smith*   *NYEJ,* August 1, 1898.

240 *famed as the country's fastest telegrapher*   "Answer No. 96," *American Mercury,* May 1926, 114.

240 *Haydon Jones, the* World's *own speed artist*   "Martin Thorn Pays the Penalty of Murder in the Electric Chair," *NYW,* August 2, 1898.

240 *scooped up by Pulitzer's crew from the* Mail and Express   Armes, Ethel, "Haydon Jones, Newspaper Artist," *National Magazine* 26 (1906): 151.

240 *his favorite Blaisdell pencil*   Ibid., 148.

241 *room was reminiscent of a small chapel*   *NYW,* August 2, 1898.

241 *"Gentlemen . . . you will oblige me"*   "Thorn Met Death Calmly," *NYS,* August 2, 1898.

241 *"the tentacles of an electrical octopus"*   *NYEJ,* August 1, 1898.

241 *"By these lamps . . . we will test the current"*   *NYW,* August 2, 1898.

242 *"The hour has come"*   *NYP,* August 2, 1898.

242 *long black rubber sash was stretched across his face*   *NYW,* August 2, 1898.

242 *"Christ, Mary, Mother of God"*   *NYEJ,* August 1, 1898.

243 *"like an overheated flatiron on a handkerchief"*   "Martin Thorn Dies in Abject Terror," *NYH,* August 2, 1898.

24. A STORY OF LIFE IN NEW YORK

244 MARTIN THORN GOES CALMLY TO HIS DEATH   *NYET,* August 1, 1898.

244 THORN MET DEATH CALMLY   *NYS,* August 2, 1898.

244 MARTIN THORN DIES IN ABJECT TERROR   *NYH,* August 2, 1898.

244 WOMAN MEDIUM COMMUNES WITH THORN   *NYW,* August 2, 1898.

244 *O'Neill was a surgeon with the New York School of Clinical Medicine*   *Medical Times and Register* 35–36 (1898): 185.

244 *sponges had dried out, causing a burn hole*   "Thorn Met Death Calmly," *NYS,* August 2, 1898.

244 *nitroglycerin, strychnine, and brandy*   *NYW*, August 2, 1898.

245 *Kemmler had been left still breathing*   Brandon, *Electric Chair*, 177.

245 *O'Neill bent over and rested the stethoscope*   *NYW*, August 2, 1898.

245 *"The law requires post-mortem mutilation"*   O'Neill, "Who's the Executioner?" 185.

246 *"the prostitution of science"*   "Electrocution," *American Medico-Surgical Bulletin* 21, no. 21 (November 10, 1898): 999.

246 Evening Journal *lavished attention that night*   *NYEJ*, August 1, 1898.

246 *front-page attacks on crooked dealings*   "The Journal Stops," *NYJA*, December 3, 1897.

246 *stoked his paper's capacity*   "The Journal's Presses—Past, Present and Future," *NYJ*, December 5, 1897.

246 THE WORST INSULT   "The Worst Insult to the United States in Its History," *NYJ*, February 9, 1898.

246 *"Have you put anything else on the front page?"*   Morris, *Pulitzer*, 339.

247 WAR! SURE!   "War! Sure! Maine Destroyed by Spanish," *NYEJ*, February 17, 1898.

247 THE WHOLE COUNTRY THRILLS   "The Whole Country Thrills with War Fever," *NYJ*, February 18, 1898.

247 "Remember the *Maine*! To hell with Spain!"   Procter, *William Randolph Hearst*, 118.

247 HOW DO YOU LIKE THE JOURNAL'S WAR?   Stevens, *Sensationalism*, 97.

247 *offered the U.S. military $500,000*   Procter, *William Randolph Hearst*, 122.

247 *now rocketed up to . . . a million and a half*   Bleyer, *Main Currents*, 378.

247 *"war news was written by fools for fools"*   Turner, *When Giants Ruled*, 135.

247 *ran news of the death of one Colonel Reflipe W. Thenuz*   "The World Confesses to Stealing the News!" *NYEJ*, June 9, 1898.

248 *newspaper publisher tearing around Havana Harbor*   Churchill, *Park Row*, 131.

248 MUST FIND THAT FLEET!   *NYEJ*, May 28, 1898.

248 *summer dessert tips for homemakers*   "Even Ice Cream and Confectionary Are Now Made to Suggest War," *NYEJ*, May 28, 1898.

248 *taking some Spanish prisoners of war*   Procter, *William Randolph Hearst*, 130.

248 *spotted at the Battle of El Caney*   Ibid., 129.

248 *Eden Musée was busy adding a score of patriotic*   advertisement, *NYT*, August 14, 1898.

248 *its baggage car disgorged a plain pine box*   "Curious Crowds Look on the Coffined Face of Martin Thorn," *NYW*, August 3, 1898.

249 *worries that freak-show promoters might try*   "Took Amperes to Kill Thorn," *NYP*, August 2, 1898.

249 *A thousand disappointed spectators had appeared*   "Thorn Met Death Calmly," *NYS*, August 2, 1898.

249 *A dozen policemen from the Twenty-Seventh Precinct*   "Martin Thorn Body Buried in Calvary's Consecrated Ground To-Day," *NYH*, August 2, 1898.

249 *undertaker barred the door*   *NYEJ*, August 2, 1898.

249 *his head still bore red electrode marks*   *BE*, August 2, 1898.

249 *brother-in-law leaned over for a word*   *NYEJ*, August 2, 1898.

249 *luxuriant display of lilies of the valley*   "Thorn Met Death Calmly," *NYS*, August 2, 1898.

249 *"Probably a woman"*   *NYEJ*, August 2, 1898.

249 *"Mrs. Nack?"*   *NYH*, August 2, 1898.

250 *inmate #269 at Auburn*   "Mrs. Nack Is Now No. 269," *NYW*, January 20, 1898.

250   *a three-inch-thick oak door*   "How Mrs. Nack Will Spend Her Term in Auburn," *NYW,* January 16, 1898.

250   *spent her day in the prison's sewing room*   *NYW,* January 20, 1898.

250   *Word was leaking out*   "State Control of Midwives," *Buffalo Medical Journal* 48 (1898): 131.

250   Journal *pounced on a damning discovery*   "Mrs. Nack Has Money in Realty," *NYEJ,* August 11, 1898.

250   *sardonic inscription of AUGUSTA NACK, SURGEON*   "Bright Editorial," *San Antonio* (Texas) *Daily Light,* March 13, 1900.

250   *"Epidemic Hypnotic Criminal Suggestion"*   "Epidemic Hypnotic Criminal Suggestion," *Massachusetts Medical Journal* 21 (1901): 512.

251   SECOND GULDENSUPPE CASE   *NYT,* October 9, 1899.

251   *third* [Guldensuppe case]   "Zanoli, Queer Man of Tragedies," *NYJA,* December 11, 1897.

251   *fourth* [Guldensuppe case]   "Murder and Butchery," *NYT,* February 9, 1898.

251   *fifth* [Guldensuppe case]   "Like Guldensuppe Murder," *NYT,* June 11, 1899.

251   *a woman's leg was found*   "Another Ghastly Find," *NYS,* October 10, 1899.

251   *her chest washed ashore on Staten Island*   "Torso of the Body Found," *NYS,* October 11, 1899.

251   *NYPD threw 200 detectives on the case*   *NYS,* October 10, 1899.

251   *Moses Cohen, the "C" newspaper*   "Murder Still His Mystery," *NYT,* October 13, 1899.

251   *captain of the barge* Knickerbocker   *NYS,* October 10, 1899.

251   *"would have appealed to Sherlock Holmes"*   "The Influence of Sherlock Holmes," *BE,* October 11, 1899.

251   *Prospect Place coal cellar of Alma Lundberg*   "New Clue in Murder Case," *NYT,* December 4, 1899.

251   *other clues proved to be the usual nonsense*   "Police at a Standstill," *NYS,* October 13, 1899.

252   *"the Great American Identifier"*   *NYT,* October 19, 1899.

252   *cuts precisely matched those on Guldensuppe*   *NYT,* October 13, 1899. NB: Although the crime was officially unsolved, police afterward believed that the victim was Kate Feeley, who went missing after answering a newspaper ad for employment. Max Schmittberger, later the chief police inspector for the NYPD, voiced the suspicion that William Hooper Young—later convicted of the 1902 murder of Anna Pulitzer—was the perpetrator. (See "Mrs. Pulitzer Is Buried," *NYT,* August 24, 1902.)

252   *a novel,* Three Men and a Woman   "A Strong Book by an Iowa Author," *Cedar Rapids* (Iowa) *Daily Republican,* June 10, 1901.

252   *"The death of Guldensuppe preyed"*   "Nack Brooded," *Lowell* (Massachusetts) *Sun,* June 23, 1903.

252   *346 Second Street sat vacant*   "For Use as a Wine-Shop," *BE,* March 19, 1899.

253   *thrown the Bualas' baseboards into a bonfire*   "Relics of Murder Burned," *NYTR,* March 24, 1899.

253   *turning them into a jaunty pair of scarf pins*   "Personal Chats," *Muncie* (Indiana) *Morning Post,* May 4, 1898.

253   *"We have already put one haunted house"*   "Join to Rout Ghosts," *NYTR,* May 21, 1904.

253   *only to die of rabies*   "Dog Dealer Dies of Rabies," *NYT,* February 12, 1910.

253   *preserving the bathroom upstairs*   *BE,* March 19, 1899.

253   *Piernot ran half-naked and screaming*   "Saw Guldensuppe's Ghost," *NYT,* December 1, 1900.

25. CARRY OUT YOUR OWN DEAD

254 *A tall, long-haired artist* "Mrs. Nack Set Free, Met Here by Mob," *NYT,* July 20, 1907.

254 *CUT HIS THROAT BY ACCIDENT and SHE HEARD VOICES* *NYJ,* July 19, 1907.

254 *story of a Civil War vet in Central Park* "Talks War to Tots and Kills Self," *New York Evening Mail,* July 19, 1907.

255 *MRS. NACK SET FREE* *NYEJ,* July 19, 1907.

255 *a train crewman stopped* "Mrs. Nack, Free, Centre of Mob on Arrival Here," *NYW,* July 20, 1907.

255 *"I am glad to be out"* "Mrs. Nack Free, Denies Identity as Murderess," *NYH,* July 20, 1907.

255 *the platform boiled over with hundreds of people* "Great Crowd to See Mrs. Nack," *NYS,* July 20, 1907.

256 *"Get away from me!"* "Mrs. Nack Free, Denies Identity as Murderess," *NYH,* July 20, 1907.

256 *"We are friends of yours"* *NYW,* July 20, 1907.

256 *Ranks of tripod cameras lying in wait on Lexington Avenue* *NYS,* July 20, 1907.

256 *"Keb?"* *NYW,* July 20, 1907.

256 *police station where she'd been interrogated was gone* "The Passing of No. 300 Mulberry St," *NYT,* September 21, 1902.

256 *the courthouse and the jury's hotel were both burnt out* "Garden City Hotel Burned," *NYTR,* September 8, 1899.

257 *she'd had to pay the driver six dollars* "Mrs. Nack, Unwelcome Patron at Hotel, Leaves," *NYET,* July 20, 1907.

257 *"I suppose I shall find things a great deal different"* *NYH,* July 20, 1907.

257 *Manny Friend, had been gone for three years now* "Emanuel M. Friend, Lawyer, Dead," *NYT,* November 2, 1904.

257 *English child of a brothel keeper* "Central Criminal Court, Sept. 20," *Times* (London), September 21, 1854.

257 *forging admission tickets* "Bow Street," *Times* (London), November 4, 1848.

257 *clerk in Blackfriars* "Central Criminal Court, June 17," *Times* (London), June 19, 1854.

257 *convicted in 1854 of impersonating* *Proceedings of the Old Bailey, Eleventh Session 1853–4,* September 20, 1854, Case No. 997, 1193. NB: While it has been suspected since at least Rovere's biography that William F. Howe had a criminal record in the United Kingdom, I am the first to discover the specific offenses and records. They seem to have also remained quite unknown in Howe's own lifetime. The revelation that Howe was the child of an accused madam, noted in the *Times* of London account of September 21, 1854, has also been previously unknown to biographers.

257 *emerged to reinvent himself across the ocean* Rovere, *Howe & Hummel,* 21.

258 *Hotel Markwell, where the manager recognized her* "Mrs. Nack Confesses!" *NYEJ,* April 20, 1907.

258 *Wilson Mizner . . . whose lobby sign read CARRY OUT YOUR OWN DEAD* Johnston and Marsh, *Legendary Mizners,* 66.

258 *"I got those knocking down dames"* Ibid., 113.

258 *signed in as "Mrs. A. Ross, Buffalo"* *NYEJ,* July 20, 1907.

258 *"I have had enough misery for one woman"* *NYW,* July 20, 1907.

258 *"I am selling this story"* "Mrs. Nack Tells of Life in Prison," *NYT,* July 21, 1907.

258 *"Remarkable Photograph"* *NYEJ,* July 18, 1907.

258 *Hearst's paper was now more squat and squarish* *NYEJ,* January 5, 1898, and

July 22, 1907. NB: Although most newspaper histories cite the 1920s as the beginning of the tabloid (along with some brief nineteenth-century forays), in reading issues of the *Journal*, it struck me that the paper was already moving in that direction years earlier. Measuring them shows that indeed it was: The height/width ratio on an 1898 issue is roughly 1.4, while on the 1907 issue it is 1.25.

258 *an outright tabloid format would be "the 20th Century newspaper"* Lee, *American Journalism, 1690–1940*, vol. 3, 274.

258 *crude wooden-type letters that were seven inches tall* Winkler, *Hearst: A New Appraisal*, 107.

259 *BUILDING FALLS; 40 KILLED* *NYEJ*, July 18, 1907.

259 *WOMAN KILLS MAN IN UNION SQUARE* *NYEJ*, July 22, 1907.

259 *fascinated by the notion of sending armed zeppelins* editorial, *NYEJ*, July 20, 1907.

259 *MRS. NACK CONFESSES!* *NYEJ*, July 20, 1907.

259 *money to move back to Germany* "Mrs. Nack Will Go to Live with Old Mother," *NYW*, July 21, 1907.

260 *she wasn't sure where to start looking* *NYT*, July 21, 1907.

260 *"This . . . is worse than prison"* *NYW*, July 21, 1907.

260 *One year later, a call came* "Mrs. Nack Calls at the Tombs," *Syracuse Herald*, September 6, 1908.

260 *"brutal" place of "wanton waste"* "Finds Gross Cruelty in Auburn Prison," *NYT*, April 28, 1913.

260 *"You do not have enough to eat"* *NYET*, July 20, 1907.

261 *"I would like to get a place"* *Syracuse Herald*, September 6, 1908.

261 *Judge Smith* "Justice Smith's Funeral," *NYT*, April 1, 1906.

261 *Judge Maddox went on to state supreme court* "Judge Maddox Buried," *NYT*, March 16, 1916.

261 *Youngs, the case was followed by a plum promotion* "Col. Wm. J. Youngs Dies," *NYT*, April 2, 1916.

261 *urge the adoption of an alternate-juror rule* "Change in the Jury System," *NYT*, January 30, 1900.

261 *only took another thirty-three years* "Extra Jurors Bill Signed by Governors," *NYT*, May 2, 1933.

261 *testifying in major murder cases* "Dr. R. A. Witthaus, Poison Expert, Dies," *NYT*, December 21, 1915.

261 *view stomach membrane . . . dazzling crystals of arsenic poisoning* Blum, *Poisoner's Handbook*, 84.

261 *"inheritance powder," as it was dubbed* Ibid., 79.

261 *under an ultraviolet light, that was chloroform poisoning* Ibid., 23.

261 *it would also turn yellow for mercury poisoning* Ibid., 110.

261 *charged the city a dizzying $18,550* "Molineux Experts' Charges Over $50,000," *NYT*, August 10, 1900.

261 *his heirs would later claim* "Dr. Witthaus's Will Attacked in Court," *NYT*, September 22, 1916.

262 *evidence ruined by drunk and incompetent coroners* Blum, *Poisoner's Handbook*, 5.

262 *bribed with, say, a nice gold watch* "Admits Trying to Bribe Juror," *Los Angeles Times*, April 29, 1908.

262 *the coroner's job was abolished altogether* "What Coroners' Exit Means," *NYT*, December 9, 1917.

262 *promptly dubbed "Guldensuppe's head"* "Guldensuppe's Head?" *NYT*, October 30, 1910.

262   *Price, rose to become one of the most recognizable detectives*   "Police Capt. Price Dead," *NYT,* January 9, 1914.

262   *O'Brien . . . went on to address the bewildering rise of automobiles*   "Ex-Inspector O'Brien Dead," *NYT,* July 3, 1913.

262   *first head of the NYPD's newly formed Homicide Bureau*   "Arthur Carey, 87, Ex-Inspector, Dies," *NYT,* December 14, 1952.

263   *teaching the homicide course*   "Detective School Faculty Announced," *NYT,* February 24, 1923.

263   *had become a standard procedure*   Cole, *Suspect Identities,* 152.

263   *"In a murder case there is no one obvious clue"*   Carey, *Memoirs,* 51.

263   *It was a warm June evening*   "Bundled Up Body, Dismembered, Found in Street," *NYW,* June 11, 1909.

264   *head was discovered under the Brooklyn Bridge*   "Murdered Man, Found Mutilated, Had Love Affair," *NYW,* June 12, 1909.

264   VICTIM CARVED UP LIKE GULDENSUPPE   *Hartford Courant,* June 12, 1909.

264   CASE MOST PUZZLING SINCE GULDENSUPPE   *NYEJ,* June 11, 1909.

264   *Scores of detectives tracked the distinctive oilcloth*   "Beheaded and Dismembered Victim of Murder Was Samuel Bersin, a Decorator," *NYH,* June 12, 1909.

264   *murdered by a jealous husband. . . . robbed for his diamond rings . . . rivals for the hand*   "Murdered Man Found Mutilated, Had Love Affair," *NYW,* June 12, 1909.

264   *Sammy was a Russian Jewish anarchist*   "Jean Pouren Case Now Figures in Bersin Murder," *NYW,* June 15, 1909. NB: Despite all the attention that it drew, the Bersin case remained unsolved.

264   *"Mrs. Nack has taken the name of Augusta Huber"*   "Murder Case Recalled," Oshkosh (Wisconsin) *Daily Northwestern,* March 4, 1909.

264   *she was in bankruptcy court*   "Mrs. Nack in Trouble Again," *NYT,* July 13, 1909.

265   *Still working the streets of New York*   "Old Morgue Inadequate," *Pittsburgh Press,* August 8, 1915.

265   *empty cabernet bottle*   "Mrs. Nack May Be Indicted," *NYT,* July 6, 1897.

265   *stabbed while naked*   *NYT,* June 28, 1897.

266   *"I last saw her"*   Van Wagner, *New York Detective,* 15.

EPILOGUE: THE LAST MAN STANDING

267   *"the first of the great newspaper trials"*   "Winchell on Broadway," *Mansfield* (Ohio) *News Journal,* September 12, 1946.

267   *a venture into writing novelty songs*   *Catalogue of Copyright Entries, part III: Musical Compositions* (Washington, D.C.: Library of Congress, 1915), 930.

267   *Ike White, went on to expose dozens*   "Isaac White Dies, Noted Reporter, 79," *NYT,* September 25, 1943.

267   *Hawthorne landed in prison*   "Julian Hawthorne, Dead on Coast, 88," *NYT,* July 15, 1934.

267   Journal *had burned through about $4 million*   Morris, *Pulitzer,* 344.

267   *He and Hearst met . . . and negotiated a deal*   Ibid., 355.

268   *their resulting agreement went unsigned*   Ibid., 359.

268   *came to admire the sober reliability of the* New York Times   Ibid., 418.

268   World*'s proprietor was rehabilitated*   Bleyer, *Main Currents,* 351.

268   *"a Coney Island of ink and wood pulp"*   Palmer, *Hearst and Hearstism,* 120.

268   *Patterson's founding in 1919 of the New York* Daily News   Nasaw, *The Chief,* 321.

268 *runs for mayor, then governor*   Winkler, *Hearst: An American Phenomenon*, 191.

268 *inevitably for president*   Bleyer, *Main Currents*, 384. NB: He never made it to the White House, but a few suspected Hearst of depriving a previous holder of the office. In 1901 his penchant for brash content backfired spectacularly when a poem by Ambrose Bierce that wished William McKinley dead ran right before the president's actual assassination. Hearst had to patriotically tack "American" to the *Journal*'s name—making it the *New York Journal American*—to set that one right.

269 *"a lark and a triumph"*   "The Hearst Boom," *Nelson* (New Zealand) *Evening Mail*, November 15, 1906.

269 *"Ah well, we were young"*   Procter, *William Randolph Hearst*, 97.

269 *That man was Ned Brown*   "Ned Brown Dead; Writer on Boxing," *NYT*, April 26, 1976.

269 *"Being a newspaperman gave you stature then"*   Liebling, *Liebling at* The New Yorker, 166.

270 *evicted from his apartment*   "Most Important Possession," *Sarasota Herald Tribune*, May 22, 1973.

270 *the case files had been destroyed years earlier*   "Queens to Destroy Noted Crime Files," *NYT*, December 7, 1949.

270 *reporter picked out a yellowed evidence envelope*   Edward Radin column (no surviving headline), *St. Petersburg Times*, July 13, 1949.

ACKNOWLEDGMENTS

It was years ago that I first chanced upon an 1897 article about some faked murder relics found in a sleepy neighborhood of Queens. From that peculiar beginning came this book—but it couldn't have been written without the love, patience, and encouragement of my wife, Jennifer, or the inspiration of my sons, Morgan and Bramwell. My great thanks also go to Marc Thomas for all his help in the twenty-first century while I was off traveling in the nineteenth.

I am especially grateful to the John Simon Guggenheim Memorial Foundation; the generous support of a Guggenheim Fellowship was vital in the creation of this book.

My many thanks as well to my agent, Michelle Tessler, and my editor, John Glusman; their wise guidance in the book's early stages led to my pursuing New York's newspaper wars as a key part of this story.

Finally, this book is deeply indebted to many librarians. My particular thanks go to the staffs of the New York Public Library, the Library of Congress, Portland State University, and the Multnomah County Library. The soul of this book is probably in room 100 of the NYPL, where I found many of the thousands of newspaper articles I used from the case, and where many more stories slumber and wait to be found. When I first stopped by to see the famed NYPL "Librarian to the Stars," David Smith, he had a surprise for me: "You just got me in time," he said. "I'm retiring in a couple of days." And so he was. I suppose I was his last new author and new book in a four-decade career of assisting everyone from Jimmy Breslin to Colson Whitehead. I hope that this book does his old library proud, and that he gets some good beach weather for reading it.

ILLUSTRATION CREDITS

Frontis: Is Any One You Know Missing?: *NYJ*, June 29, 1897. Courtesy of the Library of Congress.

Page 1: Body diagram: *NYJ*, June 28, 1897. Courtesy of the Library of Congress.

Page 43: Martin Thorn and Anna Held: *NYW*, November 12, 1897. Courtesy of the Library of Congress.

Page 91: "Mrs. Nack, Murderess!": *NYEJ*, June 30, 1897. Reproduced by permission of the New York Public Library.

Page 135: Mrs. Nack's letter: *NYJA*, October 6, 1897. Courtesy of the Library of Congress.

Page 138: Thorn's letter: *NYJA*, October 7, 1897. Courtesy of the Library of Congress.

Page 147: "Thorn Denies That He Shot Guldensuppe": *NYJ*, November 30, 1897. Courtesy of the Library of Congress.

Page 209: "Interior View of the Woodside Cottage": *NYEJ*, November 30, 1897. Reproduced by permission of the New York Public Library.

Page 273: "Mrs. Nack Tells Her Own Story of the Amazing Guldensuppe Tragedy": *NYEJ*, July 20, 1907. Reproduced by permission of the New York Public Library.

INDEX

abortion, criminalization of, 128
Aloncle, George, 262
alternate-juror rule, 261
American Medical Association, 128
Arnold, George Waugh, 35, 42, 267
Astor, John Jacob IV, 13
Astoria Model Bakery, 45, 50, 193
Atlantic Medical Weekly, 245–46
Ayer, Harriet Hubbard, 131–33, 155

Baker, Undersheriff, 130, 156
Baldasano, Agguzzo, 29
Barberi, Maria, 169–70
Barrymore, John, 186
Beane, George, 86
Bellevue morgue, New York:
  body parts delivered to, 5–7, 11, 18,
    20–21
  false identifications at, 21–22, 27–30,
    36, 62, 149–50
  legs misplaced in, 84, 86
  medical examinations at, 7–8, 19–21,
    24–25, 36, 37
  and trial testimony, 166–68
Bennett, James Gordon, 56, 108, 268
Bersin, Samuel, 264
Bertillon, Alphonse, 95
Bertillon card system, 95
Black Hand, 264
Blomquist, L. E., 157
Bly, Nellie, 17
body:
  autopsies of, 7–8, 24–25, 36, 37
  discovery of, 3–5, 10–12, 18–19,
    163–64
  dismemberment of, 41, 84, 101
  disposal of, 65, 101, 140

false identifications of, 21–22,
  27–30, 36, 47, 62, 149–50, 263
fatal wound on, 20
grand jury testimony about, 99–102
head missing, 20, 26, 57, 61, 75,
  103–5, 109–11, 117–19, 150,
  151–52, 162, 176
identity of, *see* Guldensuppe, William
legs recovered, 54, 65, 86
medical examiner's work on, 7–8,
  19–21, 24–25, 36, 37
murder weapons, 37, 59, 60, 64, 78,
  194
oilcloth wrappings, 14–15, 18, 19,
  22, 26, 40, 41–42, 47, 53–54, 77,
  176, 220, 236–37, 262
partially boiled, 24, 37, 74, 85
rewards for information about,
  32–33, 40, 84, 205, 217
rumors and conjecture about, 34–36,
  41
Boorn brothers case, 151
Bowery, New York, 12–15, 57
Bowery Boys, 13
Boylan, Johnny, 117
Boyle, Detective, 81–83
Brady, Diamond Jim, 7
Brandel, Malwine, 195
Braun, Adrian, 238–39
Braun, Ludwig, 87
Brisbane, Arthur, 145
Brooklyn Eagle, 64, 145, 169, 220, 224,
  230, 251
Brooklyn Society for the
  Extermination of Ghosts, 253
Brown, Carrie, 78
Brown, Ned, 16, 85
  death of, 270
  and discovery of the body, 18–19

ABOUT THE AUTHOR

Paul Collins is an assistant professor of English at Portland State University and the author of six previous books. His work has also appeared in the *New York Times*, *New Scientist*, and *Slate*. He edits the Collins Library imprint of McSweeney's Books and appears regularly on NPR's *Weekend Edition* as the show's resident literary detective.